PRAC̵ ̵ ̵ ̵ ̵ ̵ ̵ ̵W
AND MORALITY

Practical Reason in Law and Morality

NEIL MacCORMICK

OXFORD
UNIVERSITY PRESS

OXFORD
UNIVERSITY PRESS

Great Clarendon Street, Oxford OX2 6DP

Oxford University Press is a department of the University of Oxford.
It furthers the University's objective of excellence in research, scholarship,
and education by publishing worldwide in

Oxford New York

Auckland Cape Town Dar es Salaam Hong Kong Karachi
Kuala Lumpur Madrid Melbourne Mexico City Nairobi
New Delhi Shanghai Taipei Toronto

With offices in

Argentina Austria Brazil Chile Czech Republic France Greece
Guatemala Hungary Italy Japan Poland Portugal Singapore
South Korea Switzerland Thailand Turkey Ukraine Vietnam

Oxford is a registered trade mark of Oxford University Press
in the UK and in certain other countries

Published in the United States
by Oxford University Press Inc., New York

First published 2008
First published in paperback 2011

British Library Cataloguing in Publication Data
Data available

Library of Congress Cataloging in Publication Data
Data available

Typeset by Newgen Imaging Systems (P) Ltd., Chennai, India
Printed in Great Britain
on acid-free paper by
CPI Antony Rowe, Chippenham and Eastbourne

ISBN 978-0-19-826877-2
ISBN 978-0-19-969346-7 (pbk)

1 3 5 7 9 10 8 6 4 2

Contents

Preface

With the publication of this book, my quartet on 'Law, State and Practical Reason' is complete. I owe to the Leverhulme Trustees the opportunity to have achieved this, through a research professorship in philosophy of law that they granted me 1997–9 and 2004–8. I thank them warmly for that, and I thank the University of Edinburgh not only for administering the research professorship excellently but also for the privilege of employment there as Regius Professor of Public Law and the Law of Nature, and Nations from 1972 till 2008.

In preparing the manuscript of this book I obtained enormous help and wise advice particularly from Garrett Barden, from Maks Del Mar, and from Stephen Guest, with other input from William Twining and John Cairns, and from Flora MacCormick, who in every way supported and encouraged development and completion of the whole project as well as of this particular book. The support of many colleagues in the Edinburgh Law School and the many animated conversations of many years contributed also in countless ways to whatever of wisdom there is in this book. Claudio Michelon and Zenon Bankowski lightened other burdens for me during the later phases of writing the book, when I was somewhat hampered by illness. Thanks to them all.

I count myself deeply fortunate to have been able to bring this long project to completion and I hope it will meet with a favourable reception from readers. It is nice to achieve liberation, even from a pleasant task, on Bastille Day.

Neil MacCormick

Edinburgh, 14 July 2008

Table of Cases

Introduction

Can reason be practical? That is the central question of this book. The book itself is fourth to appear of a quartet on 'Law, State and Practical Reason'. Its predecessors have covered: legal concepts and law itself within a theory of 'law as institutional normative order'; law, state, and nation in the context of concerns about sovereignty and post-sovereignty; and legal reasoning at a junction point between rhetoric, demonstrative logic, and general practical reason. These books have left open questions about the autonomy of persons as moral agents, about the universal rather than particular quality of moral judgements, and about the objectivity (or lack of it) that attends human attempts to settle good reasons for deciding what to do in the face of serious practical dilemmas. These matters are all considered extensively in the present book.

Can reason be practical? It is an old question, an old challenge. 'No' said David Hume. 'Reason' said Hume, 'is, and ought only to be the slave of the passions, and can never pretend to any other office than to serve and obey them.'[1] He meant that all human motivation to action depends on our emotions and sentiments. That I feel grateful to you for some service rendered makes me wish to do something nice for you in return. Reasoning about matters of fact may help me to find the best way to please you with my reciprocal favour—but reason enters the picture only given my established wish, based on my sentiment of warm gratitude.

Certainly, the 'passionate' or 'emotional' or 'sentimental' element(s) in our common human nature play a key part in the way we interact with each other, and in all else that we do. People who keep their emotions bottled up can be dry, unattractive souls—and dangerously unpredictable when the bottle bursts. Those who are easier emotionally seem better adjusted to life's contingencies. Yet it will not do simply to write off reason, to make it play a purely ancillary role in human decisions and actions. A basic argument concerning action for reasons occupies Chapters 1 and 2 of the present book, so need not be further anticipated here.

Human conduct engages both reason and emotion. Acting well and wisely means acting for good reasons, and these must fully allow for our affective as well as our intellectual nature. David Hume's great friend and younger contemporary, Adam Smith, while following much of the 'sentimentalist' strand in Hume's thought, nevertheless married it to a fascinating psychological postulate, the 'impartial spectator', by reference to which people normalize or even

---

[1] D. Hume *A Treatise of Human Nature* (L. A. Selby-Bigge and P. H. Nidditch eds) Oxford: Clarendon Press, 1978) p. 415.

rationalize their emotional responses in mutual interaction. This is, I believe, a vitally important corrective to pure sentimentalism.

Its value as a corrective was certainly noticed by the great German philosopher, Immanuel Kant, of Königsberg. Kant famously claimed to have been awakened from his 'dogmatic slumbers' by the need to confront Hume's empiricist philosophy. Abandoning what he saw as the uncritical rationalism of his previous work, he devoted his later years to constructing a transcendental philosophy that explains the presuppositions implicit in, and necessary to, all possible human thought about and knowledge of everything, either in matters of 'pure reason' (mathematics, logic, etc) or of 'practical reason' (morality, law, politics, etc).

Kant's enthusiastic response to Smith's impartial spectator, or judge, is revealed in his correspondence and in some side-remarks in his great philosophical texts.[2] But there is an absence of reciprocal influence, in that Kant's work was not known by nor indeed available to Adam Smith when he was doing his great work on moral philosophy, the *Theory of Moral Sentiments*, after which he turned his attention to the political economy that crystallized in his masterly *Introduction to the Nature and Causes of the Wealth of Nations* of 1776. His final work, on jurisprudence, was unfinished at this death, so he ordered it to be burnt rather than published in an inadequate or scrappy way. (But, despite him, some fragments have survived in the student lecture notes now published as *Lectures on Jurisprudence*.)

A conviction of mine that lies at the heart of this book is that it is urgent to achieve somehow a credible synthesis of Smithian and Kantian thought in order to solve the riddle of practical reason. The proposed route to this synthesis is introduced in Chapter 3 as 'the categorical imperative of Adam Smith', or rather, 'the Smithian categorical imperative'. (The latter phrase is preferable, since the former names a non-existent object—what is needed is not *of* Smith, but *after* Smith). The idea is to see what happens if one reconstructs a version of Kant's basic organizing principle of moral thought, the 'categorical imperative', in terms that mesh with the need to give full weight to human sentiment and emotion in any judgement about how to act in human predicaments. The case for this approach is made out in Chapter 3 below. Chapter 4 continues the theme by considering the place of mutual trust in human engagements, both in relation to honesty and truthfulness in communication and in relation to good faith in contracts, promises and the like.

The idea of human practical reason cannot make sense unless we postulate a human capability for self-command or self-government in dealing with dilemmas and decisions and in making plans about what to do. 'Autonomy', in Kantian terms, is a transcendental presupposition of our capacity to be active selves in the

---

[2] See S. Fleischacker 'Philosophy in Moral Practice: Kant and Adam Smith' Kantstudien 82 (1991) 249–69; cf. C. L. Griswold, Jr., *Adam Smith and the Virtues of Enlightenment* (Cambridge: Cambridge University Press, 1999) 14, 19, 37, 94, 138–9, 196, 223–4.

world. So far as we somehow can make or find law for ourselves and mould our conduct to it, we are truly acting subjects. Otherwise, we do not 'act' at all, but are acted upon. Like tides which are pulled by gravity or like wild beasts which act instinctively, we can be understood as enmeshed in causal processes over which we have no control. To be so enmeshed is to be in a condition of heteronomy, the opposite of autonomy. To clarify the place of autonomy in the account of practical reasoning, and to connect it with Kant's idea about the 'laws of freedom' characteristic of a liberal state and with Smith's 'system of natural liberty' essential to a free market economy is the task of Chapter 5 below.

Another historical great, James Dalrymple first Viscount Stair, author of one of the greatest legal texts in English, *Institutions of the Law of Scotland* (1681; definitive edition 1693),[3] makes a brief entry in Chapter 5; prior to taking centre stage in Chapters 6 and 7. Stair's is a spectacularly clear and articulate account of the kind of rationalist natural law theory that, in their different ways, both Smith and Kant sought to transcend. For this purpose, he is simply a representative figure from whom we can gather, in small bulk, the big ideas Smith and Kant sought to surpass, Stair himself not having been a particular target for either of them.

Chapters 6 and 7, however, adopt and adapt ideas of Stair's as having continuing deep relevance for the study of practical reason. He advances three 'principles of equity', 'obedience, freedom and engagement', that delineate three provinces of practical reason. So far as concerns 'obedience', there are basic moral duties that we must fulfil to each other and that cannot legitimately be neglected or defied. So long as we fulfil the basic duties, we are otherwise free agents, morally at liberty to pursue the good as we see it—this is the principle of 'freedom'. But to limit this freedom in favour of others lies within our own power, under the principle of 'engagement'.

Through promises, contracts, and many other kinds of voluntary arrangements we can enter into obligations to others, who may also reciprocally obligate themselves in our favour. These obligations involve self-set limitations on our freedom, and yet they also emerge from its exercise. A well-planned use of freedom will often involve the need for engagement with others as they pursue their plans. Jeremy Bentham's utilitarianism is also considered in Chapter 6, as proposing a single-principle, rather than a tripartite, approach to practical reason—but Stair's tripartition is preferred.

Chapter 7 is about the application of the three principles of equity to the practical domain of positive law. In such applications they transmute into the principles of 'society, property, and commerce'. How so? First, if human beings do not mutually observe such basic duties as not to kill or harm or defame or steal from each other, they cannot together sustain a peaceful community. Yet we need to live in society, hence need institutions to back up the basic duties with

---

[3] Stair, *Institutions of the Law of Scotland* (ed. D. M. Walker) (Edinburgh: Edinburgh University Press, 1981).

adjudication and coercion when necessary. Property is the necessary domain for the exercise of liberty. People cannot act freely save with access to physical space and to material resources. Property regimes secure this. Commerce then follows naturally as the engagements people make enable them to engage in exchanges of all sorts with each other, each in pursuit of some reasonable life plan.

Justice enters this account of law and practical reason through the simple idea that justice requires securing to everyone that to which each has a right, or, in a somewhat wider way, securing to each what is due to each under some overall dispensation. Smith's system of natural liberty, Kant's laws of freedom, and Stair's 'society, property and commerce' are all, however, inadequate to satisfy the full demands of justice of which contemporary humans in the twenty-first century are aware. Issues of distributive justice, of environmental justice (and common good), and of justice among different generations escape their net. Chapter 8, drawing on famous recent work by John Rawls and Ronald Dworkin, suggests ways in which such concerns can be built on to the picture developed so far, enriching it deeply but not deleting its broad outline.

Chapter 9 then carries on into discussion of good uses of freedom. Naturally, we should all try to act for the best so far as we are free to do so—that *is* the principle of freedom. If we are free, what to do lies within our own choice, yet we want some clarity about what is good, and about what personal qualities ('virtues') we should cultivate in order to pursue well whatever is good.

Chapter 10 takes up an issue left hanging from earlier in the book. As autonomous moral agents, do we more resemble legislators or resemble judges, so far as concerns some parallel with agencies of state? The answer given here is, unequivocally, 'judges'—in which answer lies another reason for trying to adapt Kant towards Smith. So in this chapter an extended attempt is made to explore the difference and the similarity between moral and legal decisions about specific issues. I take two leading legal cases that I have discussed at good length in prior works on legal reasoning. In the context of the present book, I now discuss these cases primarily to get an answer to the moral problem that lies at their core. In one case, I suggest that moral reasoning yields a different solution to the legal one determined by the judges, in the other I find parallelism but not identity between the moral and the legal decision that seems right. Practical reason is at work, both in legal judgement and in moral judgement. But these are two species of one genus, not simply species and subspecies.

Finally, Chapter 11 concludes the book and the quartet by tying up loose ends and essaying some concluding remarks.

Can reason be practical? The case made in these eleven chapters justifies the resounding answer 'Most certainly, it can!' If, reader, you wish to test this assertion, read on. You have a very good reason to do so, namely, to find out if it is true.

1
Incentives and Reasons

1 'Nobody but a blockhead'

This book is the fourth in a series about 'Law State and Practical Reason'. This very fact has given its author certain incentives to complete it with all deliberate speed, leaving no excessive gap between it and its predecessor volumes. There are incentives that touch one's reputation—one appears foolish or irresolute if, having promised a quartet of books, one fetches up with only a trilogy. One may thus also injure the reception of the earlier books in the series if it is seen to be an incomplete one. There is also a weak mercenary incentive. Few authors of works such as this become rich through their literary endeavours, but the annual receipt of modest royalties is always welcome.

Then there are incentives that have regard to other persons. The project was supported with a research grant for five years that freed the author to undertake unimpeded reading, reflection, and writing. Good faith with the Leverhulme Trust, which gave the grant, and with Edinburgh University, which administered it, requires that the whole project be brought to its planned conclusion, even after the end of the five years. Relationships with colleagues or former colleagues, who took extra loads to let the project proceed, would be soured if it were never finished. Finally, the publisher has given a contract for four books and has backed the series with suitable publicity, and this will to some extent be wasted if the series is not completed. Indeed, there are contracts with the grant-givers, with the University, and with the publishers that would be breached if the project were abandoned. These are, however, contracts of a kind that it is pointless to try to enforce, so the risk of legal proceedings does not enter the calculation. Nevertheless, there is an ethic of contract-keeping. One should keep the contracts one makes even if there is no serious prospect of being subjected to legal sanctions for the breach of them in given circumstances. This is, quite simply, a matter of honour. Honest people keep their promises.

Another aspect of relationship with colleagues concerns membership of a particular work community. A law school or other academic department of a University when it works well works as a common enterprise of all or most of the teachers, researchers, and administrators employed there. The public standing of a Law School (perhaps even attested through formal public assessment exercises, as at present in the UK) depends among other things on its strength as a research community. Each participant's work to a degree feeds off everyone else's and the reputation of the whole is valuable to the recognition of the work of each of its members. Regard for the common good of this community is another possible element in an author's motivation. Whatever enhances the common good is also good for oneself, but not in an instrumental way.

This shades over towards, but is not identical with, what one might characterize as pure scholarly motivation. One, and perhaps the most fundamental, reason for writing and thinking about the topic of this book is to try to get at the truth concerning practical reasoning in morality and law. An author has to believe that some new truth, or some never properly grasped aspect of the truth, will emerge from her or his writing, displayed with a unique and exciting clarity. The truth is important for its own sake; and the truth about practical thinking is also useful, for understanding it can help other people (as well as the author) to make a better job of the practice of living.

Whatever concern about truth counts for in an author's deliberation, it more or less exhausts the reasonable motivation any ordinary reader (leaving aside special cases like book reviewers and student readers of set course-books) has for giving attention to such a work. If it does not contain some new insight, some better-grasped and better-articulated truth or truths, why would anyone read it at all? These are thoughts that do or should motivate an author not merely to get on with the writing, but to write well, wittily, and wisely, with the ultimate readership of the work in mind. Their good is in this way also her/his good—and here the issue of enhanced reputation again rears its head as a side-issue.

The story so far has been told in terms of 'incentives'. It is a story about the reason an author, indeed this author, has to write the book and prepare it for publication. Without some such incentives, how would any work of this kind—work of any kind, for that matter—ever get done? Yet by the time the work is in the hands of a reader, the incentives are spent. If they have been sufficient, there is a book to read, and, if not, no question arises. Incentives concern something to be done, and they either sufficiently motivate one to do it, or they do not. So after the work is done, what becomes of the incentives for doing it?

The answer seems to be that they survive as reasons either of an explanatory or of a justifying kind. They are available to help answering questions such as 'How did it come about that this author wrote this book? What reason had s/he to do it at all, what reason to do it in just this way?' As reasons of this kind, they are open to at least two forms of appraisal, the historical-biographical and the critical-rational. The former concerns their accuracy or adequacy as an historical account of a particular author's activity and achievement. Is it true that MacCormick was motivated by a some sort of pride in keeping to plans he had announced, or by a sense of honour, or of fidelity to commitments made to various parties, together with some view about the prospect of income enhanced by royalties from publication? Is that all that was to it, or were there perhaps other unacknowledged motives, or even, as a Freudian might suppose, unconscious or subconscious, motives (what sexual repression might lie behind these primly crafted sentences)?

Explanatory accuracy, whenever one really tries to come to grips with it, is a matter of history, of biography. As such, it is inherently particularistic. One examines a particular person's life and tries to figure out what made that person tick, and what accounts for the various things s/he did in a lifetime or some slice of it, to account for books written and other things accomplished. Nicola Lacey's great book about H. L. A. Hart[1] is a good example. Her skilful reading and use of his journals and other personal papers, taken together with the public record, give a vivid insight into his character. This in turn makes it possible to understand or at least make informed guesses about the reasons why he authored certain books that transformed understandings of and about law, for at least one generation of interested readers. Of course, in each real case, like that of Hart, or of Karl Llewellyn[2] as William Twining has portrayed him, one is also engaged in an exercise of interpretation and of conjecture. There is always some degree of uncertainty in this kind of explanation, however great the detail of one's account and however excellent the source materials at one's disposal. Anyway, whatever the truth of the matter may be, and whatever difficulties and conjectures are involved in trying to get at it, the truth is about a particular person and the particular events in sequence that constituted that person's life.

Critical-rational examination of reasons that are supposed to account for some actions or activities of a person concerns their adequacy as justifying reasons. That is, it concerns their adequacy towards an account of rational action, not their historical or biographical accuracy as explanations. 'No man but a blockhead ever wrote, except for money,' said Dr. Johnson. For him, only one of the reasons offered in the earlier account gives a good reason for doing the job. If you will make money by executing a piece of writing, then do it. If you will not, do not. Indeed, if the effort you must expend is incommensurate with the profit you will make, you should turn your attention to something else more profitable.

Observe that this is not a claim about any person's actual motivation. Certainly, somebody might as a matter of personal history have written a book solely out of a sense of honour, or of pride, or of commitment to the truth. Such a person is, however, in Johnson's view a blockhead. These are not good reasons at all for investing the huge amount of time and effort that is required for writing a book, or at best they give weak additional makeweight reasons for doing so. For example, in a case where the financial gain is conjectural or seems likely to be only just enough to compensate for effort expended, these might tip the balance just enough to make it rational to go ahead with the project.

[1] N. Lacey, *A Life of H. L. A. Hart: the Nightmare and the Noble Dream* (Oxford: Oxford University Press, 2004).

[2] W. Twining, *Karl Llewellyn and the Realist Movement* (London: Weidenfeld and Nicolson, 1973).

We must at once add that Dr Johnson's saying so does not make this view correct. Johnson upholds the economic analysis of authorship. But he is not necessarily right. There is an argument to be had with him. We can stand up for authorial pride, for fidelity to commitments, for honour, and for disinterested regard to the truth as valuable in itself. There are good arguments to be had in favour of—and against—all of these, and even at the end of the day reasonable discussants may well disagree about what are acceptable as good reasons for anybody doing a piece of writing (or anything else). At least, perhaps more likely, they may agree about what could count as adequate or acceptable reasons, but differ about their relative importance or weight as reasons when it comes down to a fine judgement about what to do next in one's life.

By contrast with historical appraisal of a person's reasons for doing something, critical-rational appraisal is apparently not particularistic. The pride a particular person might take in some piece of work may indeed be quite idiosyncratic, such that only s/he would see it in just this light. But we can all understand the pride of creation or of authorship or of accomplishment of a difficult task, and pride of this kind is a concept we share. It is particular in each of its manifestations, yet it is as a universal that we can include it in a catalogue of rational motives, or adequate reasons, for acting. To think about adequacy of reasons is to think in interpersonal not in idiosyncratic terms. It is not: 'what would be a good reason for *me* to do this?' It is: 'what good reason could *anyone* have to do this?' Of course, one might then go on to wonder: 'does that good reason apply to *me* in this case?' A discussion of good reasons is a discussion of an objective matter. This is so, even though it is inevitable that everyone who comes into the discussion comes in from her or his own angle, with her or his own experience of life, with her or his own particularities and (it may be) peculiarities.

It is also inevitable that, when one leaves off discussing and goes back to living, one applies criteria of judgement that express one's own view of the right answer to the objective question. If after discussion and reflection I conclude that Dr Johnson is correct, I'll stop writing save when I am paid enough for a piece of writing (or see a reasonable prospect of sufficient profit from it). I shall understand colleagues who ignore the mercenary motive and write out of pride or out of concern for the truth, but I'll think them mistaken. The true biographical account of the decisions they make, though fully intelligible even to a Johnsonian, will reveal that they acted foolishly, that is, they did what they did for personal motives that are objectively inadequate in the perspective of the economic analysis of authorship.

It is worth remarking at this point that there is an obvious mutual interdependency between historical-biographical accounts of motivation and rational-critical appraisals of it. To be able to understand what somebody did on the supposition that it was a matter of decision and in principle rational as a decision, one has to have before one some statement or conjecture about the character of the act as it appeared to the actor. The character of the act includes for this purpose the very thing (to be) done, and also this act's results, outcomes and remoter consequences so far as the actor was (or was presumably) aware of them at the time. Only something that you think could be regarded—even mistakenly regarded—as an objectively good reason for acting can enter into an account of what somebody did in the character of a rational agent.

At once it must be added that not everything that one does can be attributed to one as a rational agent. Odysseus failed to sail home directly after the Greeks' final victory at Troy. Why? Not because of any decision he made but because of a contrary wind that forced his ship off course while sailing homewards. Mariners under sail are at the mercy of the wind. Faced with contrary winds they have decisions to make about how to cope with the situation in which they find themselves (the *Odyssey* is an extended account of how Odysseus coped), and a rational account can be given of this. But things that happen to us, as distinct from things that we do, escape the rational account, or are only background elements in it. To the extent that humans suffer forms of psychological compulsion, phobia and the like, they are like sailors driven before the wind, not like oarsmen heaving determinedly into it.

Any account of a person's life is an amalgam of the things that happened to that person and the things that he/she did, taking account of surrounding circumstances and context. What a person did is intelligible only so far as the outsider(s) can understand as reasons, even if inadequate reasons, the motives for which s/he is said to have acted. Another aspect of intelligibility is concerned with things that just happened to the person, including perhaps basic traits of character derived from heredity and upbringing in some impenetrable mixture. A further aspect concerns the social context in which the person found him or herself, the milieu in which he/she moved.

Conversely, the critical-rational discussion depends on an understanding of real people as they have really acted in the past and go on acting now. Taking an objective view depends on one's being able to enter imaginatively into the lives of others. Great works of literature—novels, poetry, drama, history, biography—as well as interpersonal interactions make it possible for each of us to come to some understanding of what it would be like to be somebody else. Without empathy there is no understanding of (other) people as people. Without understanding of other people, there is no self-understanding. Without literature, empathy is impoverished. There is an always-ongoing interaction between the subjective and particularistic analysis of individual acts and motives and the objective and universalistic assessment of acceptable reasons for action under a critical-rational appraisal of them.

A study of practical reason and of practical reasoning has to be wary of giving or appearing to give an excessively rationalistic account of human activity. Not everything that a person does or appears to do is the outcome of a process of reasoning. Much that we 'do' is more a matter of what happens to us, and of not very thoughtful responses to events that unfold around us, than it is conscious action done thoughtfully, for reasons. Much that we do is a matter of our own ingrained habits. Habitual actions and activities may have started from some choice, some reasoning, but they have ceased to depend (except negatively) on any choice we make (we could, and perhaps one day will, choose to give up our habits, but that is not a thought before our mind at the moment). Habits and routines are an essential element of what enables people to conduct their lives successfully, attending only to matters that actually need their attention.[3]

Understanding human beings in the round requires attention to the passive as well as to the active voice, attention to what they suffer as well as to what they do. Practical reason is at most a part of what enters our character as human beings, though it is decisive for our status as moral agents. Some may even deny that it is a real part of our humanity at all. Appeals to conscious human motivation in accounts of what we do, some say, belong to the table-dressing (lace cloths and fine china) of self-presentation, not to the kitchen machinery within, where action is cooked up. Appeals to practical reason are matters of mere 'rationalization', a process whereby to make seem rational things that are not rational at all.

Three lines of thought that powerfully influenced much twentieth-century work in the human sciences contributed heavily to scepticism about practical reason. Sigmund Freud and his followers taught us to be aware of subconscious motivations and of the likelihood that our ostensible motivations mask deeper drives of an essentially sexual kind owing their origin to earliest infancy. Karl Marx and his followers warned of 'false consciousness' found in theories about morality and justice which were no more than masks for, or reflexes upon, appeals to one's class-interest in the class-conflict that is built into the foundations of capitalist economies. Behaviourism in psychology and sociology taught scientists to study human behaviour simply as behaviour, without reference to the self-presentation of actors in terms of their alleged rational motives. These scientific, or allegedly scientific, views of human beings were sharply different from each other, even at points mutually contradictory. Yet each contributed insights about the human condition that have to be taken very seriously, albeit in a modified form. All of them diminished faith in the idea of action ever having a purely rational motivation.

They overstated their case. There does remain a place for reasoning about reason in human affairs. There are some acts and activities that call for some kind of rational account. This is true even though they may also be susceptible to illumination in other ways, such as in terms of unconscious motivation or as some kind of response to social structural forces outside of our control and (often) our awareness. The running (and self-referring) example in this chapter is a good one. Writing a book, or even writing a substantial essay or paper, is not a discrete event that could simply happen by a kind of reflex on the spur of a moment. It is not an

---

[3] See S. P. Soosay, *Skills, Habits and Expertise in the Life of the Law* (Edinburgh: Edinburgh University PhD Thesis, 2005).

act, but an activity that is spread out over many days and weeks, sometimes even months and years, subject to many interruptions—for meals, for sleeping, for meetings with friends and colleagues, for business activities of various kinds, for leisure pursuits, and much else.

Yet it is a continuing project that one picks up after each interruption to start where one left off, or to review progress to date and reflect on what should come next. It is also a process of discovery, for as the argument develops one can see new lines along which it can be developed, and sometimes one discovers that lines originally planned have to be abandoned because they no longer seem correct or convincing. Half way through, one may realize that earlier chapters need to be considerably re-thought and re-cast to make them lead sensibly into the central arguments as these now seem to be best put. Writing is thus a reflexive, self-critical process, in which what one does is always being judged against what one has done so far, and what one thinks most appropriate to do next.

Writing no doubt has its own peculiarities, but it does have much in common with other long-term creative projects. It resembles laying out a garden and growing it to maturity, or taking on a small business—say, a newsagent's shop— and developing it into a well-going concern. (One has to improve the layout of counters, make the products on sale attractive, build up good customer relations and generally seek to get into a position of secure profitability that justifies the outlay of money and effort one has put into the business.) A similar deliberative and reflexive quality is found equally, or perhaps even more, in projects that are essentially collective and co-operative. Think of what goes into building a house or a great public building, such as an art gallery[4] or Parliament,[5] in which many people are involved in ongoing deliberation about how to phase the work and how to ensure an overall coherence in the final shape of what is created. A team of lawyers building up a case for some major litigated dispute, and finally taking it through to debate or trial, and, in the end, if necessary, to appeal, is yet another material example.

Even the more individualistic projects like the writing of a single-author monograph in fact often (usually, indeed, in successful cases) involve a lot of consultation with other persons. It may involve presentation of sections for critical reading by colleagues, or seminars for discussion of ideas that are developing but not yet pinned down in the written word. It is definitive of things that one does deliberately that they do involve deliberation. Deliberation is often more effectively conducted interpersonally than by soliloquy. We think best when we test our thoughts out with other people.

Another case in point is when one wonders whether to apply for a new job; or when, having been offered a new job, say, in a place far from one's present home,

---

[4] Consider, for example, the Guggenheim Museum in Bilbao, designed by Frank O. Gehry (see <http://www.guggenheim-bilbao.es/>).

[5] Compare *The Holyrood Inquiry: a Report by the Rt Hon Lord Fraser of Carmyllie QC* (Edinburgh: Scottish Parliament Corporate Body, 2004).

one wonders whether to accept it. Nobody can ever be sure after the event that irrational or unconscious factors may not in the end have swayed the choice one finally made. But that is no help at the moment of deliberation. For then what is needed is reflection upon the reasons that make this seem the right or best thing to do in all the present circumstances, set against reasons that tell in the other direction, against doing this at present or at all. To the extent that one becomes aware of subconscious motivations that may be influencing the decision to which one is inclined, the sensible thing to do at this stage is try to bring them into the open. One can then confront them to assess whether in the light of reason they are entitled to any serious consideration and, if so, how much, and in what direction. In all such thinking about what to do, one can be hugely assisted by consultation with appropriate friends and colleagues.

2 Types of reason

Enough has been said to make it clear that interest in practical reasoning is interest in how reasons that are justifying reasons have a bearing on how one decides to act. Reflection about them does also require reflecting about explanatory reasons, and nobody who lacks an interest in human biography or in novels, plays and movies is likely to have much to contribute to understanding practical reasoning. But critical-rational reflection on the way reasons can constitute valid incentives to action, or can guide away from certain acts or courses of conduct, is the theme of the present work, and explanatory reasons have only the necessary but ancillary part already indicated.

There are various ways in which one can differentiate types of reasons. One division concerns their directedness. Here, we identify differences between self-regarding reasons, other-regarding reasons, and community-regarding reasons. Another concerns their content: some concern what is good for us simply as animals seeking to stay alive and sustain bodily comfort, others have regard to more abstract values that matter to us particularly as human beings. Whether we pursue these in a self-directed, an other-directed or a community-directed way, they are ideal rather than material in their content. In relation to book-writing as considered in the opening paragraphs of this chapter, self-regarding motives included pride of authorship, concern for reputation, and possible economic gain through publishing. Other-regarding motives concerned commitments (commitments that were legal contracts as well as personal promises) to others, namely, the research grant-giving trust, the employing university that administered the grant, and the publisher that had undertaken to publish the quartet of books. There are also non-contractual obligations to colleagues who facilitated the project, and there is a wildly conjectural gain to persons in general if a better understanding of practical reason is achieved through the book and eventually comes to affect people's action in a positive way. The community-regarding motive concerns what is for the common good of the community to which the work makes some contribution, in this case, the community of a Law School. Research publications that will help to enhance or consolidate the common reputation and standing of the place are worth the effort. All of these have a bearing on an ideal content. This concerns pursuit of truth. To understand these things is good in itself, even if no practical outcome arises from this other than the better understanding itself.

Is it an omission not to have included the possible self-regarding motive of the satisfaction one will achieve through completion of the project? The answer is 'No'. Satisfaction can't be a motive till after the project has commenced. For it is rational to take satisfaction from completing a project only if it was a good or reasonable project to undertake in the first place, hence to contemplate ultimate self-satisfaction in the initial deliberative process would be irrelevant.

A different case is where one contemplates work in progress. Once one has started on a task of extended duration, the prospect of getting it finished and having the satisfaction of its completion is indeed a good reason to press on and get the job finished. The negative stable-mate of this is the dissatisfaction over time and effort wasted were one to abandon it half way (or some way) through. Indeed, from that point of view, the fact that a particular contemplated book is fourth in a quartet is equivocal. Shall one write it or not? From the point of view of a present moment, taken in isolation, the issue is whether to start a new activity or project. To that, the prospect of satisfaction is not yet relevant. In a broader perspective, the picture is different—for this represents the fourth quarter of a bigger project, and satisfying the wish to complete the whole quartet is one good reason to press on, though it may not be compelling, or even very strong. If, on reflection, the three precursor books have said all that is really worth saying, it is better to announce that the series is complete as a trilogy and that the original plan for four has been scaled down for good reasons, not abandoned out of idleness.

This draws to attention a different aspect of practical reasoning, namely its temporal character. We have differentiated self-regarding, other-regarding, and community-regarding reasons, and differentiated animal or material content of reasons from ideal. Now we need to observe other differences concerning phases of reasoning. Deliberative reasoning precedes decision. Circumstances frequently expose us to practical dilemmas, whether to do this thing or that thing, whether to do this thing or not do it but instead consider whether there is something else that is better worth doing. There are even occasions when it seems that everything in a programme of activity is completed and the question looms: what to do next? Graduates who have come to the end of a demanding degree course will be familiar with this type of practical problem (it is not really a dilemma, and 'polylemma' is an uninvented word, which should stay that way). At this stage, one seeks to identify possible courses of action and to ascertain what reasons can be found that make one or another worthwhile. Deliberative reasons may be of the various kinds already noticed. If one or more courses of action are practically possible, then the issue is whether the reasons in favour of doing this are good enough reasons, and in a choice between two possibilities the issue is which has the better reasons on its side. As well as reasons in favour, there can be reasons against doing something, and sometimes we review the pros and cons in a quite ordinary way. But sometimes there can be negative reasons which rule out doing this or that, regardless of the good reasons that would otherwise favour doing it. Such 'exclusionary' reasons[6] have a particular significance in law and morality.

The exclusionary character of a reason concerns its force as a reason—some reasons have exclusionary force, some not. This adds a third dimension to the earlier discussion of types of reason—as well as directedness and content, reasons have force.

Deliberation cannot go on for ever. After thinking matters out as best we can, we must decide. Sometimes we may even resort to tossing a coin when matters are clouded by uncertainty or the case seems equally strong either way, and neither is excluded by any exclusionary reason. Decision is an act of will, often signified by some overt action, like booking a flight ticket, or phoning and confirming a reservation at a hotel, or writing to accept an invitation of either a social or a professional kind. Decisions can of course be revoked, or abandoned over time. But revocation calls for a new decision guided by new deliberation. The collective or corporate parallel to the individual act of registering a decision by some act is the passing of a resolution at a competently convened meeting of the corporate or collective authority. Procedural rules usually stipulate that such decisions can be revisited or revoked only by recourse to special procedures.

After decision comes implementation. How to do it? How to phase the bits of a long project? When to pause, when to pick up the threads again? All these questions call for a kind of 'executive' deliberation and the making of choices (mini-decisions) about the best and most opportune way to go on. Whether to abandon the project altogether? Here, as noted, the issue of satisfaction at completion is one factor in favour of going on, backed up by regret over time wasted if indeed there is no useful prospect of going on to the end.

This draws to our attention the obvious fact that life can be complex. Even the single-minded author is likely to have more than one project under way. As well as writing a book one may have a family life to go on leading, a teaching or administrative job that calls for effort and attention, or perhaps some relatively menial work undertaken to keep up one's income while saving all free time for the literary effort in hand. And in between times, there may be conferences to attend, or visiting lectures to prepare for presentation, or holidays to be taken and enjoyed. Even one's grandest projects interweave with other projects or activities, some quite mundane, to which one is also committed. So there are trade-offs between one and another, and some allocation of time or effort is called for in one's deliberation, towards which, for example, keeping a diary of commitments and

---

[6] J. Raz, *Practical Reason and Norms* (London: Hutchinson, 1975), 37–45.

appointments may be helpful. The life of a self-managing person is complex and calls for regular reflection and deliberation about how one is getting along with all one's projects and activities, and this may call for executive decision-making in relation to ongoing projects and deliberation about possible new ones. In terminology popularized by John Rawls's, one has to have some overall 'plan of life'[7] within which one's activities and current projects are somehow integrated.

3 Is this too self-centred a picture?

The rational deliberator portrayed so far must seem a terribly self-absorbed person. She is wrapped up in her life-plan with all its component projects and activities, he in his, and so on for each individual there is, setting aside, of course, those projects that are corporate or collective—but that in turn may exemplify what is simply corporate self-absorption. Yet that is not all. As rational deliberators, she and he are also moral agents, and that implies a non-self-absorbed attitude.

Practical reasoning in morality certainly concerns my plans for myself, but it even more saliently raises the issue of the calls other people have to make on me. What about my children, my spouse, my friends, my colleagues, my employer, my fellow citizens, and indeed all my fellow human beings with all their sufferings? How do they figure in my plans? More urgently, how should they? Isn't that the very essence of every moral problem? What do we owe to others? How do we respond to them? Is not the unreflective response of kindness and good will to the stranger in misfortune the most obvious example of morally good action, by contrast with all the calculation and deliberation that we typify as practical reasoning?

These points have much weight, but they are far from foreign to the discussion so far, which has insisted on the place that other-regarding and community-regarding reasons have among the components of deliberative (and also, it may be presumed) of executive decision-making. It is obviously true that only you can think out what you are going to do, certainly from the perspective of agency and action. I can wonder what you will do, I can reflect on what would be wise or right for you to do, and can give you my opinion on that if you want it. But only you can decide what is most worth your doing at this point, what is the thing you ought to do above all others. Practical reasoning is in this sense always self-directed and self-directing, whether the reasoning be individualistic or corporate in a given case.

Self-directed does not, however, mean self-regarding. The author who decides she simply must embark on writing a certain book and see it through to

---

[7] J. Rawls, *A Theory of Justice* (Oxford: Oxford University Press, 1972) 407–16. J. Finnis also considers possession of an adequate plan of life to be a basic requirement of practical reasonableness. See his *Natural Law and Natural Rights* (Oxford: Clarendon Press, 1980) 103–5.

completion by a certain deadline might consider her obligation to a publisher or a grant-giving body to be a good and sufficient reason to get on with the job. She could hold this to be a compelling reason, regardless of any economic or non-economic reasons of a self-regarding kind that she might also think have a bearing on the case. This would become obvious if the situation were imagined to be a little more complex. A potentially enjoyable and prestigious visiting professorship has been offered to her, but must be taken up within the coming twelve months, or not at all. These are the twelve months in which the book has to be written in order to fulfil the agreed deadline. So far as concerns self-regarding reasons she might well think that postponing or abandoning the book for the sake of the visiting professorship would be the right course of action from her 'selfish' point of view. But the obligations to the third parties trump these considerations, so she regretfully declines the invitation and gets on with the writing.

'Morality' in one of the narrower senses of the term is used to draw attention to the other-regarding elements of practical reasoning. The demands of morality are demands on behalf of persons other than the one who is deliberating. Moral motives or reasons are those that compete with self-regarding ones. Each of us is perennially at risk of favouring herself or himself too highly. One's self-regarding reasons for doing something can appear in vivid light, and seem blighted by the shadows of the demands that we have characterized as 'other-regarding reasons'. Moral virtue requires at its foundations a steady and even steely determination not to over-value what regards oneself against considerations that regard others. Impartiality between oneself and others is difficult to cultivate, but it is fundamental to morality.

This is true and important. Yet it is only one sense of the term 'morality'. Moreover, attending too much to this can push one over into an opposite error. It is true that everyone has a tendency to selfishness in the sense of a propensity to overvalue the self-regarding as against the other-regarding among motives to act, and we should be on our guard against this. Over-correction is also possible, however. Making oneself a doormat or a martyr in favour of others' relatively trivial needs is as much an error of judgement—of moral judgement, indeed—as its opposite. It can also have morally undesirable effects, as in the case of parents who, fearful lest they neglect their children, end up by thoroughly spoiling them and effectively encouraging them to become selfish brats. Here, as in many matters, there is a golden mean, and deviation from the mean in either direction leads one into moral error, notwithstanding that the tendency to err is normally skewed somewhat in the self-regarding direction.

A distinction is sometimes drawn between 'prudential' and 'moral' reasons for action, on the footing that the prudential ones are self-regarding, while the moral ones are other-regarding. This is a very undesirable usage. 'Phronesis' in Greek translates as 'Prudentia' in Latin and 'Prudence' in English. It means practical wisdom, exhibited in one's mature ability to deliberate in a sound and balanced way taking account of all that ought to be considered and setting aside irrelevant considerations. 'Prudence' in this sense does not concern only that which is self-regarding. It consists in giving just value to self-regarding, other-regarding, and community-regarding considerations in any context of weighty deliberation. Wise counsellors of those who are troubled by difficult practical problems are ones who can help to guide (not control) the deliberations of the person beset by difficulty.

Hence we shall not treat 'morality' and 'prudence' as mutually exclusive virtues. Prudence leads to morally sound decision-making, and decision-making is morally sound to the extent that it gives just or proper value to other regarding considerations whenever these compete with self-regarding ones. The question then is one that concerns 'just or proper value'—how are we to evaluate reasons in order to achieve practical wisdom in decision-making? One apparently circular answer has been popular through the ages—learn wisdom by observing and trying to imitate persons who are already wise. You become a good decision-maker by learning from someone who is already wise. Likewise you learn to carve wood well by being apprenticed to a good craftsmen, to sail a boat well by learning from a good skipper, to write well by modelling yourself on established good writers and attending to the criticism of good critics, and so on. This is tricky, though. Wise people make the right decisions. I learn how to make good decisions by following the words and example of the wise. But how do *they* know? Alternatively, what enables the less wise to be so sure that, judged by the rightness of their decisions, this exemplar they regard so well is really wise, is really a right-minded decision-maker? The rightness of his decisions proves his wisdom, but the decisions are right because he is wise. Surely they are reasoning in circles here?

Perhaps the solution is not unlike that which we apply in the case of lesser practical skills that are learned by example. The master-craftsman can show you what to do, show you what is going wrong in your attempts, give you helpful criticism of your efforts, explain what effects one is looking for in applying the skill, and so on. Practically wise people do not only issue delphic assurances as to what is right, they explain why it is. They show the reasons that seem most relevant and why one is valued for more in a given context than another, and so on. The wise person draws to your attention aspects of the situation you might not have noticed or whose relevance you might not have realized. Wisdom comes with experience, and the wise have experienced more than the novices, and have learned from their experience, an experience of mistakes as well as successes. They are not infallible oracles but they are invaluable guides.

True as this is, it has not brought us much closer to resolving the problem from which we started. How do we assess the different value of differing reasons? What kind of thing are reasons? The first answer to this, is 'reasons are not things at all'. Aspects of a situation and aspects of relationships between persons are relevant to human concerns. That a course of conduct is possible and that I find this course of conduct desirable in itself or for its probable outcomes is a reason for me to do it. That I have promised you not to enter into such a course of conduct if it will turn out to your detriment, makes it necessary for me to check if the relevant detriment is probable in the given case. If it is, then there is a reason for my refraining from that course of conduct. If it is not, then I am free to engage in it and should do so unless some more valued option becomes open, or comes to my attention. Reasons to do things are facts, not entities. Facts are what true statements state. The world as humans apprehend it consciously is a world of facts.

This gets more and more puzzling. Some say there is an unbridgeable gap between facts and values, but it seems that facts (and only facts) can give us reason to act, that is, can make it worthwhile to do something. What it is worthwhile to do has value. So facts have values after all. Yes, but value in a relative sense—value for humans. This relativism is not incompatible with objectivity. Facts that have value have it for any human being relevantly situated. (In justificatory reasoning, remember, reasons are universalistic, by contrast with explanatory or biographical reasons.)

What we have discussed as 'other regarding reasons' are facts of a particular kind, namely facts concerning relations between persons. Calpurnia and Caesar are spouses; Brutus is Caesar's friend. Brutus loves the Roman republic and regards Caesar as a danger to its survival. Cassius is jealous of Caesar for his military success. Caesar commands troops who can intervene if merely political means are manipulated to halt his machinations. Caesar can be killed when he appears at the Forum. Thus might conspirators come to the view collectively that the best course is to assassinate Caesar when he goes to the forum. Reflecting on this risk, Calpurnia might implore Caesar to avoid the forum today, and thus might Caesar be found in a dilemma—he owes it to Calpurnia not to go, unless her fears are groundless. He considers it essential to his role as a statesman that he attend at the Senate meeting in the Forum. The conspirators get their chance, and take it. Nobody in this situation, we may conclude, reasoned well. Caesar ought to have given more attention to his wife. Brutus ought to have spared his friend, and indeed should have warned him off himself, finding a way of doing so that would not betray the other conspirators. Nobody ought to have taken part in a bloody murder, even if Caesar was threatening to establish a new monarchy with every prospect of tyrannical rule. All this is arguable—but what is not arguable is that such relationships between persons, and such facts about people in relation to other people, are material to judging what to do—if we are one of the actors. Secondarily, it is material to our critical assessment of what is done, if we are merely spectators. So what makes relationships count as reasons in this way?

4 The legislative will

As human beings, we both act and reflect upon our actions. We react to events, and sometimes that reaction is a reflective one, preceded by deliberation what to do. This has been the theme of the present chapter up to this point. What is it then that we come to see when reflecting on relationships between ourselves and others or between persons generally? The best answer is that we see the need for some kind of a law-like response to the situation. Caesar is a human being who is exposed to my dagger's point if I do but strike at him as he enters the Senate. But shall I? All tyrants ought to be resisted; no human beings ought to be killed save in necessary self-defence. In this situation, unless the threat of tyrannical rule is so grave and immediate and incapable of deflection by any other means, the exception for self-defence does not apply, and the norm against killing ought to prevail. It ought to prevail, that is to say, in accordance with what I propose to you as being an acceptable element of a universal code of conduct. This proposal is challengeable, and a discussion could well ensue concerning the problem of tyrannicide[8] and the issue of what is necessary to protect persons who are endangered other than Brutus (or whoever). Issues of fact might be challenged as well—how certain is it that Caesar intends to take on tyrannical powers and destroy the republic?

It is easy to see that it may be questionable where exactly one draws the line in respect of justified exceptions to the norm 'thou shalt not kill', in ways that could be relevant to this case. But one could not imagine any possible human community in which it was not acknowledged that one person's wilful act of killing another is in all ordinary circumstances unacceptable in the highest degree. Exceptions, if any, need to be defined with great care. If anything deserves to be considered a 'universal law of nature', in Kant's famous phrase,[9] this surely does. A 'society' whose members acknowledged no normative restraint on extreme interpersonal violence is not conceivable as a society—for society implies some minimal level of mutual civility and mutually trusting interaction, however guarded such trust may be. A Hobbesian war of all against all is the antithesis of society.

Kant and many of his followers, including recently Christine Korsgaard,[10] represent the way in which we subject our active selves to the rulings of our reflective selves on the analogy of a legislature. Killing is wrong because there is a law against it, and the law is enacted by the will of a moral agent guided by practical reason, being a law because it applies objectively and universally to all acting persons. We are all moral legislators and the law of our rational nature depends on our common universal legislative will. This, however, makes morality seem somehow an arbitrary affair. An alternative and preferable analogy, it will be contended throughout the present work, is one that looks to the judicial rather than the legislative function. Nobody comes to reflection about right and wrong

---

[8] Garrett Barden has reminded me of the important discussion of this in Cicero. M. Griffin and M. Atkins (eds), M. Atkins (trans) *Marcus Tullius Cicero On Duties (De Officiis)* bk III. Cicero and Julius Caesar were, of course, contemporaries.

[9] The second formulation of the first version of Kant's categorical imperative is: 'Act as if the maxim of your action were to become through your will a universal law of nature'. See H. J. Paton, *The Moral Law* (London: Hutchinson, 1948) 84.

[10] See C. Korsgaard, *The Sources of Normativity* (Cambridge: Cambridge University Press, 1996) 97–103.

in the context of practical deliberation save in the context of a learned and inherited practical code. People are brought up to know and understand simple moral rules, like not to tell lies, not to break promises, not to be violent, not to bully, not to steal things.

In the gradual process of achieving moral maturity, one typically comes to endorse such already operative norms, although on occasion one may wish to challenge and revise them. One embraces autonomously what was originally inculcated heteronomously. But this is not like the solemn re-enactment of a whole criminal and civil code. It is more like the position of a judge confronting problems that arise in the context of an already ongoing legal system, but in a context in which always new interpretations may be called for in order to achieve proper justice under law. One embraces the law in a new and improved understanding of it.

The analogy is only a weak one (though we shall have cause to return to it in greater depth later). Judges within a state system of law have a strict hierarchy of sources of law. They may be bound by precedents of superior tribunals, as they are also bound by acts of the legislature that make many and often labyrinthine provisions about weighty matters in civil or criminal law, or public law.[11] By contrast, there are no hierarchies of moral authority (outside certain religious traditions, that is to say). There are not carefully recorded precedents, nor codes of detailed law, nor year-upon-year statute books containing acts of the legislature on a multiplicity of topics. There is no moral code-book,[12] though there are popularly recognized summaries like the Ten Commandments, and there are numerous tomes of moral philosophy and works on natural law that state broadly accepted propositions by way of moral rules or commonplaces, and by way of moral principles more generally. As judges of what we ought to do ourselves, and as judges of the conduct of others, we have to extrapolate beyond the simple guidelines we have inherited or been brought up with and gradually work out what seems acceptable if universalized. The maxim of an action that one must will universally is much more like the *ratio decidendi* of a common law judgment than it is like an article of a civil or criminal code or a Commonwealth or American statute.[13] Anyone making a decision assumes a background of prior judgements and accepted moral commonplaces that are the framework for the present decision and with which it must cohere. Judgement is, however, an act of will not solely of reason: it is a question of what one is to count as acceptable by way of universalizable maxim—not of what is already accepted. In that sense the rational will is indeed engaged in the process of settling the moral relevance of relationships.

---

[11] On the use of precedents in many legal systems, see N. MacCormick and R. S. Summers (eds) *Interpreting Precedents: A Comparative Study* (Aldershot: Dartmouth, 1997).

[12] On the significance of the absence of a rule-book of morality, see J. Dancy, *Ethics without Principles* (Oxford: Oxford University Press, 2004) 130–32.

[13] Compare N. MacCormick, *Rhetoric and the Rule of Law* (Oxford: Oxford University Press, 2005) ch 8 'Using Precedents' 143–61.

This argument draws attention to two different kinds of judgement. Sometimes one's judging is merely contemplative, trying to reach a conclusion about what is or is not the case. I may wish to form a conclusion on the question what is causing the brown patch to appear on my wallpaper. Is it damp, and, if so, where is it coming from? Or I may contemplate the course taken by the war in Iraq since 2003 and the circumstances of the years 2001–2003 that led up to the attack by the USA and the 'coalition of the willing'. I may wish to evaluate these events against the standards of international law. Was this military action a legal war or an illegal act? This is a question about a practical issue, but for me, as a mere matter of contemplation, the issue is not a practical one. Of course, if I am about to vote in a relevant election, or if I am considering whether to participate in some protest or another, the judgement about the war's legality will be important in the context of my practical deliberation, how to vote, whether to join the protest.

Had I been a member of the UK Government, or of the UK Parliament, in February 2003, considering the issue of the legality of the war, the same factors would have been relevant to answering it as in the contemplative case. But the deliberation would have been a matter of practical reasoning, not of pure contemplation or speculation. It would have been material to my deliberation on the issue whether to remain in the government and back its war policy, or the issue whether to vote 'aye' or 'no' on the question whether to approve the military action or not. (As it happened, my own position at the time was that of a Member of the European Parliament, where I put my voice and vote on the side of resolutions deploring the decision to embark on war in the then-prevailing circumstances.)

This distinction follows from the proposition already established, that it is facts that can be constitutive of reasons. Whether or not a certain fact exists is not itself a matter determined by practical reasoning. Whether the fact, if it exists, is a good reason for action to be taken after due deliberation by a person is dependent on how that person is placed. Facts can be reasons-in-relation-to-action, but only for a person to whose contemplated acting this fact and others are relevant. Whether they are relevant depends on whether they figure in a governing maxim or norm of action, the universalization test always being decisive in this matter.

There is also a place for more wide-ranging essays in critical moral philosophy. A famous case in point is H. L. A. Hart's *Law, Liberty and Morality*,[14] and another is its great exemplar and precursor, John Stuart Mill's *On Liberty*.[15] Such works do address legislative reason and propose principles of legislative practice on moral grounds. They have great practical value, but they are not exemplars of ordinary moral reasoning.

---

[14] London: Oxford University Press, 1963.   [15] Harmondsworth: Penguin, 1985.

5 Reciprocity and the protected domain

Other-regarding reasons in deliberation are (or include) moral reasons of the kind generated by the rational will in the manner discussed. These are essentially inter-personal and relational, hence they have a certain built-in reciprocity. The wrong-ness of my attacking you to the danger of your life entails the equal and similar wrongness of your attacking me, and so on. Whatever the soundest version of 'thou shalt not kill' may be, it is universal, so if it binds one it binds all. The same goes for not stealing, not bearing false witness, not lying, not breaking prom-ises, to take suitable hackneyed and non-controversial examples. My duty not to attack you is matched by your duty not to attack me, and so on. Conversely, therefore, each of us has a right against all others not to be attacked. We likewise have a right not to be robbed, to suffer perjury, or to be deceived, or let down by breach of promise.

These and other basic moral duties are thus dual in aspect. On the one hand, of course, they amount to self-imposed restrictions that limit what we can rightly permit ourselves to do. Conversely, however, they demarcate a domain of moral liberty, where we are free to act as we think best once we are satisfied that this will not involve violation of a duty, or, to put it another way, an invasion of some right of someone else.

When we consider practical reasoning in its self-regarding mode, directed towards choosing and engaging in projects and activities within some broader plan of life, the significance of this becomes clear. In deciding deliberatively or in an executive way about what to do or how to get on with an adopted project (for example, writing a book) we are in the first place and in the main deliberat-ing about the good. We are asking 'What is a good use of my time, what among various good uses is currently the best?' Again, this involves not only an acquired sense of what is worth doing, but also the development of that sense through autonomous reasoning. The judgement of what is worthy of our care, concern, attention, and action is a judgement in the realm of the 'ought', though not in the realm of 'duty' as such. It is universalistic in a weaker way than the judgement of duty. What is worthwhile for me must be worthwhile for anyone—but not for everyone. People have different talents and predilections and arrive at maturity of decision making after a variety of courses of learning, schooling, training or whatever. Each must be able to see what makes another's ends worthy, or their worth is gravely in doubt. But not everyone does, should, or could adopt identical projects. This is another essential feature of moral liberty. Different people have different goods and different perceptions of the good. One person may consider another's project to be a serious waste of time, but that is no warrant for interfer-ence (as distinct from friendly criticism and advice). People who stay within their rights are morally free to pursue their own ends, and indeed from time to time to make their own mistakes.

These reflections show the good sense in the idea that duties to others can be side-constraints[16] on one's deliberation. They are 'keep off' signs, like 'keep off the grass'. One who is willing to respect the directive to keep off the grass is given no instruction where to go or in what direction to walk—walk wherever you like, just so long as you leave this beautiful lawn untrampled. Another terminology in which to express this is that of 'exclusionary reasons'[17]—that you have a duty to keep off the grass is a reason to exclude from deliberation all courses of action that involve walking on it.

Certainly, that is not all that there is to it. Many duties enter deliberation as part of what delineates the good one may choose to pursue. A dutiful daughter or son may set about planning a holiday that will include an elderly parent and enable her or him to visit some long-hoped for resort, such as Venice, or the Grand Canyon. Such deeds are not done out of pure duty and against inclination—they are done for pleasure and out of love, and can be deeply rewarding experiences. This does not, however, exclude that a part of one's motivation in opting for such a holiday trip is a sense of filial obligation or duty. This is also significant in the sense of justifying what one does not do—perhaps there is another old person among one's acquaintance for whom it would be an even greater treat to make this trip than it is for one's parent. But there is a prior obligation to the parent, so the issue simply does not cross the threshold of deliberation. In the mundane example of writing a book, we have seen that considerations of what one owes one's grant-giver, one's university, one's colleagues, and one's publisher can be a part of the amalgam of motives—or reasons—that one adopts as justifying the project.

6 Custom, convention, morality

If it is true that human beings as rational and active creatures have to be considered to be in some sense the autonomous creators of their own moral norms and values, it has been true for a very long time. In the twenty-first century of the Common Era, we humans have a respectable antiquity as a species, though relative newcomers compared with turtles or crocodiles or others. This makes it unlikely that, in the present or any recent generation of humans, the autonomy of each human person will have entailed the radical originality of any. Most possible versions of credible moral values and moral norms will already have been proposed, tried out, refined, abandoned at some time or place. Moreover, precisely

---

[16] The idea of a side constraint was proposed by Robert Nozick, in *Anarchy, State and Utopia* (Oxford: Blackwell, 1975). Comparable is F. Schauer's concept of the 'entrenched generalization'— see F. Schauer, *Playing by the Rules* (Oxford: Clarendon Press, 1991) 38–52. Raz's 'exclusionary reasons' are a third variant, here preferred. See next footnote.

[17] J. Raz, *Practical Reason and Norms* (London: Hutchinson, 1975) 37–45; for certain purposes at least, Raz has subsequently revised his terminology, substituting the term 'protected reasons'. This change is not important for present purposes.

because of the reciprocity entailed in the acknowledgement of binding norms governing human relationships, it is likely that most people who interact to any great extent with each other will have come to at least some kind of provisional understanding of what each owes everyone else.

Hand in hand with this general reflection goes the more particular need for various kinds of conventions that facilitate mutual co-ordination. Common systems of time-measurement and time-telling are pretty well essential in industrial and post-industrial societies based on high technology. The very languages we speak are a fantastic co-ordination device enabling the exchange of meaningful utterances and thereby information, warnings, imprecations, threats, jokes, and everything else we communicate to each other. The internet depends on conventions and standards wholly unknown to most of its users. Astonishingly, it works. Indeed, it works astonishingly.

We have therefore no grounds for surprise if we find that in most relatively stable communities of persons interacting within some wider societal framework many moral duties and rights are also enshrined in the custom and convention of the community. We share many moral rules and principles, not in any very exact formulation, perhaps, but with a necessary community of understanding. People wouldn't be able to make promises or set up appointments or hold parties or do anything much else were this not so. The use of the richly varied vocabulary of the 'language of morals'[18] as a commonly understood and much-used part of our repertory of interpersonal communication is proof of this, were proof of the obvious required. But it is the repeated endorsement of this in the reflective judgements of the autonomous agents who comprise a moral community that gives normativity to the customs we observe—where normativity is lacking, only social pressure (sometimes quite intense, no doubt) motivates obedience.

7 Ideals and ends

The disapproval of the people with whom one lives and works is disagreeable to most people, and the weight of the disapproval increases the pain one suffers from it. Disapproval may even shade over towards coercion and threats of violence in some cases. All this means that people always have a self-regarding motive to conform to customary morality, at least to the level of paying lip service to it, but usually going the length of actual compliance, at least where non-compliance would be easily detected and much disapproved. Likewise, legal sanctions provide people with self-regarding motives to do what the law requires, at least when

---

[18] This phrase deliberately echoes the title of R. M. Hare's *The Language of Morals* (Oxford: Clarendon Press, 1952). Both personally and by his writings, Hare triggered my interest in many of the matters discussed in the present book, though my ideas about them have come to depart some way from his.

detection is likely and prosecution or litigation probable. In other cases, like the purchase of land and houses, the desire to secure an unimpeachable title to what one purchases provides a strong motive to ensure observance of the conditions and burdens the law places upon such transactions.

Such motivation partly resembles economic motivation (in a wide sense of the 'economic' it *is* economic motivation). A person may write for money or for other economic advantages that may result directly or indirectly from literary success. Here, as in the case of one who acts morally to avoid disapproval or acts legally to avoid sanctions or other legal disadvantages, the goodness, such as it is, of one's acting is merely instrumental. I act well to avoid disapproval, or I act well to become better off financially. Neither of these is or seems like an end in itself. Doing the right thing because it is right, is another matter. Securing an income in order to sustain a home and possibly some form of family life in that home is more intelligible—as is, indeed, securing a sufficient income to be able to stay alive and comfortable without exploiting the generosity of others. Implicit in all serious deliberation is the question of what are the ultimate goods that make instrumental goods what they are, and give them their intelligibility as motives. The next chapter will give attention to the good, that is, to what is of value and what it means to 'have value'.

There can be reluctant and in some way enforced compliance with morality or law, as we have seen and see every day. By contrast with such compliance, one who believes in and takes guidance from a conception of what it is good to do, or what it is right and wrong to do, thereby expresses allegiance to a value that has ideal rather than animal content. Where the contrast of 'right and wrong' is applied, the reasons to which one appeals have the exclusionary force that was noted above. In what follows, Chapter 2 deals mainly with the good, then Chapters 3 and 4 deal with the foundations of rights and wrongs.

2

Values and Human Nature

1 The importance of language

It is an old belief, still held by many, that human beings are creatures who owe their existence to an all-powerful and wholly benevolent God. Jews and Christians and Muslims all hold, in different ways, but with the same root source, that some human beings in history were, through prophets (and for Christians, through God's incarnation in Jesus, and thus from Jesus' teachings), granted a revelation of the laws God made binding on humans. Yet it was observed by believers that even those who had not received the divine revelation that was recorded in holy scripture nevertheless seemed to live, albeit very imperfectly, according to similar tenets. They had some idea of the principles expressed in the Ten Commandments, with or without the further interpretations added to these by the New Testament. Divine law, according to such believers, is specially revealed in the Bible (or the Tanakh or the Qu'ran). But even without revelation, humans have some access to it. Here is a foundationally Christian way of putting the point: 'For when the Gentiles, who have not the law, do by nature the things contained in the law, these are a law unto themselves, which showeth the works of the law written in their hearts; their conscience also bearing them witness, and their thoughts in the meanwhile accusing or else excusing one another.'[1] Similar observation that common points of law were observed in many communities despite local variations in things like coinage and weights and measures and forms of governance had similarly led ancient Geek philosophers to the conclusion that some things are right or wrong by nature, not only by enactment. Thus it seemed that there was in some sense a 'natural law' common to all human beings as such.

To persons alive in the early twenty-first century, the metaphor of 'writing in the hearts' of human beings has acquired a new resonance. For contemporary life-scientists, both in their frontier work and in their popular accounts of what they are doing, tell us to think of the human genome as a book. This book contains an elaborate code of biochemical letters and words, which function as a kind of recipe for proteins to build themselves into the elaborate molecular clusters of which we

---

[1] *Paul, Epistle to the Romans* 2,14–15.

(like every other living thing) are made up.[2] 'In the beginning was the word' says the opening sentence of the Gospel of Saint John. Actually, a word, or rather a book of words, is in the beginning of each living thing, each with its own genetic coding written in the matching pairs of bases in the double-helix of its DNA. The writing is not, rather it is not only, in our hearts, but in every cell of our bodies. But this is not itself a moral code, or anything like one. What it may be, on the other hand, is a precondition of any possibility of any moral code, and much else besides.

Whoever can read and understand the preceding paragraphs must have recognized them as an exposition of ideas in the English language. Of anyone who has got this far, it is possible to make a confident inference. Each such person has a properly working gene known as 'FOXP2' on chromosome 7. 'Th[is] gene is necessary for the development of normal grammatical and speaking ability in human beings, including fine motor control of the larynx.... When it is bust, the person never develops full language.'[3] Of course, genes that are necessary for speech are not sufficient for it. They are themselves switched on through the exposure of the human being between infancy and puberty to the environment of a speech community, and the language one develops is the language of that community—a language translatable, however, if with imperfections, into any other natural human language. Profoundly deaf persons may never learn to speak with their vocal cords. But manual signing can be just as complete a mode of linguistic communication, and can be complemented with the use of written—or electronically encoded—language just as can a vocally spoken language.

As Thomas Reid long ago and Ludwig Wittgenstein much more recently pointed out, a private language is inconceivable.[4] The power of speech is one of the irreducibly social powers of the human mind. The conditions of learning and using speech depend absolutely on a common adherence to the common norms of grammar and the like that structure our speech. As will be argued more fully in a later chapter, these must include a norm favouring truthfulness and sincerity over falsehood and cheating, for a community without such norms would either never develop a language or swiftly lose the one they have. That lying and cheating are wrong is not itself written in the genome. But abilities that can be developed by bearers of the human genome do depend on most members of a speech community treating them as wrong most of the time, and refraining from them especially in front of learners.

Let us add to this a recognition of the connection between language as speech by vocalising or signing and the invention and development of writing. First written, then printed, and now digitally encrypted language messages create an

---

[2] See Matt Ridley, *Genome: the Autobiography of a Species in 23 Chapters* (London: Fourth Estate, 1999) 1–15.

[3] Matt Ridley, *Nature via Nurture* (London: Fourth Estate, 2003) 214–5.

[4] See Thomas Reid, *Essays on the Active Powers of Man* (Edinburgh: Printed for John Bell, and G.G.J. & J. Robinson, London, 1788); L. Wittgenstein (trans. G. E. M. Anscombe), *Philosophical Investigations* (Oxford, Basil Blackwell, 1968) 269, 275.

extraordinary human facility that has progressively distinguished us from our closest relatives, the chimpanzees and bonobos, whose gene code is astonishingly close to our own. This is our capacity to communicate at a distance both in place and in time, and to accumulate knowledge generation by generation, becoming ever more specialized in the branches of knowledge we can master and thus almost inevitably undergoing an ever more advanced social division of labour. This implies a capability to develop a more and more extensive civil society, in turn requiring an extension of at least provisional trust across an ever-wider range of people who are not personally acquainted with each other. This idea is familiar to any reader of Adam Smith.

The civility of civil society, and the impersonal trust it both requires and underpins, is a remarkable achievement to the extent that humans manage to achieve and sustain it. In recent times, at least, it has depended on the construction and maintenance of constitutionalist states, states with some constitutional distribution of powers that facilitate checking and balancing of different power holders over time. Only in constitutionalist states of that kind has democracy been a long-term possibility. None of this is dictated by the gene code, of course, nor was its construction achieved by reasoning a priori. It does nevertheless remain true that such developments have been possible for human beings given the nature that we have, and given that we are capable of learning how to improve what has evolved with us. The fragility of civility and civilization always confronts us, and the lesson of events such as those in Iraq between 2003 and 2008 warns us how much easier it is to knock down than to rebuild. The impulse to destroy is also a part of our nature, but one against which our institutions can help us to guard.

The example of human language from which these brief reflections commenced is an important one. We all speak some language, perhaps more than one. Languages are highly normative.[5] Yet their norms were not made by any human act of will clad with some form of institutional authority—even the *Académie française* has a comparatively subsidiary role in respect of the great language it cares for. We cannot write the grammar of a language until we are already well equipped with that language and with skill in using it. We have no grammar to write about unless we are already speaking the language into whose grammar we choose to inquire. In studying and constructing grammar, we are finding out the implicit norms of correct communication that we are already using. The moral is that we humans are norm-users before we are norm-creators, or legislators. If so, it follows that our sense of duty and obligation to each other is and has to be prior to any authoritative imposition of rules upon us. Were it not so, civil institutions could never have developed.

It is not a merely contingent fact about some particular human being here or there that he or she speaks some language. It is no more a contingent fact than

[5] For a strong view on the normativity of grammar, see G. Pavlakos, *Our Knowledge of the Law: Objectivity and Knowledge in Legal Theory* (Oxford: Hart, 2007).

it is a contingent fact that cod are aquatic animals. There might never have been any vertebrate aquatic animals, and the species codfish might never have evolved as it happens to have. To that extent, the cod's aquatic character is contingent. Likewise, featherless bipedal terrestrial animals with a capability for speech might never have evolved. To that extent, humans' existence as speaking animals is contingent. But evolution having taken the course it has, those animals that humans can recognize as belonging to their species have necessarily a capacity for linguistic communication, and (as we now know) there is genetic coding for this in human DNA. Beings that have most human characteristics but lack this are sadly defective in the most characteristic feature of our species. They deserve profound care and attention, but they are not fully or normally human. This has a profound implication. Since speech can develop only in a human community, membership of a community is essential for the realization of the most fundamental human capacity. To live in community with others is thus of fundamental value for human beings.

2 Humanity and animality

Humanity here is not in radical contrast with animality.[6] Speaking animals are indeed animals. There are therefore things that are of value to us simply in virtue of our animal nature. Being a member of a speech-community is one of these, but there are others.

Staying alive is preferable to suffering an untimely death. Health is preferable to sickness. Having shelter is preferable to sleeping rough. Friendship is preferable to enmity. Love is better than hate. Sound limbs are better than broken or rickety ones. Plentiful food is better than starvation rations. Clean water is better than brackish or polluted water.

What should I say to somebody who doubts these statements, or who tells me they only express my subjective values? There is not much to say but 'nonsense!' A human being in any situation imaginable does not merely prefer the one of these pairs to the other, but if conscious and of sound mind considers the one objectively preferable to the other. It's not just I who prefer—anyone would, and if somebody claimed not to, we would need to hear a special reason why.

Circumstances alter cases, of course. When Ronald Ross was working on his theory that malaria was a blood-borne disease spread by insects, he inevitably became exposed to mosquito bites and thus to the disease whose cause he was trying to discover. He willingly exposed himself to disease, and acted reasonably, if also heroically, in doing so. What Ross did is intelligible, however, not as expressing a preference for sickness over health, but the reverse. As a physician, a healer,

[6] A point shared strongly with Martha Nussbaum. *Hiding from Humanity: disgust, shame, and the law* (Princeton, N.J.; Oxford: Princeton University Press, 2004).

he wished to establish the cause of a disease with a view to pursuing better treatment and prevention of it. He risked his own health for the sake of improving human health more generally. All sorts of other instances can be found of those who one way or the other risk their own life and limb for the sake of comrades or even for the sake of endangered strangers. They do so not because they think death better than life or injury better than wholeness, but for the sake of those very values in the lives of others. Love is better than hate and life is better than death, so risking one's life for the love of another or others is not an instance of denying the value of life to a reasonable person. It is acknowledging that sometimes one value yields before another.

Religious ascetics may also consider that renunciation of all the ordinary comforts of life is necessary in order to focus the mind on devotion to God and to express the exclusiveness of that vocation. This does not say the goods I mentioned are not good, but that sometimes sacrifice of them promotes a higher good. Perhaps this line of thinking can make intelligible even the conduct of the suicide-bombing terrorist who thinks that witnessing the truth of her or his religion, or vindicating injustices done to a whole people, calls for nothing less than self-sacrifice and random killing of strangers. But if this is intelligible, it is nevertheless wrong. The weighing of values is totally wrong here, though one can see how a mistaken belief in their relative weights could motivate a person to act in this radically inhumane way. By contrast, the religious ascetic, however bizarre her or his values may seem to other people, at any rate harms no other person in pursuing them.

Sexuality is also part of animality and satisfaction of sex drives is good. The expression of this in heterosexual unions is also the means to continuation of the species in general, and within any human community the guarantee of its continuation as a community through generations. Care for the young and their defence against disaster, disease, and attack by other humans or other animals is of value to us as it is to all animals. It is part of the good of life.

Community is essential to realizing the character of a human being as a speaking person. The securing of other such essentially animal goods as we have been considering here is also possible in the context of community with other humans, both in narrower family units and more widely, how much more widely being a contingent matter dependent on societal development here or there. Among the ways in which community with others is of value to humans we must include the possibility of co-operative mutual defence against the evils to which we are exposed. Yet it is a part of the duality of our nature that other humans are capable of being the authors of those very evils, up to and including the greatest imaginable of them, as any visitor to the death camp museum at Auschwitz can appreciate with ghastly clarity. Humans are capable of communal co-operation and mutual support. They are also capable of inter-communal as well as intra-communal cruelty, deceit, exploitation, murder, and much more. Indeed, it is community that makes possible the forms of collective strength through which these evils can be most effectively perpetrated.

The safety humans can have in numbers depends on the terms of co-existence of those numerously brought together. Only given shared—and respected—norms against mutual violence and cruelty is community preferable to solitude—and yet community under acceptable norms is essential to human development. Unequal terms of social co-existence may prove better than no co-existence at all from the point of view of those at the losing end of inequality. These are the very persons who—as in the case of slaves, or, in many social settings, women and children—have no option of exit from community as well as no effective voice in it. Human societies can be as readily loci of natural evils as of natural goods.

This does not mean that the good where and for whom it is realized is anything other than good. To repeat what was said once already: Staying alive is indeed preferable to suffering an untimely death. Health is indeed preferable to sickness. Having a home is indeed preferable to sleeping rough. Friendship is indeed preferable to enmity. Love is indeed better than hate. Sound limbs are indeed better than broken or rickety ones. Plentiful food is indeed better than starvation rations. Clean water is indeed better than brackish or polluted water. Those who have access to all these are indeed well off. Those who have not are indeed unfortunate. Their misfortune may be directly caused by or at best callously un-remedied by the well off. That makes yet worse their misfortune, for they suffer not only natural evils but also human injustice.

The issue of the moment, however, is simply whether there are goods and values natural to humans, some of them goods for other animals too, some specific to humans (with the corollary that, however they may come about, there are also in both categories genuine human ills or evils, by way of absence or deprivation of that which is good). The answer is that there are, and that denial of this would be impossible to entertain seriously.

That these are goods has an important implication for a study of practical reason. That a state of affairs or a state of being is good in one or other of the ways we have been exploring means that it is a reason for activating oneself in appropriate circumstances. Faced with a danger to life, one has reason to take avoiding action, faced with dirty water one should seek a clean source or find a method of purification, faced with a leaking roof one should try to mend it. People behave reasonably when they take account of the risks of matters turning out badly in any such way, and take precautions that seem suitable to forestalling the risk in question. All this concerns what we called self-regarding reasons for action in the previous chapter.

3 Other-regarding reasons and 'sympathy'

Now let us turn to other-regarding reasons. The fundamental place of friendship, and its close kindred in the way of love in a sexual union, and parental love for children, possibly also children's love for parents and among siblings and cousins, gives rise to a natural concern with the animal wellbeing of others. One's friend's, one's spouse's, one's children's or parents' or siblings' wellbeing in the basic animal ways is a part of one's own good. That is what is in the nature of friendship and of family connection. In wider senses, the community's good is also a part of one's own good. But it cannot be subdivided into shares that each could enjoy alone. If the residents of an area work together to tidy up the neighbourhood park, everyone is better off as a result, but the park remains a common asset that everyone can enjoy, those who helped and those who did not.

Humans also have, as Hume and Smith pointed out, a yet more extensive capacity for sympathy with others of their own kind.[7] We are capable of feeling, and indeed we simply do in appropriate circumstances feel, the pain of others. We do so, for example, witnessing a road accident, or a physical assault by one person or another, or a TV clip of a suicide bombing and its aftermath, or one of the planes flying into the Trade Towers—albeit less acutely than the direct victim(s). We can also feel in a pallid way, except when masked by pangs of envy, the joy of those who are happy, when we see or envisage the occasion of their happiness. Out of sympathy (or 'empathy') we can take others' good as a part of our own good, and have thus natural other-regarding reasons for action which yet have also an element of the self-regarding in them.

A different, though not altogether unconnected, aspect of the other-regarding among the reasons we can have for acting or refraining from action concerns norms of conduct dictating how we ought to behave towards each other. It can be wrong to treat people in certain ways and right to act towards them in other ways. To refrain from this because it would be wrong towards somebody, while doing that because it is the right way to treat somebody else is indeed a good reason for one's actions. Anyway, it is not hard to see why everyone regards as evils attacks on their physical and psychological integrity. Nobody likes to be hurt by somebody else, far less to be the subject of a murderous attack. That a course of action is one that will avoid hurting someone else is a genuine reason in favour of undertaking that course of action. The difference between right and wrong is principally considered in the next chapter.

Humans are not only a species of animal subject to similar risks and causes of death and pain as other animals. They are passionate animals, capable of a range of feelings brought on by their circumstances, including the side effects and consequences of their own actions. To suffer evil in any of its forms is painful, pains being of different kinds depending on the cause of suffering. A broken limb hurts in a different way from a broken heart. To suffer contempt is painful but different from suffering indigestion or a beating. Pains that have purely physical causes can usually be cured or alleviated by taking suitable physical measure. Pains arising

---

[7] D. Hume, *A Treatise of Human Nature* (L. A. Selby Bigge and P. H. Nidditch eds) (Oxford: Clarendon Press, 1978) 317–22, 369–86; A. Smith, *The Theory of Moral Sentiments* (D. D. Raphael and A. L. Macfie eds) (Oxford: Clarendon Press, 1976) 9–15. Theirs is an extended concept of sympathy, as it covers any 'feeling with' another.

from mental or psychic ills are harder to alleviate. Avoidance of direct and simple pains is a basic self-regarding reason for action.

Not all pains are in the relevant way direct and simple. One can feel guilt over a wrong one has done and got away with, the consciousness of wrongdoing being essential. One can feel shame over having done wrong and being detected and held up to blame by others. One can feel remorse over wrongs done or harms caused, where one sympathizes with those who suffer from one's deeds and misdeeds. One can feel resentment towards others who have or whom we believe to have caused us harm, especially where the harm was deliberately inflicted, but also when it results from neglect or negligence. We can also feel disgust and repulsion from filth, including human filth, and correspondingly desire facilities for washing and for waste and sewage disposal, all the more urgently when we live in the crowded conditions of great cities.[8]

Conversely, happy experiences make us feel joy or elation, love for friends and helpers, warmth of community with whoever else is involved in the happy activity, gratitude towards benefactors, and the sheer pleasure of exercise and activity when in good health. We have aesthetic pleasures in scenes of natural beauty or in fine works of art, great music, fine architecture. We can rejoice in the satisfaction of curiosity when we find or learn how others have found the solution to some deep and significant question. The Crick-Watson discovery of the 'double helix' and the way this transformed understanding in biology and particularly in genetics is one specially striking example from the last half-century.

We need not here follow philosophers like David Hume who have carefully itemized and classified the passions. They are many and various, both those which have positive connotations for us and those which have negative ones. They can feature in our reasons for action. For the prospect of positive feelings is one reason for undertaking activities, both in a self-regarding way when our own good feelings are in issue, and, when those of others whom we seek to benefit are in issue, in an other-regarding way. Likewise, the avoidance or warding-off of evil is a reason to act both where self-protection is in issue and where other-protection is. It seems wholly implausible, however, to construct a hedonistic system according to which the only motives for all action are the avoidance of pain and the maximization of pleasure. The greatest pleasures arise as side-effects from activities of a complex kind undertaken for a complex of reasons that either do not include or only in a subsidiary way include seeking for pleasure, or, indeed, happiness. It may be true, for example, that many people find deep happiness in a marriage partnership with a single other person, each of whom seems reciprocally the one right person to the other. But a marriage is a complex relationship that develops and evolves over time, always calling for joint and several 'executive deliberation' how to keep working together well, in a context in which each partner has many

---

[8] Martha Nussbaum, *Hiding from Humanity: disgust, shame, and the law* (Princeton, N.J: Princeton University Press, 2004).

other activities and interests to pursue. Aiming to be happy all the time would be a good way of making such a relationship grind to an unhappy halt. That good marriages generate great happiness is one reason why unmarried persons might hope to or even seek to find the right other person for them. To get married just in order to be happy would, however, be a great mistake, one which many have made.

4 On ideals

What then about ideals? Is it true that the scholarly pursuit of knowledge in some domain or another is good in itself? Is it true that the building of beautiful buildings, the construction of opera houses and the financing of opera companies, the development of great football teams which compete successfully with other teams to the delight of countless fans are worthy objects of endeavour? Can one who admires the sun setting over a beautiful landscape take satisfaction just from the beauty of the scene? Most people are passionate about some ideal or ideals. But are ideal goods then simply the objectified objects of passions we find ourselves to have?

John Finnis has famously applied a 'retorsive' argument to refute or at any rate to confound those who deny that knowledge is good in itself, and better than ignorance.[9] To produce and deploy an argument in support of this denial makes sense only if it is worth getting at the truth of that matter. This implies that it is, after all, at least in this case, worth while to try to establish the truth rather than remain in ignorance of it. But if that is true in this case, why not in others? Of course, one who solves a problem or makes a discovery or who finally comes to understand some well-known but difficult piece of mathematics or physics or philosophy or literature gets pleasure and satisfaction in the discovery or in achieving the understanding. Pleasure in this achievement of one's own may also involve pride. But the pleasure, the satisfaction, the pride seem to presuppose that the facts or points of theory were worth knowing in their own right. If not, what would be the pleasure in discovering them?

Considerations of this kind seem to me to be highly persuasive in the way of establishing that, for humans (and to that extent relativistically) there are some ideal goods that are good not just as expressions of animal wellbeing or even as means to the satisfaction of passions. They are also and principally good in and for themselves as matters of standing interest and concern to humans as thinking, speaking and social animals. There is here an element of relativism. These are matters of *human* good, and their goodness is relative to the present and continuing existence of our species. If some catastrophic nuclear incident or collision with an asteroid were to reduce life on earth once again to the microbial level,

---

[9] J. Finnis, *Natural Law and Natural Rights* (Oxford: Clarendon Press, 1980) 59–80.

there would be nothing to which such goods would be good. Among human beings, however, no special pleading needs be made for the existence of certain ideals as objective goods *for any of us*. The place of such goods in practical reasoning both intersubjectively and from each individual's point of view can be taken as sufficiently well-grounded to need no further argument.

The conclusion of this part of the argument is that there really are objective human goods, of a kind which it is rational for anyone to take as good reasons for decisions, acts, activities and grand projects within some plan of life. Whatever we do, and whenever we wonder what to do, reflection on the presence of such reasons may enable us to come to what seem to us sound decisions about the things we should do or be doing. Of course we can be mistaken. The facts may turn out to be otherwise than we thought. Matters that were uncertain at the commencement of a course of action may clarify themselves in a sense adverse to our project. The promising geology that seemed to justify opening a coal mine at a particular place may turn out to have been deceptive if an unexpected fault appears, distorting the coal seam and making it economically unworkable. Our own capability for or interest in a particular line of activity or endeavour may prove insufficient, and a career-change may be the most sensible course of action, even after much time spent acquiring the qualification one no longer feels comfortable using. Reasonableness and rationality require a continual 'executive' monitoring of one's activities to ensure they continue to be supported by either the very reasons that initially supported our deliberative decision(s) or other supervening reasons that turn out to be more satisfactorily supportive of one's activity.

Anyway, there clearly can be genuine reasons for doing things, for there are genuine objective values. Their character does indeed depend on our human nature, and understanding them is part of what is required to understand human nature. 'Practical reasoning' is not an oxymoron. It can be directed at all of self-regarding, other-regarding, and community-regarding reasons, having as their content human goods that are either animal or ideal in character. What remains obscure is what it means to weigh or evaluate such reasons and discriminate between more and less important ones, or ones that cancel others out or override them or exclude them from present deliberation. To understand such matters requires thinking about practical reasoning, especially relevant as that is to the other-regarding reasons of which only a rather thin account has so far been given, but which will form the focus of Chapters 3 and 4.

5 Deciding what it is best to do

If there are facts that have value, such that we have reason to do things, how should we carry out this reasoning process? What is involved in trying to act for the best, whenever this is the question we have to decide? These are the questions to consider now. For the moment, the discussion will artificially exclude or downplay issues concerning duties, or what is right and wrong—sometimes called 'exclusionary reasons'. These will arise for discussion in Chapter 3. Suppose that an agent faces a choice, between two apparently reasonable courses of action, and is not duty-bound to exclude either of them, what kind of deliberation should that agent undertake, and how should deliberation come to a conclusion?

One frequently proposed but not very helpful line of argument to explain this concerns 'weighing' and 'balancing' reasons. Let us say that the choice is between doing A and doing B. The assumption is that each of A and B is a good thing to do for at least one reason. It is a further assumption that if there is any reason against doing either A or B, it is not an exclusionary reason. Clearly, if the pro-reason or pro-reasons in respect of either A or B are not stronger in some way than whatever the anti-reasons, at least one of A and B can be eliminated on that ground. But it may turn out that both are eliminated, and that there is no third possibility C. In this case, the choice between A and B will now present itself in the guise of a choice among evils. Then the reasonable thing will be to try to reach a conclusion on which is the lesser of the evils, and decide for that.

The issue of choice of evils can be postponed. Let us simply focus on the idea that one must choose between A and B, and that both A and B are supported by good reasons. Should one then envisage a deliberation in which one lists all the pro-reasons for each of A and of B, and ascertains the strength or weight of each such reason, then aggregates the total strength (or weight) of them all in each case? If pro-A reasons are greater in cumulative strength than pro-B reasons, then deliberation reveals that A is the better course of action among those available. It will be most rational to decide to do A, not B. If it were otherwise, then B would be the thing to (decide to) do. This would be clear enough if we could account for how to calibrate the 'strength' or 'weight' of reasons. Do we find this somehow inherent in the facts and the values they embody? Or is it more that we assign relative weights as part of the very process of deliberation? Only in the former case would 'strength' or 'weight' give an independent and objective basis for evaluation. Yet it is difficult to see what is the source or means of measuring such deliberation-independent weight or strength.

A further difficulty concerns commensurability. Earlier, it seemed reasonable to identify self-regarding, other-regarding, and community-regarding types of reason, and to differentiate in terms of content between animal and ideal goods. How should I then choose between something I very much want for myself, and something that will be very much appreciated by my friends (but not something that I owe them or am in duty bound to them to do)? How do I choose between two aspects of the good of communities to which I belong, or between what is good for one community and good for another? There is no obvious *a priori* scale of goodness that we can read off here. Utilitarians might suggest that in each case we try to add up the total of happiness or preference-satisfaction that each brings with it, or that it seems likely to bring, making due discounts for relative degrees of probability. That is a possibility we shall return to in Chapter 6 but, for the meantime, let three objections be registered here. The first is that the ordinary person's ability to calculate such things, if they are calculable at all, is at best restricted, given all the problems of probability and the difficulty of measuring interpersonal intensity of pleasure. The second is that it may involve re-posing the question in new terms rather than answering the original question. Even if we can translate the options into net units of prospective pleasure (all the pleasures minus all the pains) or some other net units, it is an unwarranted assumption that what constitutes the goodness of the goods we start from is simply their productivity of pleasure or some other such common basis of measurement. The third concerns preference-satisfaction. Practical reasoning concerns what it is rational to prefer in a situation of choice, hence is presupposed by, not answered by, preference-satisfaction utilitarianism.

It seems better for the moment to pause and cast doubt on the whole 'measurement' project and the ideas advanced about 'strength' and 'weight'. Real deliberation seems to be different from this kind of exercise. To explain why this seems to be the case, it may be worth indulging in a modest excursus into autobiography.

6 A real choice

In 2003, at the age of 62, I was a Member of the European Parliament (MEP), to which I had been elected in 1999. At the time of my election, the University of Edinburgh had granted me five years' leave of absence from the Regius Chair of Public Law, on the understanding that I might return to my academic post after serving one mandate as MEP. The alternative would be that I continue in office as MEP, but as of the beginning of the next mandate I must resign my University post finally. By June 2003, it had become necessary for me to decide whether to announce that I was available as a candidate for re-election in the elections of June 2004, or not. There were highly convincing reasons to suppose that if I did go forward as a candidate I would almost certainly be re-elected as one of two (or, just possibly, three) representatives of my political party (the Scottish National Party) to represent the constituency of Scotland again for the years 2004–9.

I was very conscious that I was thus in an unusual position, and indeed an unusually lucky one. At a time in life when few people have any choice at all about a job to do, I had a choice between two jobs that were both very attractive indeed to me. Both were quite well paid, at about the same level of financial reward, in the middle to upper range of public service pay, though well below the rewards available to those who succeed in business or the practice of law. In terms of material needs and desires, including the desire to be able to help members of my family if needs arose for them, I was in either case as well-off as I had any wish to be. I had an income that I could comfortably live within, while saving a modest surplus for contingencies.

I took great delight in my work as MEP. It is a sustained thrill to represent one's fellow citizens in a great democratic assembly, trying to solve problems for individuals, and trying to secure good outcomes in projects with impact at the level of communities or whole societies. In the process one engages in quite searching debates in specialist parliamentary committees and in deliberations of one's Party Group where decisions are taken about the Group's collective line on important issues arising in Parliament. One can express one's position in great but rather formal and often thinly attended debates in the plenary sessions. One interacts regularly with civil servants, both at the all-Europe level of the European Commission and at one's own national level, through representatives both of the UK government and the (currently devolved) Scottish government, and often one encounters those from other member states as well. At home base, one's staff members maintain active contacts with individuals and interest groups and there are important points of contact with the political party as an organisation and with its representatives in local councils and parliaments (Scottish parliament and UK parliament, in this case). One makes many visits to party branches at local levels throughout the country, and through them meets other public representatives and activists in various organisations with political issues to air concerning the politics of the EU. One has to do also a good deal of travel within Europe to keep in touch with the activities and concerns of sister parties in other nations and regions whose cause one collectively represents in the European Parliament. All this is hard and demanding to do, but to a person of a certain cast of mind, extremely fulfilling and (in that sense) rewarding. It is a matter of finding one's own good and self-fulfilment in activities that serve what one takes to be really important aspects of the common good and of justice affecting communities at many levels within the great confederation of the European Union.

In addition, I had the exceptional good fortune in the years 2002–3 of being elected to take part in the 'Convention on the Future of Europe'. This august body drafted a possible 'Constitution for Europe' in the form of a draft Treaty offered to the European Council in July 2003 for possible adoption by the European Union. In the end this was only a partial success, in ways for which I have accounted in other writings.[10] Succeed or fail, to take part in a continent-wide constitutional convention is for a person with my personal intellectual background and history an exceptional and fascinating opportunity, and I considered myself to have some stake in trying to progress the ideas and ideals expressed in the Convention's output.

A negative aspect of the role of MEP, for me, had proved to be that it almost entirely precluded having time for serious reading of legal and political philosophy, even works with close relevance to my ongoing work. For the same reason,

---

[10] N. MacCormick, *Who's Afraid of a European Constitution?* (Exeter: Societas/Academic Imprint, 2005); 'The Convention and its Constitution: All a Great Mistake?' in Hanne Petersen, Anne Lise Kjær, Helle Krunke and Mikael Rask Madsen (eds), *Paradoxes of European Legal Integration* (Aldershot: Ashgate, 2008).

it became progressively harder for me during my years as MEP to contribute to high-level debates in these disciplines. I did a fair amount of journalism, but relatively little substantial scholarly writing. I had assumed at the time of my first election that it would be possible to pursue a balanced timetable with room for scholarly interests built into parliamentary work. The day to day demands of parliamentary work falsified this expectation, leaving very little time for the kind of reading and reflection needed in scholarship.

The physical demands of the job were also considerable, with frequent flights often starting at very early hours of the morning and all the wear and tear of contemporary long-distance travel. There were some signs that this was beginning to take some toll both on my own health and on that of my wife.

As for the idea of returning to the Chair in Edinburgh, there also were strong attractions, in part alluded to in Chapter 1. I had unfinished business that was important to me in the way of completing a lifetime's contribution (of whatever quality) to the philosophy of law, the present book being the conclusion of that effort. The fellowship of academic colleagues both in Edinburgh and beyond it, and the contact with students and contribution to their learning counted for a great deal. An enhancing factor arose from the coincidence that the third centenary of the foundation of the law faculty or law school fell in the year 2007. Indeed, it was specifically associated with my own rather unusually entitled Chair of 'Public Law and the Law of Nature and Nations' established in that year by Queen Anne on the advice of the then Scottish government. It also seemed possible that I could contribute in a different way to some at least of the wider, even Europe-wide, goals and ideals with which I was engaged as MEP from the different standpoint of a senior academic and member of various learned societies. Also, returning full-time to my home in Scotland would facilitate making a continuing if diminished contribution to Scottish politics.

I knew that whatever I did, some good friends would be disappointed, on the ground that they would have preferred me to take the other course. On the other hand, my wife and my family would be pleased to see me give up the gruelling weekly travel to and from the seats of the European Parliament in Brussels and Strasbourg. Their view on this was based partly at least on the fact that I had suffered some heart disease during 2001, though in what seemed a once-off way.

Let these paragraphs suffice by way of a brief historical-autobiographical account of my dilemma. It is as accurate as I can make it. The conclusion was my decision to tell party officials that I would not go forward for re-election, and to inform Edinburgh University that I intended to return after my leave of absence and to seek renewal of my grant from the Leverhulme Trust. In due course I did return, surprised indeed that the Trust had responded favourably to my request.

At no time in the deliberation process, which I found agonisingly difficult, did it seem possible to reduce the problem to a mere list of pro-reasons and anti-reasons, followed by an assignation of weight to each and a mathematical calculation of the winner. Certainly, I tried writing each of the pro- and anti-considerations down in two lists in parallel columns to try to compare whatever was comparable. This gave quite a lot of help, though the lists were in the end pretty long. It helped to ensure so far as I could that I was really taking everything into account and comparing like with like, while also allowing for incommensurable and divergent considerations affecting one side or other of the dilemma. It was also material to ask how far and in what ways values that obviously supported one option might be pursued or realized, if to a lesser extent, if I chose the other option.

I discussed aspects of the problem with people very close to me, especially my wife (whose personal preference was for my returning to the University), and returned to conscious reflection about it all several times over a week on holiday on the Costa Brava in Catalunya.

In the end, having broken down the choices into components and pro- and anti-considerations, one has to put everything together again. What I faced was the choice between two whole packages which amounted to two significantly, though only partly, different ways of life that were to occupy the closing years of my full-time work before indulging in the pleasures of retirement. (Making a choice in one's sixties, one is wise to reflect on which way of life tapers off most readily into part-time engagement, then further reductions of commitment, with final complete abandonment of work. Academic life has notorious advantages on this score, but for me in 2003 they were not decisive.)

Choice among partially different ways of life might be in terms of what they express or what they are instrumental towards. As for instrumentality, in this particular case the financial rewards were much the same either way, and in either case amply sufficient to my needs and modest luxuries, and to fulfilling my various obligations. Always, a rational decision-maker ought to have in mind the needs of survival and reasonable comfort and capacity to help those who need one's help and have some call on it. If one is fortunate to be able to treat this as already established, grounds of choice move to what is of intrinsic value (by way of ideal good) in the options for choice, or to whatever they are expressive of.

'Justice is the first virtue of political systems as truth is of systems of thought,' said John Rawls.[11] In a way, that expresses the kind of choice I was making. The governing value of academic work is truth, in the sense of pursuing a good understanding of a domain of inquiry. The governing value of political endeavours is the pursuit of justice in society according to some well-thought out conception of justice and the common good. In public representative office, this is of course subject to compromises at several stages, since one cannot act effectively in a representative assembly (or even be elected to one) without participation in a party. This complexity is even greater inside a complex parliament like the European Parliament whose members are elected through national parties in many member states, and who therefore have to work in party groupings that involve working alliances with other parties. A degree of compromise, a willingness to fall

---

[11] J. Rawls, *A Theory of Justice* (Oxford: Clarendon Press, 1972) 3.

somewhat short of the perfect truth about justice and the common good as one sees it, is the price one pays for effective engagement in the exercise of power. It may be all too easy to let this become an excessive price that increasingly corrupts one's capacity for acting honestly and yet in a spirit of compromise. But that is not inevitable.

By contrast, while academic life contains some pressures towards compromise and cutting awkward corners for the sake of achieving publishable results and meeting publication deadlines, and even sometimes pressures against pursuing uncomfortable truths, good universities and like institutions jealously protect the right of the scholar or scientist to pursue her or his vision of the truth, her or his path to good understanding. By this test, Edinburgh University was and is a good place to work. Where one's domain of inquiry includes matters of justice and the common good, one can pursue one's conception of the truth about these in an uncompromised and uncompromising way (though not in a way that is insensitive to competing conceptions of others). But the price of freedom from compromise is that one has relative, or even complete, lack of influence on the conduct of public affairs, at least in the short run and probably in the long run as well.

I do not deny the propriety and legitimacy of compromise in political life. It is essential to working democracy. I am glad to have over the years and in various capacities played my part in this, within my own home places. Indeed, I am proud of having done so, at considerable cost in free time and enjoyment of the quiet life. To be engaged in public life is a part of civic virtue that everyone has some reason to cultivate. Yet finally, for me, when it came to deciding the right way for me to spend the last period of my fully active life, I finally favoured giving priority to the scholarly virtues, with a subsidiary continuing political engagement and without disparaging the political virtues. This was how I justified my decision to myself, taking all things into account. It is how, in an autobiographical way, I now characterize the decision I took in 2003 and with whose consequences I am still living—very contentedly, let it be added. In some way, one's large choices express commitment to aspects of the good life, that is, to virtues. There can be different ways of life that exhibit genuine but different virtues, and one has to choose in the light of one's own character and predilections. One's choices also over time have a character-forming effect. One becomes what one does. The same goes for vicious ways of life, unfortunately.

This part of the discussion may have been too idiosyncratic, based on one particular and extremely unusual situation of choice. Perhaps one can say some things of more general import as well.

Some human values are shared animal values, to do with staying alive (*perseverare in esse suo*) rearing a next generation of one's own kind, avoiding sickness and exposure to injury and disease and the like. These come first, not necessary in importance in themselves, but simply as the condition of achieving all else that is of value. Where these are in danger, or simply taking a long-term prudential view of future possible risks, it is reasonable to attend to these first, for one's own sake and for those that are close to one either physically or emotionally or through family relationship or close friendship. For fortunate people, this is not difficult in itself, and often one can take for granted in decision-making that these values are for the time being under no threat.

Beyond that, decision-making deals with self-regarding, community-regarding, and other-regarding reasons for action that are at least partly ideal in content, and it seeks to establish a best course of action taking account of all that is at stake. Where there are strong reasons of a self-regarding kind for pursuing one course of action, it is an essential question whether one is morally free to pursue this course of action. If exclusionary reasons apply, and make it on some account wrong to pursue the contemplated course of action (or wrong to do so unless some path-clearing way can be found), then one ought to close down that possible course of conduct. (It is not the case that one always does so—but that just says that we sometimes act wrongly through illegitimate self-preference. That is almost too obvious to be worth saying.) The issue of 'right and wrong' is taken up in the next chapter, not here.

Within the sphere in which one has moral freedom to act, acting for the best does call for a broad plan of life. In this, a person pursues a multiplicity of values in a reasonable and balanced way over time, in accordance with some conception of virtue or goodness in action and character. We have considered this in a preliminary way above, and will subject it to further consideration later (in Chapter 9). A key balance to strike is between what one does for the sake of one's own enjoyment of value in its various forms, and what one does for others or as a matter of common good. Selfishness is always a risk, and yet self-respect calls for attention to self-regarding reasons to a reasonable extent. How we can judge what is reasonable falls for discussion later.

7 Choices in the public domain

Public authorities seek to co-ordinate the actions of many persons in the cause, presumptively, of justice and the common good within the community where they have authority. To achieve such co-ordination it is necessary to have some clear statement of the values or 'mission' of the authority. A case in point is that of the Scottish Government that took office following the Scottish Parliament election of 2007. This example is a convenient one, since much material for evaluation, and concerning evaluation, is available through that government's website. From its earliest days, the Government announced five 'strategic objectives' as its guiding values, in the following terms:[12]

'To focus Government and public services on creating a more successful country, with opportunities for all of Scotland to flourish, through increasing sustainable economic growth.

[12] See Scottish Government website (<http://www.scotland.gov.uk/>).

1. WEALTHIER AND FAIRER
Enable businesses and people to increase their wealth and more people to share fairly in that wealth.

2. HEALTHIER
Help people to sustain and improve their health, especially in disadvantaged communities, ensuring better, local and faster access to health care.

3. SAFER AND STRONGER
Help local communities to flourish, becoming stronger, safer places to live, offering improved opportunities and a better quality of life.

4. SMARTER
Expand opportunities for Scots to succeed from nurture through to life long learning ensuring higher and more widely shared achievements.

5. GREENER
Improve Scotland's natural and built environment and the sustainable use and enjoyment of it.'

It is open to argument, of course, whether or not this is a complete and sufficient list of values for a government to pursue. Have they left out something of great importance, equal to those that they have listed, or even more important? If so, their progress in government will either fail in its aim of making the country for which they have responsibility a better place for its citizens, residents, and visitors, or it will at least fall short of what might have been achieved. A better framing of the strategy of government might have led to better outcomes for all or most people affected. That is not a matter for further exploration here, but will be a topic of political controversy in Scotland now and in the times to come. For now, let us take the statement as a serious and noteworthy attempt to set a framework for governmental action, and consider how it works as such.

Most obvious from the point of view of our attempt to reflect on practical reasoning about questions of value is that no single action by government and no single policy initiative can equally serve all these ends. Some will be focal for some policy initiatives—obviously, 'healthier' is engaged most closely by health service policy. But efforts to diminish public drunkenness in the context of the 'stronger and safer' objective will also have beneficial public health effects, and that will be relevant to their justification. So there is no one-one line-up between strategic objectives and single departments of state. There can also be competition between objectives. Not all ways of increasing economic activity and economic growth are compatible with the 'Greener' objective. The strength of a criminal justice policy can easily come to be at odds with its fairness. The effort to create a smarter society may enhance economic competitiveness without increasing distributive fairness. And so on.

Issues of practical efficacy also arise. For example, the 'Greener' objective may seem well served by schemes to develop renewable energy, including wind energy. There may be suitably steady wind-flows over bog lands in the Outer Hebrides. Yet use of such land may be itself environmentally damaging by prejudicing the capacity of the land to continue acting as a 'carbon sink'. Moreover, in terms of preservation of natural habitats for animals of endangered species, there may be further environmental considerations that tell against use of such a site for a wind farm. Meanwhile, there may be a strong case under the 'wealthier and fairer' objective for encouraging industrial development of this kind in a remote area of the country where there are few employment opportunities. In any such deliberation, it is important to reflect on the whole range of probable effects brought about by construction of a large-scale wind farm, and to assess these with a view to estimating the balance of advantage between this and alternative possible means to develop renewable energy sources. Moreover, if there is an obligation on government (e.g., under the EU Habitats Directive) to give an overriding priority to habitat protection, this may operate as an exclusionary reason excluding further promotion of this possibility. So applying the guiding value 'Greener' requires complex reasoning both of a probabilistic cause and effect kind and of an evaluative kind. This may include quantitative elements but in the end calls always for a qualitative conclusion, that justifies a decision.

Modern government involves highly complex and interactive processes with many collaborative participants. Business is always making progress through the conduct of the bureaucracy, under the overall guidance of elected Ministers dependent on the co-operation (normally) and advice (always) of their civil servants. A democratic parliament and its members are charged with the task of securing governmental answerability for decisions, and for showing that decisions do serve the announced values, and are not a cover for more sinister objectives or interests. In such a multi-player activity, some statement of strategic objectives such as the ones listed above is essential to any kind of coherent administration of government, and to satisfactory democratic accountability. For any proposed legislation or set of executive actions, it is material to ask: which of the established strategic objectives does this promote? Are there any that it supports in a subsidiary way? Are there any towards which it is unhelpful? Are there any with which it is directly in opposition? The task of government as a whole, led by a First Minister and Cabinet, is to see to it that there is a satisfactory balance in the pursuit of all, none abandoned in the face of the others, and none subject to direct opposition from acts aimed at others. To the extent that one can list five numbered strategic objectives, there is obviously some quantitative element to this. But the overall task is, again, more qualitative than quantitative. If no objective is sacrificed for the sake of the others, and if none comes to be treated as merely subsidiary to one or more of the others, each provides a fulcrum on which to balance the achievement of each of the others. The wise statesperson seems to be again the benchmark for success in qualitative judgement and practical reasoning in government. Wisdom is the supreme virtue of governance, but it is achieved by doing other things well, not by pursuing it as an independently specifiable value.

The tentative or interim conclusion is that good reasoning about what it is good to do, both in individual decision-making and in collective (e.g., governmental) decision-making has a quantitative element. One should be able to produce some summary statement of the values that guide one's action. It has a probabilistic element, to the extent that one always has to calculate the likelihood that steps taken in pursuit of a certain goal will actually achieve it. One may wish to use check-lists of all the factors telling for and against one course of action or another. But there is no simple algorithmic additive way of totting up plus points and subtracting minus points to reach a conclusion. Taking all the quantified or quantifiable features of the choice-situation into account, one finally makes a qualitative decision guided by some commitment to preferred values of private life or of public life.

3

Right and Wrong

1 Norms and contexts

That an act is wrong is a reason not even to consider performing it. What is wrong can be wrong from one or another point of view, in one or another context of judgement. In association football, it is wrong to play the ball with your hand unless you are goalkeeper and are within your goal area. In rugby football, anyone may pick up the ball and carry it, but only a player carrying the ball may be tackled or physically obstructed. Tackling a player without the ball is wrong. Not so in American football, where blocking an opponent off the ball is permitted. In law, it is wrong to drive a motor vehicle in excess of the speed limit on a given stretch of road, or to drive on any public highway with excess alcohol in your bloodstream. Morally, it is wrong to behave with contempt for the health and safety of other persons with whom one is in contact. All monotheistic religions regard it as gravely wrong to commit blasphemy against God, or to defame His prophets. Each of these contexts of judgement is a 'normative order', in a sense to be explored more fully through the present chapter.[1]

The wrongness of an act is what has earlier been called an 'exclusionary reason'. It excludes that act, or any such act, from deliberation as an available course of action by anyone committed to the normative order within which it is wrong. To contemplate doing so, far less doing so, is to waver in, or fall short of, that commitment. Adverse consequences may follow—a penalty against one's team in one or other species of football, or a sending-off; or a legal prosecution and punishment; or moral blame by others and feelings of guilt on one's own part; or excommunication. Wrongness thus presupposes a standard of judgement, a ground for judging wrong the conduct in question in the context in question.

Not merely are wrong acts wrong in a context of normative order, they are wrong under a description. 'Playing the ball with one's hand, but not as goalkeeper [in a soccer game]'; 'Obstructing a player [in a rugby game]'. 'Driving in excess of 30 mph on a stretch of road subject to a 30 mph speed limit [set by the Road Traffic Act and Regulations made under it]'. 'Showing contempt

---

[1] The account of right and wrong given here in terms of context-relative norms or commandments is based on that developed in N. MacCormick, *Institutions of Law* (Oxford: Oxford University Press, 2007) chs 1 and 2.

for the wellbeing of one's neighbour who is in danger [morally speaking]'. 'Committing blasphemy by insulting the one true God [according to Judaism/ Islam/Christianity]'. Each of these can be given an imperative or a normative formulation. 'Thou shalt not handle the ball/obstruct another player/exceed the speed limit/show contempt for your neighbour/commit blasphemy'. 'No one may handle the ball except when goalkeeper...etc'. Acting wrongly entails violating such a commandment or infringing such a norm. Setting aside the possibility that there may be unstated exceptions or qualifications, including exceptions not hitherto expressly recognized, to any such commandment or norm, one can see that each necessarily applies to every act performed within a relevant context to which that description properly applies. In that sense, such negative commandments or norms are universal in character.

There may also be commandments or norms that it is natural to express in positive terms, rather than as prohibitions: 'Respect the referee's decisions [in soccer/ rugby/American football].' 'Make an annual return of your income for taxation in the form prescribed by currently valid statutes [in the state of S].' 'Treat your minor children with care love and attention, helping them to develop autonomous moral agency [as a moral person].' 'Worship God and honour Him always' [according to your religion]'. The same character of being contextual and being universal within the context is found in the case of such positive injunctions as in the case of negative ones.

Even in the case of the positive injunctions, one can appropriately apply the terminology of the 'wrong'. The first list was a list of wrong, or wrongful, acts. From the second we can derive a list of wrongful omissions: 'It is wrong to disobey the referee or ignore his decisions.' 'It is wrong to fail to make a tax return annually.' 'It is wrong for parents to neglect the upbringing of their minor children.' 'It is wrong for believers ever to fail to worship and honour God.'

Acts and omissions, then, can be wrong or not-wrong. They are wrong in a context of normative order and, in that context, they are wrong under a description. The description is in terms of logical universals, and whenever a particular act or omission does, or would if carried out, instantiate the universal(s) in question, that act or omission is, for that context, wrong. Wrongness presupposes a context-relevant norm or commandment, but not necessarily an explicit or positively enacted or publicly declared norm or commandment. There may be explicit or implicit exceptions, so that a *prima facie* judgement of the wrongness of an act may be defeasible.[2] But exceptions and grounds for defeasance are themselves generic in character and hence also universalistic in the same way as the norms we have used as examples above.

---

[2] On defeasibility, see N. MacCormick, *Institutions of Law* 163–66 and *Rhetoric and the Rule of Law* (Oxford: Oxford University Press, 2005) 237–53; also R. H. S. Tur 'Defeasibilism', (2001) 21 OJLS 355–68.

When conduct is not wrong, what to do is at the actor's discretion. Provided I am not handling the ball in a game of football, I may choose to pass forward towards the opponents' goal, or to try to dribble the ball past my immediate adversary, or to pass back to my own goalkeeper. All non-wrong options are open to me. Certainly, for any given context there may be a large catalogue of wrongful acts that one may be capable of committing and occasionally at least tempted to commit. But provided that no act or omission you commit or contemplate committing is wrongful in the context, you are necessarily free to do as you choose. You are not necessarily able to do it, not necessarily unimpeded in doing it, but are guilty of no wrong in doing it or trying to do it. We have in this sense 'negative liberty' to act or refrain from acting as we choose, just so long as we do no wrong (which includes avoiding wrongful omissions).[3] Here, this will be called 'normative liberty'. The sphere of normative liberty of action and omission contains every act and omission that is not wrongful under any reasonable description of that act/omission. What that sphere contains in the way of possible acts and omissions depends on the presupposed context, and of course each context defines its own sphere of normative liberty. (From the point of view of soccer, I am neither at liberty nor not at liberty to break the bank at Monte Carlo. Soccer in no way defines or recognizes any such act, either positively or negatively. It is not a possible act in the context of football. Betting on your own side to win or lose in a league competition is, and is prohibited.)

There is a connection between doing something wrong and doing something bad, but 'wrong' and 'bad' are not equivalent concepts or terms. It would indeed be strange to mark as wrong an act that one did not consider in any way bad, and thinking that an act is a very bad thing to do is a paradigmatic reason for deeming it wrong. 'Bad' and 'good' are grading words, and the spectrum from best to better to worse to worst covers the range of grading conceptually open to us on any given scale of valuation. Analytically, one always has reason to prefer the better to the worse, and to prefer good states, acts and outcomes to bad ones. This emerges from the earlier discussion about values.

People are passionate creatures who are also rational valuers. The very idea of acting rationally is intimately connected with values held by the actor. It is rational to try to bring about what seems good, irrational to try to bring about what seems bad. This is so, because in regarding something as good or bad respectively one evinces a view about what is preferable to bring about or to prevent coming to pass, so far as this lies within one's power.

In human experience, however, though there are some unmixed goods and some experiences that seem to us wholly good without any accompanying ills or drawbacks, this is, in experience, relatively rare. In most of our deliberating and acting we are engaged to a greater or lesser extent in the art of compromise. We

---

[3] I. Berlin, 'Two Concepts of Liberty', in his *Four Essays on Liberty* (London: Oxford University Press, 1969) 118–172, on 'negative liberty'.

put up with some of what is bad for the sake of greater good, where it appears that there can be no total elimination of what is bad within the compass of the possible actions among which we deliberate. We have to do, literally, the best we can, acknowledging that unalloyed good is rarely realizable in human affairs. Great difficulty surrounds choices where one can do a very little good, without any adverse concomitants, or far greater good with more attendant evils, but where these seem more than compensated, and the great good seems vastly preferable to the small alternative.

Here is precisely what gives the 'wrong' its special significance. Not everything can be accepted as open to trade-off. Some things that are bad have to be ruled out altogether, excluded from all reasonable deliberation, though temptation may often let one's mind range over the forbidden territory and sometimes the will may be weak. The conceptual point of 'wrong' is to mark off that which is excluded from reasonable deliberation, not that one's actual deliberation is always reasonable by the standards of a given context of discourse. And, of course, one may reject the standards of a particular discourse, and actively embrace the 'wrongs' it condemns, as in the case of persons in the USA who in the ante-bellum period assisted fugitive slaves to escape from the control of their masters.

2 Normative orders and conventions

It is time to reflect further on different discourses, or what we earlier called the 'context' of a judgement about what is wrong. Each such context is an instance of 'normative order'. All sports—e.g., the different kinds of football mentioned above—are forms of normative order. So is the law of a state. So is international law. So are religious codes of behaviour. So is morality, but in an overarching way. Each of these is a domain in which people active in that domain act on the basis of reasons that include consideration of what is right and wrong, in football, under positive law, under international law, according to the true religion, according to morality. The grounds of rightness and wrongness can be formulated as commandments or norms in the way we noted earlier. In institutionalized normative orders, these are often positive norms enunciated and promulgated by a person or body claiming authority to do this, their authority being recognized on some ground or another by other participants.

Morality, however, on at least some conceptions of what it is to be moral, and certainly on the conception advanced here, is non-institutionalized. Yet it is clearly one context of normative judgements, and indeed is the most comprehensive of all, having the whole universe of moral agents for its subjects, not separated out according to difference of preferred sport, or religion, or state-with-its-law. The moral context is the unbounded context, unlike all the others—or so the rest of this book will argue. That it is non-institutionalized, however, does not mean either that it cannot contain a great deal in the way of conventional norms and practices, nor that it ignores the domains of institutionalized orders—far from it. What counts as cheating at football or at chess depends on the rules of the game in question. What (if anything) is wrong with cheating can be answered in the context of the game itself, for it undermines the game when done clandestinely, just as the cheating move would disrupt it if done openly. What is wrong with cheating also raises a moral issue, however, and this is the more fundamental question. This subject is taken up again in the concluding section of Chapter 4.

One strategy to start understanding conventional norms, which I have used elsewhere and still think fruitful, is to think of ways in which people can achieve a kind of ordered co-ordination through the way in which they orient themselves towards each other in some particular aspect of their conduct. *Gulliver's Travels* contains a marvellous imaginary description of a watch written by highly intelligent people who had no such artefacts themselves.[4] They can see the hands on the face of the watch, they can discover that the glass covers them and covers the evenly distributed figures inscribed around the perimeter of the circular surface within. They hear the ticking of the clockwork. They could if they wished open up this 'marvellous engine' and see the gearwheels and spring and gradually work out how the hands are driven.

None of this meticulous observation and description involves or gets its writers close to understanding a watch as a time-measuring device, nor to understanding the time-measurement conventions that make all this possible, reckoned against the construct of a twenty-four hour day, having hours of even length. Now think: How would we explain this measuring business to an ignorant person? How do we explain it to each new generation of children as they grow up?

Again, think of people standing in a line.[5] Sometimes they are standing in a line because they are queuing up for a service or opportunity of some kind. Maybe it is a bus queue, or a queue for a train. Sometimes there are managers or officials ensuring that people take their turn properly. But often there are no such managers or officials, and yet despite their absence people simply form a queue spontaneously and in a self-regulating way. How do we account for that?

The answer is in terms of mutual beliefs of the persons. Each thinks each other is ready to take her or his turn, and to yield to whoever is ahead in the queue. Each thinks this is how he/she and the others ought to act, and thinks the others

[4] 'Out of the right Fob hung a great Silver Chain with a wonderful kind of engine at the Bottom. We directed him to draw out whatever was at the End of the Chain; which appeared to be a Globe, half Silver and half of some transparent metal; for on the transparent Side we saw certain strange figures drawn and thought we could touch them, until we found our Fingers stopped with that lucid Substance. He put this Engine to our Ears which made an incessant noise like that of a Water Mill. And we conjecture that it is either some unknown Animal, or the God that he worships; But we are more inclined to the Latter Opinion, because he assured us...that he seldom did anything without consulting it. He called it his Oracle, and said it pointed out the time for every Action of his life.' See discussion in N. MacCormick *Legal Reasoning and Legal Theory* 2nd edn (Oxford: Clarendon Press, 1994) 275–92.

[5] In N. MacCormick, *Institutions of Law* chs 1 and 2, the queue is a running example of a norm in action, that may be either purely conventional or in other contexts quite highly institutionalized.

think much the same about who ought to go first or next to the point of opportunity. These beliefs can be expressed in gestures in gestures of mutual deference,
and in gestures of, or words of, disapproval, and even in acts of obstruction, when
someone threatens to jump the queue. For each, or for most, of those present
'first come, first served' sums up what is both a pattern of preferred behaviour
and believed to be a pattern of shared preference. Where all or most people have
such beliefs and these are (therefore) well-founded, there is an orderly mounting
of the bus at the bus-stop or approaching the counter for service in the shop. One
kind of order that can exist among humans, and here is an example, is normative order. It exists where all or most people are successfully orientated towards
a common but possibly quite non-explicit pattern of conduct towards each other
as a norm. The same applies, in a rather more complex way, to the case of using a
watch to tell the time, and all the more complicatedly to the idea of using watches
and clocks in conjunction with timetables to run a railway or the classes in a
university.

Implicit in this is that people can have in mind a pattern of conduct that it is
possible for each to observe. They think that all or most others share a common
understanding of the pattern. They are willing to act in accordance with the pattern so long as (most) others do. They expect others to take the same view; each
believes that the others (or most of them) share this conditional belief about what
others will do and share this attitude of approval or disapproval towards their following or violating the pattern.

This is one context in which use of the language of 'right and wrong', 'ought and
ought not', is in place. What each believes (or nearly everyone believes) is that everyone ought to take her or his turn on the basis of 'first come, first served'. What
each believes is that everyone ought to have set their watch according to a common
standard and ought to signify the time according to the 'minutes past/minutes
before the hour' or 'on the hour' for each of the 'hours' marked on the watch. This
comes into play particularly in the context of co-ordinated activities like a programme of university classes, or the keeping of individually made appointments,
or the running of a railway in accordance with a train timetable. What use of the
'ought' and its cognates does, is to appeal to a common norm of this kind, whether
it remains implicit or becomes explicit in some particular context.

The 'ought' or the 'right/wrong' is then the marker for a pattern of conduct
envisaged as a basis of mutual expectation, where each person supposes a common will for conformity and to encourage or even enforce conformity by others.

Someone might object that this kind of preliminary account works all very well
for contexts involving mutual co-ordination to solve 'co-ordination problems',[6]
but this is only one domain of the 'ought' and by no means the most important.

---

[6] D. K. Lewis, *Convention: A Philosophical Study* (Cambridge, MA: Harvard University Press,
1969) esp 5–35; cf G. Postema, 'Co-ordination and Convention at the Foundations of Law', *Journal
of Legal Studies* 11 (1982) 165–89.

Clock-using and queuing are instances of conduct that makes sense only on the basis of common and indeed mutual understandings. I can take my turn only when others are also taking their turn. That I ought to take my turn presupposes that others are doing likewise and would make no sense otherwise.

3 Co-ordinating non-violence

Not using deadly force to attack my neighbour seems a different matter. Refraining from unprovoked violence and murder is always justified, even if no one else seems to see it that way. It makes sense to have and to support norms against rape and murder even if there is no presupposed common pattern of behaviour supported by relevant mutual beliefs. Surely one ought not to kill even if there is no conventional norm against killing? In conditions of chaos and anarchy and deadly mutual violence, a Hobbesian war of all against all, would there not still be good reason to refrain from descending into mayhem oneself? Would there not be good reason to try to maintain a sense of respect for the lives of those others one might be able, if so minded, to hurt or even kill, with the possible exception of absolutely necessary self-defence? If there were not such good reason, how could any civil war ever come to an end, how could reconciliation ever follow conflict?

The answer to these questions has to be one that favours peace. This is so, indeed, for more or less the reasons Hobbes himself gave. We have basic self-regarding reasons to seek peace and try to maintain it, given our need for communal co-existence with others. Our capacity to conceive of the pain of others as though it were our own is a reason not to inflict such pain even though we may not always be capable of self-restraint, or the circumstances of self-defence may make it unreasonable to do so. To secure communal peace or diminution of communal strife is always a rational motive for action, and everyone who reflects upon human life is likely to acknowledge this. These reasons hold good without regard to any suppositions about mutual beliefs among people, or attempts at co-ordination around such beliefs. In this imagined condition of things, one would still be far from able to assert or rely on a common or shared norm against mutual violence, subject to certain exceptions (just punishment, reasonable self-defence).

The context for asserting and relying on a norm against violence would in fact strikingly resemble, or indeed be the same as, that which we envisaged in the pure co-ordination cases. My belief that you believe that you ought not to use violence against me so long as I believe I ought not to use it against you, and act on that belief, can be matched by a like belief on your part. Among several persons each may have essentially the same set of beliefs about all the others. Then they have a common norm against violence. That it is wrong for anyone to use interpersonal violence save in the understood exceptional cases is then a customary or conventional norm among us. Each can appeal to the 'ought not' in dialogue with the

others, and the norm-abiding may be able to join together to convince or if necessary coerce the recalcitrant.

This line of thought in no way presupposes or involves appeal to any kind of
implausible 'contract' scenario, and that is just as well. For contracts presuppose
norms about trust and reliability, as will be seen in the next chapter. People who
had not yet got round to accepting mutual restraints on violence would not be
likely to be in a position to develop any conception of a contract or even of a
unilateral promise. Even if they were, why would they keep it? Thomas Hobbes's
scenario of the war of all against all may be a useful heuristic for considering what
are the strong reasons we have for securing or sustaining relative peace among
humans. But his suggested way out of the difficulty is less attractive, and attempts
to water the 'social contract' down into a mere 'idea of reason', as Kant and his
later followers attempted, seem like hopeless question begging. If a real contract
in these circumstances is inconceivable, why would an unreal contract in circumstances of like inconceivability be of any greater use to us?

It may be recalled that Hobbes in effect used the apparent impossibility of the
contract to introduce the device of the sovereign. 'Covenants without swords are
but words'—any agreement among participants in the totally warlike state of
nature would be of no value to any of them, for each would violate it whenever
he/she could with impunity. So everybody must agree with every other that each
shall surrender all his/her natural right to the sovereign, entrusting to the sovereign the task of upholding the social contract and keeping the peace by use of the
now-collective force of the society. The sovereign is thus instituted by the contract
but is not a party to it. Hence the sovereign is not bound by any of its terms. Only
such a fully-empowered and thus unlimited government, argued Hobbes, could
succeed in first establishing peace and then governing in accordance with the
precepts of a law of nature that would otherwise have been no better than a pious
wish-list of good behaviours. Real laws among human beings are then nothing
other than the enforced commands of such a sovereign. 'Ought' counts only as a
marker for such real laws.

A part of the perennial appeal of this line of thought may go back to this very
issue of the 'ought', which is a long-standing puzzle in practical philosophy. Once
you have commands backed by powerful sanctions, the question, 'What does it
mean, this ought?' seems to receive a simple and effective answer. Sovereign commands tell us what the ruler says we *shall* do. Why should we do this? We have to,
to avoid the sanction threatened, and we have to, since we acknowledge that this
sovereign legal order is our only alternative to endless war. The sovereign's is the
only will that can be imputed to the whole polity, and as members of that polity
we are ourselves therefore participants in the common will.

But why thus have recourse to what is either a fictitious will, or a merely
self-regarding account of what ought to be done (obey, and avoid the risk of sanction)? The simpler account says that the raw self-regarding and other-regarding
motives that humans have for getting out of universal mutual violence (if such

a disaster ever occurs) themselves show reasons for seeking a new common understanding among persons. What is needed is to cultivate relevant mutual beliefs among those who are willing to give peace a chance. For them, there is a common 'ought' that no one is to use violence against others except in exceptional cases, and each is aware of others who share the mutuality of this belief. This is for them a good reason for peaceful conduct and for developing peace-preserving schemes. It does not, perhaps, bring everyone within its ambit in the sense of willing participation and co-operation in a shared mutual belief. But those who hold that no one may use violence need not restrict the range of application of their norm to the set of people who actively participate in the required mutual beliefs. They can hold to a belief in it universally, even though they know that some of those to whom they hold it applicable do not in turn acknowledge its binding character. In this one respect, moral commitments of this sort are not so very much different from the positive laws of almost any state you can think of or even imagine.

Where does the will come into this? The answer goes back to the idea of people equipped with reason and will in combination. They wish to act for reasons, and are aware of motives that rationally govern their action. They have a will to act as it is reasonable to act. Such a will can surely embrace these 'oughts' that are grounded in mutual belief about patterns for conduct. These are highly significant among the other-regarding motives we can have for acting and abstaining from action. Many fortunate human beings may live in circumstances in which a norm (or several interconnected norms) against violence is (are) relatively taken-for-granted. For them, it is an almost taken-for-granted side-constraint on other plans they may consider laying and pursuing. But there are contexts, for example that of Northern Ireland between 1968 and 2008, where the project of trying to create conditions for mutual trust and mutual non-violence in and between the communities that composed the larger society was an arduous and demanding task. It was one to which many reasonable people gave huge amounts of time and effort over many years. Peace among people is always an ideal for humans. It is in many local circumstances a different matter to achieve a condition of mutually acknowledged positive norms that condemn violence and that everyone respects (or even that most people respect).

What is special about the situation in which commonly acknowledged norms exist among people is that they can be the ground of mutual, or reciprocal, demands. If I call upon you not to attack me or defame me, what I consider to justify my demand against you would justify exactly the same demand by you against me if the roles were reversed. It is just the same as when I demand that you wait your turn in the bus queue. We have both self-regarding and sympathy-based other-regarding reasons for seeking and supporting societal situations in which mutual or reciprocal demands are possible and are considered legitimate. What I ought to do for you is whatever you could justifiably demand my doing should I fail to do it unasked. It is not so much the case that we have a common will as that we have wills that are mutually cross-referring and reciprocal. When that is so, I have to go along with what you demand, or (with however ill a grace) acknowledge your condemnation of any fault on my part, and in the converse case you would be in the same position.

The idea that conduct by one person toward another can be 'obligatory', not simply beneficial or desirable, depends, it seems, on this concept of the justified demand. Or is it the other way round? Are demands for a certain line of conduct justified in case the conduct is obligatory, with some ulterior account of obligation remaining to be elucidated?

4 Ideal morality

One possible way forward, of the broadly Kantian kind introduced in Chapter 1, would be to suggest that we have to go beyond actual norms currently or possibly endorsed by people in this or that social setting. We should think instead of an ideal order, that would suit the nature of humans as we have assumed it to be. The issue is not what demands people actually make of each other, and actually think justified. The issue concerns a comprehensive ideal order such that everyone would be subject to norms of conduct that all could fully endorse as fairly accounting for everyone's interests and ideals. 'Act as if the maxim of your action were to become through your will a universal law of nature.'[7] True obligation attaches to acts mandated by such an ideal normative order. The demands of our fellow humans that are justified demands are ones that would satisfy that test.

Kant's case for this thesis rests on the view that a being with free will could be satisfied with (and bound by) nothing less than this ideal normative order. For freedom of the will implies acting as a non-caused cause—one causes events in the world, but one's own free decisions are not themselves caused by events in the world. This he thought conceivable only if the content of the will is universal and law-like—the normative laws set by the free will have to match the universality and exceptionless character of the natural laws of physical causation. Only the ideal set of norms that everyone could freely assent to could possess this universal character, and thus be capable of being willed as a law for all, by all.

Like many people, I find this line of thought an inspiring ideal as the basis for a critique of actual moral practices and social institutions. As an account of our actual sense of obligation, or of the judgement of right and wrong, it seems too abstract. It dodges the issue of motivation by simply asserting the freedom of the will and the necessity for the possessor of the free will to will just thus and so, and in no other way. Whatever we think the contents of our will may be, it turns out that, to the extent we are practically rational, we actually will what we would will if we reflected long enough and hard enough. This is implausible, not because

---

[7] This is the second formulation of the first statement by Kant of the 'categorical imperative'. See H. J. Paton, *The Moral Law* (London: Hutchinson, revised edn., 1958) 84.

the ideal is implausible taken strictly in ideal terms, but because its use in the present context merges actual and ideal and blurs the distinction between them. Meantime, we should reflect on whether any more naturalistic account of the problem before us promises to help solve it. The problem, it will be recalled, is the chicken-and-egg one of the priority question: Is the idea of a justified demand the idea that accounts for obligation, or is obligation what makes certain demands be justified—and, if so, how to account for obligations?

5 Turning to Adam Smith

Adam Smith's *Theory of Moral Sentiments*[8] is a good starting place in searching for an answer less abstract than that of Kant, and more grounded in our earthly nature. As already noted, both Adam Smith and David Hume sought to root our understanding of morality in a naturalistic account of human passions and sentiments. Both gave close attention to the idea of 'sympathy' ('empathy' might be a more accurate contemporary term for what they had in mind). Things that happen to human beings, and, in particular, things that happen because of the actions of other human beings, are of great interest and concern to them. They feel pleasure and pain and many more complex passions in response to the events that affect them, and indeed according to the way their own doings affect other people. They can also, however, be affected by the perception of others' feelings. I wince as the blow falls on your head. I cower behind my steering wheel when I see your car heading apparently inexorably for a head-on collision. I feel distressed at the sight and sound of someone else's weeping, especially if I know, for example, that she laments a child drowned by a tsunami, or caught in some other catastrophe. Most 'western' human beings who saw it in real time, or even those who saw only recorded video-clips, the sight of the aircraft crashing into the Trade Towers in New York on September 11, 2001, followed by the engulfing of the buildings in fire, and the sight of people leaping to their death to avoid incineration, to be immediately accompanied by a roller-coaster of vicarious emotions. Shock and pain felt along with aircraft passengers and tower occupants. Horror that this could happen in a great city. Then anger at the perpetrators.

Smith found in sentiments such as these the foundations of our capacity for moral judgement. Moral judgement, he argued, is based on a sense of approval or disapproval of our own conduct and that of others. Since approval and disapproval are sentiments of our own that can move us to action, the practical character of morality is sufficiently guaranteed by its having this sentimental basis. The acts I consider it obligatory for me to do are those I approve of my doing, where failure to do them would arouse my own self-disapproval. The shared sympathies

---

[8] A. Smith *The Theory of Moral Sentiments* (D. D. Raphael and A. L. MacFie eds) (Oxford: Clarendon Press, 1976).

of humankind make it probable that you will, or would if you were aware of all that is relevant, approve and disapprove similarly (and everyone else, too). Moral motivation is a matter of avoiding disapproval, both by the agent and by others in the vicinity.

But how do we get from sympathy with others' pain and distress to moral approval and disapproval? According to Smith, this comes about through reflection upon raw sentiments. One person's act that causes harm to another gives the other pain. That the pain arises from another person's act, especially if the act appears to have been deliberately aimed at causing pain, causes anger on the sufferer's part. S/he is angry with the other person. S/he resents this treatment, and resentment motivates retaliation, hitting back, at least where this is possible—or it leaves one with a frustrated wish to have hit back, where it is not. Conversely, good deeds please us, and pleasure in the case where someone confers a benefit, apparently intentionally, amounts to gratitude, and gratitude motivates at least thanks and possibly future favourable acting towards the benefactor.

Each human being is an observer of the social scene as well as a participant in it. Each has social impulses that lead her/him to seek to live on good terms rather than terms of hostility and enmity with their fellows. The capacity for sympathy extends not only to the feeling of the pain, say, at the impact of the plane on the tower. It extends also to the resentment felt by those directly affected. Not merely do you desire to hit back at whoever so violently hurt you, but I share in that sentiment too. This is not a matter of reflection, in the first instance. It is simply a matter of basic human psychology that we can and do share immediately in the feelings of others. The capacity for sympathy is built into the social character of humans. We can be sociable because we can sympathize. We have sympathy because we live socially, not in mutual isolation.

Pain shared in sympathy is, however, less acute than the original pain of the sufferer. Sympathetically felt sentiments mirror first-order sentiments, but with less vividness. This can give rise to an interpersonal sense of proportionality in reaction. An incident that has enraged you, who were the target of malevolence, arouses sympathetic anger in me, not blind rage. This is a fact of which all humans come to be aware. It has an effect in mitigating reactions to hurtful actions. Those who are direct victims wish to respond in ways that others will go along with. They have to moderate their initial response to bring it in line with that of a spectator. Original and sympathetic sentiments can thus to a degree converge, and can provide a basis for a suitably measured response, probably in the form of a lawfully administered punishment. But punishments also cause pain and we sympathize with the victim of the pain. A contemporary audience watching a re-enactment of the decapitation of a traitor or alleged traitor in the days of the Stuarts or Tudors feels a shock at the impact of the axe—and, perhaps for the great majority, an abiding sense of sympathy with the sufferer. Even if punishment was merited, this is over-punishment. Instead of sharing the sense of justice done, such as must have been desired by those who devised and inflicted the punishment, we have a sense of injustice for the excessive violence or barbarity of the response.

Thus sympathy can provide a measure both to account for a response to injurious conduct and to account for an upper limit on the appropriateness of a given response to that injurious conduct.

To come to a fully moral appreciation of these matters, Smith calls for two further corrections. First, human beings are much involved with each other, they have family and friends and associates, and this is true of nearly everyone. No one is naturally impartial where friends and family are involved. Likewise, when enemies or adversaries are involved. We sometimes feel *Schadenfreude* and gloat over the harms done to our enemies, rather than feel sympathy with their affliction. If there is to be any objective moral judgement among us, beyond the very narrow range of family and friends, it must be on the basis of a cultivated impartiality. We either must find an actually impartial spectator and put the case to that person as vividly as we can, or must cultivate a capacity for abstraction from our own partisan involvement. We can make ourselves be impartial, or act on the basis of our best efforts at a kind of feigned impartiality. That is the first corrective to the response of mere sympathy.

The second concerns knowledge. The motives and intentions from which and with which a person acts towards another have a considerable bearing on our response to the act, and to the person acting. There is all the difference in the world between a pure accident that occurs despite a person's best efforts to prevent it, and the same physical damage done by careless acts, by reckless action, and by acts done with the intention to do this harm. Perhaps only the actor and (given the human capacity for self-deception) perhaps not even the actor can be totally well informed about all the circumstances of action and activity. However, as moral judges of our own conduct and that of other people we have to seek to be as honestly well informed as possible.

We can construct our judgements by the model of an ideal and impartial spectator. Right and wrong are matters of which we judge, by filtering immediate responses of the sentiments by reference to the sentiments we think imputable to somebody situated as we are but possessed of perfect impartiality and complete knowledge. What then leads us into attempting to cultivate 'ideal spectator' sympathies, rather than simply act on the basis of raw feelings? The answer Smith gives is in terms of our social character. We find it disagreeable to have reactions that are out of keeping with those of others. The 'ideal spectator' response to an incident, because it is impartial, and is well informed, can be everyone's response. To sustain fellow-feeling and solidarity in a moral community, everyone has reason to accept the spectator's response and adjust her or his own raw feelings accordingly. This is so, even though one who adopts the position of the ideal spectator implicitly accepts that her or his own immediate interest will not unquestionably prevail in the dilemma under consideration. At this point, it seems, we move beyond simply felt disapproval or approval to a judgement of what is wrong or improper, or right and proper. Being fully aware of the complex feelings that make a case morally significant, we come to a judgement about an appropriate equilibrium among them, and that is our judgement of what is right or wrong in the case.[9]

Not everyone can achieve a capacity for judging or a high degree of skill in moral judgement of this kind. It calls for education, reflection, and some degree of leisure from unremitting toil. Those who have it can use it as the basis to inculcate simple rules into the minds of those unable to achieve this; children, certainly, and (in Smith's day and Smith's opinion) members of the labouring poor. Those who have been taught well in childhood can learn in adulthood how to progress in good judgement and moral wisdom. Those who have made some progress will be able to identify those who have made greatest progress and are truly wise in moral matters, and can use them as models for their own self-improvement.

One special virtue is called for in the development of the mature moral perspective as Smith perceives this. It is the virtue of *self-command*. Being properly in command of oneself involves restraining oneself from hasty or impulsive responses to the unfolding drama of daily life. It involves a capacity to stand back and consult 'the man within the breast', the ideal impartial spectator, before rushing to judgement. It involves a firm determination to respond as severely or as leniently to events as sound judgement dictates, not as the cry of the mob or the surge of fellow-feeling may prompt in the heat of a heated moment. The fully mature moral person starts from sympathy with all fellow-humans, but refines judgement by attempting rigorous impartiality and maximal self-knowledge, together with attention to whatever can be found out of the facts of any matter coming under moral scrutiny. S/he then relies on the judgement of the ideal impartial spectator as s/he conceives this to be and acts on her/his own judgement, not deferring to the say-so of anyone else.

One decided merit of this view of Smith's is that it involves no assumption about a pre-existing or complete moral rule-book. Smithian moral judgement starts with a specific problem situation and the raw emotions it evokes, as well as the sympathetic responses that are secondarily evoked. So far from forming judgement on the supposition that some rule or norm already applies, self-commanding agents make their own judgements and take their own decisions on the strength of them. According to Smith, moral rules, or 'rules of natural law' (a phrase Kant countenanced, but Smith did not), are rules that we gradually

---

[9] It is not clear to me that Smith would approve of this reading of his theory of 'moral sentiments' at this point. It does, however, seem obvious that the filtering of felt responses by appeal to an ideal impartial spectator necessarily involves an active judgement, not a merely passive response to the ebb and flow of emotions. Anyway, I wish to develop his theory in this way (if it is a development) or to adopt his theory (if it is not). I acknowledge a huge debt for my understanding of Smith to Tom D. Campbell in his *Adam Smith's Science of Morals* (London : Allen and Unwin, 1971) and to Charles L. Griswold in his *Adam Smith and the Virtues of Enlightenment* (Cambridge: Cambridge University Press, 1999). I impute to neither of these distinguished authors endorsement of my reading of Smith.

work out by induction and generalization from frequently recurring problem situations and from the judgements one arrives at in such cases. Examples might be cases such as wilful deceit, or physical assault, or breach of a promise, or harm negligently caused by one person to another. Considered judgement always has priority over rules, however, in the sense that when one's inductively established rule supports one answer but one's considered judgement supports a different answer in a practical dilemma, it is the rule that has to be revised or abandoned, not the considered judgement.

Even for his own purposes, however, Smith's theory of moral sentiments does not cover the whole range of morally significant issues. In his *Lectures on Jurisprudence*[10] Smith makes a distinction between 'natural' and 'adventitious' rights. The former concern issues of personal and bodily integrity, where no particular societal form seems to be presupposed in the objection people have to wanton violence, wholesale deception, and the like. Adventitious rights are those that come to be ascribed to persons under conventional (normally positive-legal) rules. Central among adventitious rights are rights of property and similar or ancillary rights. No such rights can exist except if there are already some rules about allocation of property in a community. These, it might be said, are grand instances of rules that are aimed at solving co-ordination problems, in particular, the problem of co-ordinating access to physical resources. The justice of any particular distribution of property rights is clearly a matter of moral concern, but 'spectator' reasoning can contribute nothing to discussion of this. Certainly, once property rights exist and people own particular things or the produce of particular tracts of land, the resentment of property-holders in the face of acts of wilful theft or trespass can indeed be filtered through the spectator judgement. This judgement enables one to reaffirm the owner's right to reparation or restitution, and to justify punishment of thieves and violent trespassers. But what justifies the property regime itself cannot be brought successfully within Smith's theory of moral sentiments—it is in his jurisprudence and his political economy that he deals, at least partially, with this issue.[11]

Here, like his friend and forerunner David Hume, Smith is driven back into a kind of rule-utilitarianism. In different phases of societal development different forms of property come to be recognized, and, in his view, commercial society as it was emerging in his time was an order in which market interactions would in ideal circumstances help ensure that the overall lot of members of the society would come to be as prosperous as it could be. Any critique of property institutions has to be in terms of some overall improvement of the general wellbeing, not

[10] A. Smith *Lectures on Jurisprudence* (R. L. Meek, D. D. Raphael, and P. G. Stein eds) (Oxford: Clarendon Press, 1978), 399–401 on 'adventitious rights'.
[11] See A. Smith *Lectures on Jurisprudence*, and *An Inquiry into the Nature and Causes of the Wealth of Nations* (R. H. Campbell and A. S. Skinner eds with W. B. Todd) (Oxford: Clarendon Press, 1976).

some particular gripe about the apparently unfair working of one element of the whole property system.

6 Strengths and limits of sentimentalism

Whatever may be the best account of moral normativity and moral obligation, there must surely be a parallel moral psychology that explains how human beings come to be able to frame moral judgements at all. Such an account will have to show how feelings and reason come together in motivating our judgements, our decisions and our actions. We can be confident that wholly dispassionate creatures would be unable to comprehend human beings or to construct a normative order within which humans could live at all. If nobody cared about being hurt, why would it be necessary to have moral norms or legal rules about hurting people or about assault and battery? For the same reason, people who had no sense of sympathy with the feelings of others would be apparently unable to form their own moral judgements, though perhaps able to go along with any rules that were publicly enunciated to the extent that their self-interest dictated. So-called 'psychopaths' seem to have exactly such a disability in respect of fellow-feeling, moral judgement, and moral action.

Certainly, a causal account of how we come to have certain judgements would not itself say anything about the validity or soundness of the judgements. To know in what conditions humans acquire a capacity to understand and perform mathematical calculations is not to explain which mathematical calculations are correct and which erroneous. The issue about the content of sound moral judgements is different from the issue of our having or acquiring a capacity to form them—except, of course, if such 'judgements' are no judgements at all, but only expressions of emotion. Among many objections to purely expressive theories of morality a particularly telling one concerns the possibility of disagreement. If you feel cold or angry while I feel warm or calm, we do not disagree about anything. We just have different feelings. If you think we should light the fire, while I think you should simply put on more clothes, we disagree. If you consider yourself justifiably angry about some bad deed by our friend Bill, while I think he did not act very badly at all and mild reproof is the most that is called for, we disagree. Such judgements are formed in response to our feelings, but are not simple reports of them.

Moreover, what is attractive in the Smithian account is the way it facilitates the move over from understanding the feelings people have to explaining a basis for the judgements they make. For the 'spectator' perspective effectively universalizes the initial mere reaction to an incident. What I immediately feel, either as victim or by sympathy with the victim, is, so to say, re-calibrated in accordance with an imagined common point of view, impartial between doer, sufferer, and interested or disinterested bystander. The right response is the one that everyone can go along with (not that everyone necessarily does, as a matter of fact—disproportionate grief and anger are daily phenomena on the human scene).

Smith was a forerunner of Kant, and, at least indirectly, was one of the targets of Kant's rejection of empiricism in ethics (Hume was the main target). They have very different theories, and different beliefs about the role of theory. Nevertheless, it is interesting to see what happens if one tries to re-state Smith's idea in a somewhat more Kant-like way. Had he been in a position to read Kant's *Groundwork*, he surely could not have failed to be in some measure impressed by it. In a way, what Kant does is to transform the 'golden rule' (of which, however, he was himself somewhat dismissive), that is to say the rule that you should act towards others as you would wish them to act towards you, if you were in their situation and they in yours. To the extent that one can formulate the 'maxim' of the action that you are minded to take towards those others, the question arises: could that be a rule for everybody? If it could, then the golden rule is satisfied, if not, not. There is not here a supposition that there is a pre-existing moral code-book or ideal code of 'natural law'. On the contrary, the issue is whether we can convert our inclination to act into a possible rule of action, that everyone could act on as a common rule. Only if one can will one's maxim universally in this way is it right to act according to this inclination. The question then remains an open one on what footing we decide what we 'can will as a universal law of nature') that is, as a rule for everybody. Kant was very hostile to the idea that at this point it would be appropriate to investigate the emotions of those affected. Emotions are contingent and variable, and belong to the animal nature of human beings. Morality concerns reason and universality, not emotion and contingency.

Again, one must acknowledge that it is controversial just how stringently rationalistic Kant intended to be on this point. On this, since the present work is not essentially a work of exegesis, I do not wish to get involved in argument. The aim here is to establish what seems to be the truth about our capacity for moral judgement and indeed for the moral life. The case to be made is only that the truth lies somewhere in the middle ground between Kant's and Smith's ideas as I have expounded them here (perhaps over-simply in each case). One may learn from one's predecessors as much by adapting their ideas as by attempting to adopt them in prefect exactitude.

7 A Smithian categorical imperative

Let us therefore imagine something that never happened. Imagine Smith re-thinking the 'impartial spectator' theory and using his insights to give a revised account of Kant's categorical imperative, one that properly allows for the way in which ordinary people come to moral judgements in the context of their interaction with others and their mutual reactions. The question would be whether the moment of judgement in the 'spectator' argument could be represented through some variant on the 'categorical imperative' propounded by Kant. To achieve that, one would have to distil a 'categorical imperative' out of the materials found in Smith's argument. It does not seem too puzzling to do this. Here is a possible version of such a categorical imperative

'Enter as fully as you can into the feelings of everyone directly involved in or affected by an incident or relationship, and impartially form a maxim of judgement about what is right that all could accept if they were committed to maintaining mutual beliefs setting a common standard of approval and disapproval among themselves.'

That then leads on to a subsidiary imperative:

'Act in accordance with that impartial judgement of what it is right to do in respect of the given incident or relationship'.

Henceforward, I shall call this construct the 'Smithian categorical imperative', and shall adopt it myself on the grounds of its attractiveness, whether or not it is a fair portrayal of Smith's own ideas, and whether or not a Kantian purist could extend to it a moment's credence.

Surely it does offer a very attractive way forward. It creates a comprehensible linkage between feeling, judgement, decision, and action. We start with bare feelings, we reflect, we judge, we decide, we act. That feelings are specifically taken into account makes this more not less attractive as a putative 'law of nature'. Nothing could be willed as a 'universal law of (human) nature' that did not accommodate our emotional as well as our rational character from the ground floor up.

It is a further point that nothing here would mandate a flat unchanging standard of judgement *sub specie aeternitatis*. If we take seriously the condition that moral judgements hold good among persons who are 'committed to . . . maintaining a common standard of approval and disapproval among themselves', this will enable us to note that times and societies change. Hence, what is a tolerable or even taken-for-granted common point of view in one generation can come to be seen in a very different light in another. Smith has a taken-for-granted view of the rightness of capital punishment for grave crimes—and even, sometimes, on merely utilitarian grounds, as in the case of the army sentry who fell asleep on his post in time of peace, and was executed for it. Recent intergenerational differences about sexual orientation and homosexual conduct are another obvious illustration. This categorical imperative is indeed categorical and universal in form, but the concrete judgements it would mandate are contextually variable in ways that ring true and seem intuitively right.

Another attractive aspect of the Smithian categorical imperative is that it focuses on judging rather than legislating. Kant prescribes our acting as though we were universal legislators making or confirming a law for everybody. But we are not, and there are great difficulties in conceptualizing the activity of this ideal law-maker. Speaking from relatively transient experience as a law-maker

(I was a MEP 1999–2004), I would say that the legislative process is at some considerable remove from pure moral deliberation. It involves arguments between individuals and between parties (also within parties). It calls for compromises and then compromises upon compromises, and then finally there is a vote on a text which is nobody's ideal text, but the best that can be put together at the time in question. When it is adopted (if it is) there is a minority—and often a substantial minority—in the legislature that votes against it. None of these features seems to me to be regrettable. Pluralistic democratic political systems generate just such processes. However, as a model for personal moral deliberation, it seems far from the mark.

Within the legal realm, the judicial rather than the legislative branch of government affords a more credible parallel for moral deliberation—deliberation which, it will be admitted, typically reaches its conclusion in judgement rather than in lawmaking. 'Moral judgement' is by no means a misnomer. While one should be wary of pressing too closely the analogy between what the judge in a law court does and what a person resolving a moral dilemma does, we can also attend to genuine similarities. Dilemmas are situations in which, we have in the end to do something. Even inaction has consequences, so we do one thing or another or do nothing, and all three possibilities have their effects and possibly some longer-run consequences whose probability we can quite realistically assess at the time of deliberation. The moral agent is thus faced with the need to come to a judgement—what is it right to do, or best to do in the circumstances in which she finds herself? The point of the judgement is to facilitate decision—'so that is what I'll do', followed sooner or later by actually doing that thing rather than an alternative (not all decisions are for immediate execution).

Judgements of this kind are not made in a vacuum, as if everything had to be worked out from scratch every time. We are aware of former judgements of our own that tackled similar problems (and we can reflect now on the quality of the decisions and actions that then seemed right—do they still seem so?) Especially if we have consulted friends and colleagues about our problem, we will also have some awareness of the kinds of judgements others have made or would make were they in our shoes. They may have drawn to our attention, or we may be all too clearly aware, that people of our acquaintance regard the matter in issue as being covered by an oft-stated rule or principle ('Always tell the truth'; 'One ought to treat everyone with due respect'). It may be a rule or principle we have somewhat unthinkingly relied on in the past where no obvious difficulty surrounded the issue before us, it may even be one of our own Smith-like inductive generalizations from previous judgements. Impartiality is an important virtue to cultivate in reaching moral judgements. Everyone is only too likely to have a bias in their own favour, and it is well known how easily one can fall into the trap of making special exceptions for oneself.

None of this exactly replicates the situation of a judge in the high court of this or that jurisdiction or state. But there is a real similarity in the way one may find oneself reflecting on 'precedents' from one's own and others' experience. One may draw analogies with and distinctions from other decisions previously reached, even sometimes consciously 'overruling' a previous judgement, even if it is now too late to reverse the effects of what one did in time past. One reflects on rules and principles that are relevant, even though these are at best pretty fragmentary, and there is no authoritative legislature to make such rules binding. Moreover, one has to reach one's own interpretation of their meaning and relevance to the situation that lies before one. Crucially, one seeks to be impartial in weighing different persons' interests as one's decision and action will or may affect them.

It is not so much that the moral agent is the law court judge writ small. The converse is nearer the truth. It is more plausible to think that the good moral agent is the model that well-designed judicial systems seek to institutionalize. Legal judgement is moral judgement writ large, but with specialities that arise from the large writing. Judicial institutions have to enshrine formal safeguards for impartiality and for fidelity to official rules of law, and much else besides. This counter-weighs to some extent the risks of abuse of the power judges wield, including uses of coercion and punishment that lie (rightly) beyond the scope of ordinary moral decision-making. (For two specific examples of judgements worked out both in moral and in legal terms, see Chapter 10.)

8 What about autonomy?

The considerations we have reviewed do indeed argue in favour of a 'judgement-oriented' rather than a 'legislation-oriented' version of the categorical imperative. But then, what becomes of autonomy? Kant and his followers rejoice in the idea that the free moral agent is a 'law unto herself/himself'. The law binds us because it is we who make it under the constraint of being able to will the maxim of our action as a universal law of nature.

In fact, the judgement-oriented version fully accommodates autonomy. You have to reach your own judgement of what to do. Others sometimes advise you, but their advice, however helpful, is not binding. Sometimes others can force your hand, but then you are not author of your own action—no decision was made by you on the basis of your own judgement. At most, you could be blamed for having let yourself get into a position in which you were exposed to such coercion. You may have regard to 'precedents' and to 'rules' or 'principles', but these are not binding on account of any external force. Your attention to them is a matter of your own integrity as a decision-maker, your own need to view this decision as compatible with a whole way of life. Moreover, the way of life has a context. 'Enter as fully as you can into the feelings of everyone directly involved in or affected by an incident or relationship, and impartially form a maxim of judgement about what is right that all could accept if they were committed to maintaining mutual beliefs setting a common standard of approval and disapproval among themselves.' You have to take full responsibility for your judgements and decisions, and this is a responsibility you cannot off-load or dump on to someone else.

The concept of 'being a law unto oneself' originates from a phrase in St Paul's *Letter to the Romans* in the early seventeenth century translation given in the 'King James' Bible, or 'Authorized Version'. Paul picked up a relatively commonplace theme from ancient philosophy and early discussions of natural law, and drew this to the attention of his addressees, people steeped in the Jewish tradition of revealed law as this was being re-conceptualized by early Christians. The Gentiles, he said, never received the revelation of the Mosaic laws. Yet for all their notorious badness, they were not completely anarchic, not bad through and through. They behaved as though they had the law within themselves, in an imperfect way, though no revelation had been given (yet) to them.

'For when the Gentiles, who have not the law, do by nature the things contained in the law, these are a law unto themselves, which showeth the works of the law written in their hearts; their conscience also bearing them witness, and their thoughts in the meanwhile accusing or else excusing one another.'

It seems to me that the translation here may be a little questionable. It might have been better to say that they are 'the law' unto themselves, not just 'a law'. For clearly St Paul makes here the assumption of a revealed divine law, the standard of all sound human judgement. That is what the Gentiles find 'written in their hearts'.[12] This is not the place, however, to engage in amateurish biblical exegesis. The point is that it is in their judgements and decisions, their acting according to conscience, that Paul finds evidence of the law-like disposition with which they act. I am 'the law unto myself' or (in contemporary idiom) 'I am my own law' to the extent that I judge my conduct in a principled way and seek to sustain some coherence in judgement and conduct over time, having regard both to precedent and to principle. The kind of autonomy that is possessed by the person who seeks to exercise self-command, and to judge, and decide in the way mandated by the Smithian categorical imperative, is the very autonomy that seems worth asserting. This in fact seems to capture well our capability to act and to judge each for herself/himself, while maintaining, at least in aspiration, shared maxims of judgement as common standards of (dis-)approval, not a set of solitudes or some grand but self-justified solipsism.

Wherever well-understood co-ordination norms have emerged in some societal context, there is every reason why a Smithian moral judge would normally seek to judge and act compatibly with these. Using the twenty-four hour clock in

---

[12] The *New English Bible*, though it omits the sonorous phrase 'a law unto themselves' sounds more clearly in contemporary ears: 'When Gentiles who do not possess the law carry out its precepts by the light of nature, then, although they have no law, they are their own law, for they display the effect of the law inscribed on their hearts. Their conscience is called as witness, and their own thoughts argue the case on either side, against them or even for them....' *Romans* 2, 14–15.

making appointments and catching trains, or simply taking your turn in a queue that has formed at a bus stop or a theatre box-office is something that calls for much reflection and deliberation. But disrupting expectations, or disowning mutual beliefs, except if there is some very strong countervailing reason in favour of doing so, is apt to give rise to a certain resentment, and in the absence of some clear reason this resentment is well-justified.

It seems that the problem upon which this chapter centred is amenable to solution. To find yourself in a situation in which some act can justifiably be demanded of you is to be in a position that is either covered by a conventional rule or that is open to judgement under the categorical imperative in the Smithian version of it. Where it would properly be judged wrong on your part to fail or refuse to do a certain act or refrain from a certain other act, then it is obligatory that you so act or abstain. It is sometimes questionable what the proper judgement would be, in any difficult dilemma with strong reasons telling in favour of incompatible courses of action. To reach a conclusion safely, you should (if time and social circumstances permit) deliberate openly with other people, especially those most affected, and should be ready to account for the factors that lead to your final judgement. As a person of self-command, or an autonomous agent, it can only be your own judgement that you apply in coming to a decision and acting on it. Sometimes this can feel lonely and unpopular, but persons of independent mind have to put up with that.

What if you come to a certain judgement, but cannot steel yourself to go through with the action it favours? Perhaps the weight of what you think is popular opinion, or peer-group opinion, scares you off, and you decide to go along with an opinion you truly consider misguided or downright wrong. In one sense, this is still your decision, and you are answerable for it; but it is not your authentic will. What this shows is not that there is no motive to judge or to act morally, but only that the motive is not always strong enough. The reason for doing what would be mandated by the categorical imperative is an ideal one, that of life in a community in which a fair and authentic consensus could prevail. Strength of self-command is what one needs if one is to remain faithful to that ideal. But not everyone has always sufficient such strength. Sometimes, there may be supporting self-regarding motives that help to keep us on the right road, but this is not always so. Sometimes they pull the other way, and indeed sometimes prevail in that direction. It is all down to self-command in the end.

4

Questions of Trust

1 Lying and deceit—betraying trust

That telling lies is wrong few people doubt. Dishonesty is a vice according to almost any popular conception of morality. There is usually no need for reasons to back up such an obvious opinion. Nevertheless, in the context of an inquiry into practical reason it may be worth giving some attention to the questions what if any reasons seem convincing in this matter.

To tell a lie is to address a false statement to another person knowing that it is false or not believing that it is true, or being reckless as to its truth or falsity. The circumstances must be such that the other person regards the statement as seriously made (not in jest, or in a game of 'let's pretend' or in the context of some form of openly acknowledged fiction, or in a context in which the addressee's interest in the matter is wholly illegitimate). Indeed, the speaker must intend the statement seriously, or at least realize that the addressee or addressees will reasonably assume that it is being made seriously.

The suggested conditions have the effect of linking the concept of lying to that of deceit (though of course one can also be deceived by ruses and gestures, not only by false statements). A person to whom a lie is addressed is at risk of being deceived, that is, of being deliberately led into a false belief. This may have adverse consequences, sometimes very serious ones. Even apart from adverse consequences that result from the addressee's acting detrimentally on the basis of the false belief, the very fact of suffering deceit arouses resentment of a kind that would attract 'impartial spectator' endorsement. At a deep level, no one wants to entertain false beliefs, so it is an injury to be led into them.

Let us consider why this should be so. First, it is necessary to consider in what circumstances it is possible to deceive somebody by lying to them. The two speakers must share a language, in the sense of being competent speakers of and hearers of sentences in the language, perhaps by virtue of both being native speakers, but not necessarily so, for language learners are also exposed to being deceived, indeed are particularly exposed to it. In some minimal conception of community, both must belong to the same language community, as a condition for there being any possible linguistic communication between them. Secondly, the addressee must be in a position of reposing some trust in the speaker. Somebody who mistrusts someone else has no reason to believe, indeed typically does not believe, what that other says—certainly not simply on the basis of the person's say-so. Thirdly, the addressee must be (relatively) ignorant about the subject under discussion, and must for some reason regard the speaker as better informed on the subject. One has no reason to believe what another person has to say on a given topic unless one has some ground for supposing that the other person does know about it, at least knows more than the party of the first part. Thus, in a minimal sense, a person has to be in some way an authority for the other person about the topic in issue. If I have mislaid my watch and need to know the time, and if I notice that you are wearing your watch, I'll probably ask you if you can kindly tell me the time. At this particular instant, you are for me an authority concerning the time of day.

I ask you the time, you tell me it is half past two, and I hurry off to keep an appointment I have made for quarter to two. All is well. You have spoken truthfully, my trust has not been misplaced, and you have exercised your authority of superior knowledge properly. If you tell me it is half past three, knowing I will believe that I have missed my appointment, this is an act of ill will, whether or not any further adverse consequences ensue for me. You shake my trust in you, now and for the future.

Trust between persons is of basic value among humans. Trust in relation to information is one important form or aspect of trust, though there are others. For example, someone may leave valuable property with you for safekeeping, or entrust you with business assets to enable you to act for them in a business capacity, or engage you to act as a babysitter for the evening. As for information, each person needs to have access to more of it than she or he can possibly find out for herself or himself. Other persons pass on to us much of the information we have and require for our daily lives or in employment or professional work, and this is information that we have to take on trust. The greater the division of labour, the more is this so.[1] Hence different people acquire different stocks of knowledge, and enjoy the informational authority that goes with specialist knowledge. When my computer or my lighting system or my car start to malfunction, I need someone who can tell me what is (probably) wrong and how it can be fixed, if it can. Also, I need someone who can fix it.

In a huge variety of settings, therefore, different people can come to have in respect of other people and some domain of information the 'authority of superior knowledge'[2] to which reference was made above. Nobody is an authority on everything, and some people are authorities on very little if anything at all. But those who have authority of this kind are persons to whom others look for information at occasions of need.

---

[1] Adam Smith indeed conjectured that the origins of language lie in the same human propensities as also give rise to the division of labour.

[2] See also N. MacCormick 'What is Wrong with Deceit?' *Sydney Law Rev* 10 (1983) 5–19, esp at 8–14. This paper explores the 'authority condition' and the 'trust condition' for serious utterances in the context of speech-act theory.

The exercise of such authority engages trust. In the normal context, the receiver of information has to take it on trust, at least for the moment. He/she has no information-base of her or his own on the basis of which to check the adviser's advice. Sometimes, there is time for a second opinion, sometimes encyclopaedias and the web can be searched at leisure to confirm the advice received. But in the first instance, the most reasonable course is to trust the chosen adviser on the basis of presumed authority and on the footing that people are more often than not truthful, especially in domains in respect of which they have an established reputation for knowledge and wisdom.

Deceit in this setting thus involves abuse of informational authority by betrayal of trust. And what is wrong with that?

Suppose that we try the answer 'nothing'. If this were taken to be an openly and generally acknowledged answer, it would imply that every person can freely consider her- or himself normatively at liberty to lie and deceive at will. However great the stock of one's authority, however intense the trust of another person, one may use it as one pleases, to reward trust with truth or to betray it with deceit. So let us suppose the existence of a community in which this is a known and publicly avowed norm of conduct: 'everyone is free to lie and to deceive anyone else'.

In this case, it is difficult to see how anyone could come to be considered a trustworthy source of information, since trust could never be rationally reposed by anyone in any other person. What you tell me might be true or it might be false—I'll have to check for myself as best I can, anyway. Each of us has to fall back on whatever stock of knowledge and information he or she could amass. Even if some are better informed than others, the idea of their having 'informational authority' could never arise. The situation thus depicted would be a grim one, and the only way out would be for small circles of trust to form, perhaps extending their range gradually over time. But such circles of trust would work only if their members did acknowledge among themselves a norm prohibiting the abuse of authority with a view to deceit.

Hence a universal norm prohibiting deceit is rationally preferable in any community of language-users to the alternative. This need not be an exceptionless norm (there is always room for jokes, for pretences, for fiction in all its forms, and the small hypocrisies of social interaction—white lies—are both tolerated and reasonably tolerable). Moreover, in practice the extent of those over whom it ranges might be variable in different social contexts, e.g., in tribal societies with internecine warfare and intertribal mistrust, or in highly competitive capitalism with cut-throat competition in emerging markets, one may have good reason to mistrust rivals. There may even be cases where it is actually right to lie to someone, for example one who is pursuing illegitimate and intrusive inquiries into somebody else's domain of legitimate privacy.

However, if one envisages a community that comprises all rational agents owing each other mutual respect as such, the exceptions would be relatively few, and would themselves have to be universalizable, and the range of the norm would be over all rational agents in linguistic communication with each other. The norm: 'Thou shalt not deceive thy neighbour' is rationally preferable to the contradictory: 'Thou mayest at thy own choice deceive thy neighbour'. In other words, 'Lying is wrong' is preferable to 'lying is optional'.

In any actual human community in which this rational preference is acknowledged, it is possible for extensive relationships of trust to grow and flourish. Then large numbers may be able to take advantage of stocks of specialist information that only a few can possess on the basis of direct inquiry and personal verification. Nothing can save the members of such a community from occasional fraudsters and agents of ill-will who cultivate trust and then betray it. But there is every reason to share in a practice of condemning fraudsters and cheats. In commercial contexts at least, there will be good reason for states to develop rules of positive law that both prohibit as crimes certain forms of fraudulent activity and provide for appropriate penalties. In civil law, norms against deceit (perhaps more extensive than the criminal laws) will establish forms of delict or tort that can be remedied by awards of damages or by other appropriate remedies.

There are further considerations that can be advanced in favour of this line of reasoning. Certain kinds of serious statement could be neither made nor understood to have been made in any society whose members accepted a general norm of liberty to lie. As both Thomas Reid[3] and Immanuel Kant[4] argued, a norm of truth-telling is necessarily built into the norms that make up a language. It is a norm forbidding certain (ab)uses of our power of speech, not one of the many norms that are constitutive of speech by way of semantics and syntax. This seems close to being, if anything could be, a fundamental law pertaining to human beings as rational agents. For, as was argued in Chapter 2, human beings are speaking animals. By speech and writing and electronically, they communicate through the medium of language. Their language is irreducibly and essentially public. Reid and Wittgenstein have completely demolished the idea of 'private' or 'solitary' languages.[5]

To communicate in a language involves the production of articulate sounds or of other written or electronically coded symbols that are reciprocally intelligible to utterer and receiver of utterance. This depends on shared grammar, syntax and semantics. Grammar is normative, differentiating right from wrong ways of speaking, correct, and incorrect uses of words to refer to objects or describe them, or whatever. These are implicit norms, not enacted or codified ones—language has to be in existence before norms can be formally enunciated and issued in

---

[3] T. Reid, *Essays on the Active Powers of the Human Mind* (with introduction by B. Brody) (Cambridge, MA and London: MIT Press, 1969) at 443 (Essay V, ch 6) 'Without fidelity and trust, there can be no human society'.

[4] Kant on lying and false promises—see H. J. Paton, *The Moral Law* (London: Hutchinson, revised edn. 1958)) 67–8.

[5] See T. Reid, *Essays on the Active Powers*, Essay V; L. Wittgenstein (trans. G. E. M. Anscombe), *Philosophical Investigations* (Oxford, Basil Blackwell, 1968) 269, 275.

authoritative form. It is possible for some norms of language to be explicitly formulated, taught, even enacted. But not all can possibly be.

When we speak about anything that is the case, we at the same time observe norms about how we ought to speak. Uttering an 'is' sentence presupposes some 'ought' sentence(s) that we could formulate concerning the proper use of the words and sentences through which we stated what was the case. To this extent, 'is' depends on 'ought'.

Languages can be learned only by animals with appropriate genes and bodily organs. Humans alone have these genes. They are activated only by socialization of humans as babies and young children up to the age of puberty in a community of speakers. A condition of their successfully learning to speak is that those from whom they learn speak consistently and truthfully. Hence not only co-ordination conventions about correct uses of words and formation of sentences are presupposed norms of speech. The norm that deceit is wrong is also presupposed among speakers. It is never perfectly observed, and it may be subject to exceptions. But a norm negating the norm of honesty 'No one need ever tell the truth' could not possibly be an accepted norm in a speech community. Over time the community would cease to exist as such. Such a norm is capable of being spoken but not of being accepted as a governing norm of speech.

2 Promises, contracts, and reliance

Lying and deceiving are not the only violations of trust with which a moralist concerned with honesty has to contend. Promises and contracts are also of concern. Speaking generally, there are many kinds of commitments into which people may enter, concerning their future or ongoing conduct towards, and relationships with, others. Here again, what is involved is some combination of authority and trust. Each person has to some extent authority concerning her or his future conduct, to the extent that our conduct is a matter of our own free discretion. Somebody who has authority over her own future conduct is in a position to undertake various sorts of commitment, both unilateral and bilateral, towards others. Those others may place trust in assurances about the commitment undertaken. Again, however, this trust can be betrayed. The party committed for some reason chooses to repudiate or violate the commitment. Such deeds are daily occurrences.

They are not, however, typically regarded as permissible, nor ought they to be. The reasoning is more or less the same as before. If we assume an openly acknowledged social norm that permits a person to renege on commitments whenever she or he chooses, there is no rational basis for trust in the first place. Commitments of any serious kind would wither, or never come into existence, in such a society. Co-operative activity and collaboration among individuals would be at best fragile. Envisage by contrast a universal norm that requires everyone to uphold and honour commitments seriously made to or in favour of others. This creates a possibility of extensive trust and successful co-operation, to the extent that people act in accordance with the norm. In any society of rational agents capable of reflecting on such considerations, these agents would endorse a norm in favour of universally honouring commitments as being preferable to that which treats them as always optional. This endorsement of the norm would be both individualistic, each for him or herself, and collective, all in respect of all. The temptation to violate it, which can arise in so many ways, would be accompanied by awareness of general disapproval in any case of detected breach.

This may too weakly make a point. In a society in which people have no conception of the wrongness of deceit and breach of promise, it is difficult to see how the concept of promising (or making commitments of other kinds) could have any application at all. To promise is to undertake to do some deed and to communicate the understanding that one's very act of promising will make wrongful one's failure to do the deed at the appropriate time for performance. Promising is a matter of subjecting oneself to a norm that prohibits ratting on freely entered commitments. Were there no such norm, there could be no act of subjecting oneself to it, hence no promising.

This may extend even into the idea of 'information'. Information is what I gain from serious statements other people make to me, in speech or by writing or however. But I gain information only when the statements are honestly made and true. There would be no reason to believe others' apparently factual utterances except in the context of rational trust as described above. It might even be hypothesized that there is a kind of collateral warranty that goes along with serious utterances. 'It is 2.30 p.m. (and I promise you can rely on what I say).' Certainly, in the gravest situations when people are called upon to tell the truth, as when giving evidence in a legal trial, the law requires a solemn promise or oath by the witness, to tell the truth the whole truth and nothing but the truth. 'Thou shalt not bear false witness' draws attention to a specially weighty instance of the duty to tell the truth.

Trust and reliance are parallel conceptually. If I trust you, I am inclined to rely on you. That I rely on you for something shows that I trust you at least in that respect. Reliance involves a willingness to take steps that are potentially damaging or risky, except if the state of the world is as someone else has reported it, or if the person on whom one relies takes appropriate reciprocal action. I rely upon the skills of the pilot and the good performance of maintenance crews every time I make a flight in an aeroplane. I rely on my insurance company to indemnify me in the event of my incurring heavy financial liabilities in the case of a car accident in which I damage a third party.

In the simpler cases considered above, the person to whom an assurance is given may rely on the accuracy of the assurance by acting on the assumption it is true. I ask a life-guard by the sea shore whether bathing conditions are safe, and he assures me they are. So I go in swimming at that beach. This will be unfortunate for me if he is either lying or simply inaccurate. If he says: 'You'll be quite safe. I shall be on duty here for the next two hours'. I may then find myself relying on his performing as he says. I have elsewhere suggested that the most conceptually primitive form of promising occurs where one person invites another to rely upon the former's acting in the future in a certain way.[6] This entails that he manifests to her an intention for her to treat his solemnly saying so as a ground for her acting in reliance on the performance in question. This does not necessarily presuppose that the promiser is acting with reference to some norm already explicitly formulated or even acknowledged that one must keep promises. Yet in such a context there is reason to hold that proto-promiser actually does wrong if he/she fails to keep the proto-promise, and lets the other person down, with potential severe detriment. It is thus possible to understand the evolution of a promise-keeping norm that people do invoke when making promises to each other, putting themselves under the potential stigma of being judged a wrongdoer if the promise is broken.

3 Laws?

Practical reasoners use reason to guide their will. Reasoning and reflection about what to do must lead in the end to some decision. To be able to act for one's own reasons, not under the compulsion of another person or persons, is of the essence of human freedom. Reasonable action is thus free action. According to Kant and Korsgaard, the will necessarily acts according to law, and law is intrinsically universal. My acting in a certain way for a certain reason expresses a 'maxim of action'. My decision to embark on writing a book to fulfil a promise to my publisher has the maxim: 'The book is to be written in fulfilment of the promise to write it.' Universalized, this becomes 'Whoever makes a promise to write a book must fulfil the promise by writing the book'. That in turn can be subsumed within the also universal but much more general: 'Whoever makes a promise to do anything that may legitimately be done must fulfil the promise by doing the thing promised'. One might restate this as 'It is always wrong to break a promise to do a legitimate act except where some special exception or qualification exists'.

Let us note again what Kantians think of this. They consider that the test for rational acceptability of such a universal is whether one can or cannot will it as a 'universal law of nature'. The course of reflection which we pursued earlier certainly seems to support willing the promise-keeping norm as a universal law— yes, every person must keep her or his promises unless some relevant (universally

---

[6] See N. MacCormick, *Legal Right and Social Democracy* (Oxford: Clarendon Press, 1982), ch 10, partially revising N. MacCormick 'Voluntary Obligations and Normative Powers' *Aristotelian Society Supp. Vol.* 1972. Compare T. Scanlon, *What we Owe to Each Other* (Cambridge, MA: Belknap Press of Harvard University Press, 1998).

justified) exception applies to a given promise. The importance of mutual trust and reliance in any human community makes this seem obvious. Indeed, one may argue that human nature is essentially revealed in our very capacity to be speaking animals and to live in communities of fellow speakers, and to rear our children to become competently speaking members of our own community. In this sense, the promise-keeping norm is a law essentially built into our nature, as indeed is the norm that lying and deceit are wrong. It seems that by being a rational human being one does ineluctably will these as 'universal laws of (human) nature'.

Yet if I look at this only in terms of what I for my part can will as a universal law of nature, that does not seem enough. Nor does it seem enough if I envisage that each and every other person wills the same norm, each for her or his own part. For the point of truth-telling and promise-keeping norms lies in their being shared norms, commonly held and observed norms supported by mutual beliefs, not simply coincidental wills of people who happen to share some social space. Each of us might decide that smoking is a foolish and deleterious habit, and each might resolve to stop, considering (universally) that no one ought to smoke. Then public places like bars and offices may become less smelly and disagreeable and public health will slowly improve. But this will not be the same thing as a common agreement on a common smoking ban in public places, or as an act of public legislation banning it.

What one wills in the Kantian sense is or (as it seems to me) ought to be a will for there to be a common norm, reciprocally endorsed among all rational people that no one shall lie, or break a promise, or (perhaps) smoke tobacco in an enclosed public space. The vital character of the first two norms to the viability of a speech community depends on there being a basis of mutual beliefs and expectations, conditionally willed by each on the condition of all the others exhibiting a reciprocal commitment.

Let us now therefore ask whether there would not be merit again in accounting for this by reference to what the previous chapter introduced under the name of the 'Smithian categorical imperative'. The suggested form of this is:

'Enter as fully as you can into the feelings of everyone directly involved in or affected by an incident or relationship, and impartially form a maxim of judgement about what is right that all could accept if they were committed to maintaining mutual beliefs setting a common standard of approval and disapproval among themselves.'

A subsidiary imperative is annexed as follows:

'Act in accordance with that impartial judgement of what it is right to do in respect of the given incident or relationship'.

What difference would it make if we used this line of approach to cases of deceit, breach of promise and violation of obligations, rather than the essentially Kantian line pursued so far in the present chapter?

The most obvious difference is that we would not start with speculation about what could possibly be a society-wide, far less humanity-wide, universal rule. It may be, indeed it obviously is, true that a viable speech community could not exist if there were not widely observed constraints against lying and deceiving. Yet that does not fully capture one's sense of what is wrong or outrageous about cases of cheating and deceit. 'Nobody ought to lie, therefore I ought not to lie' does not capture one's sense of abhorrence about falsehoods one is tempted to tell. We must return to the ideas of trust and reliance. The person to whom I can lie is the one who trusts me. The ones who trust me are those most ready to believe me. They will stake a lot on their belief in me, and will do so more or less unreflectively and without calculation of the odds.

So for some reason, I lie to them. I see some advantage that can't be obtained if they know the truth, to which I have privileged access. Or I feel too troubled by an inconvenient or embarrassing or shaming truth to be willing to disclose it, and choose to lie or evade or suggest what is false while suppressing what is true. Their sense of hurt and outrage if—when—the truth emerges is huge, the more so the deeper the trust that has been betrayed. The guilt I feel even when my lie is undetected (to say nothing of the shame I feel if or when it is uncovered) is in the same proportion, assuming I am an honest person who has weakly given way to temptation this once, or on this very rare occasion. Hardened fraudsters may feel no such guilt or shame. But they are the very persons who assiduously work up a relationship of trust intending from the start that they will betray it. The Smithian reckoning in this case will include indignation at the act of engendering a false trust. All ways round, the judgement one reaches under the Smithian Imperative is one of unhesitating disapproval, with a degree of weight proportioned to the depth of the trust betrayed and the severity of the deception involved—what exactly was the false belief into which the innocent person was led? The maxim of judgement is that such a deception must be condemned, the action that follows is one of condemnation in terms of appropriate severity. For the liar in person, the action called for is to apologize, to seek to make amends, and to put up with living under a cloud of unhappy suspicion and suspended trust. This will continue until such time as he or she has worked a passage back into restored (if never quite so deep or unthinking) trust. To be one who has forfeited trust in this way is itself a perpetual source of grief and shame, for, as Smith observes, it is a very common human characteristic to wish both to be trusted and indeed to be worthy of trust.

This, certainly, is a much less bloodless way of reflecting on the wrongfulness of lying than high speculation about how societies might fare were there to be a universal toleration of deliberate deceit. Neither approach undermines the other, however. It is good to consider the immediate judgement of anger, resentment and the spectator response, and after that to review the universalization of the maxim of judgement. The judgement of the individual case under the constraint of impartial spectatorship leads one into a universalization—'such lying is intolerable'—that one can indeed further test applying Kant's 'universal law of nature' formula. One should not treat the two as operating in sharp disjunction one from the other. It does however seem right that from the very ground floor one should write into one's criteria of judgement ordinary human emotions wishes and needs of a kind that can be shared among persons. They are, to be precise, shared among persons 'who are motivated to maintain mutual beliefs setting a common standard of approval and disapproval among themselves'.

All appropriate elements thus come into view. Always, as moral deliberators we are primarily concerned with judgement about our own conduct and that of others in our vicinity, and about what to do in the light of such judgements. We have to presuppose some universal common standard, and it has to take account of all feelings, those of the potentially deceived and those of potential deceivers, and it has to be a possible basis of workable mutual beliefs. There seems no reason to doubt that anyone applying this as a procedure of justifying judgements would reach the conclusion that confirms what is the ordinary judgement of conventional morality. In this case, at least, this is a strong but not conclusive point in favour of the Smithian justification procedure.

4 On obligations

In positive law, commitments of various kinds—for example, unilateral promises (under seal, or in writing, with or without necessity of witnesses according to different legal systems), long-term contracts such as insurance contracts, or contracts of employment, or loans made in consideration of some security such as a pledge or mortgage, or marriages or civil partnerships—give rise to obligations. Obligations are complex normative relations between persons.[7] They entail a congeries of mutual duties and rights, and long-term mutual expectations of various kinds. The duties and rights arise, and can be discharged from time to time during the long-term relationship—think of the mutual duties of employer and employee over a working day or a working week, to say nothing of a working year. Much of the detailed content of this is quite particular to the two parties. For it depends both on what they have expressly agreed and on the tacit understandings implicit in their working relationship, as well as on what additional duties the law imposes or rights it confers quite apart from the terms agreed by the parties. The norm of law or of morality that one must fulfil one's obligations is universal— everyone should fulfil all the obligations he or she has. The specific conduct that at any moment becomes mandatory depends on particular prevailing facts and circumstances and on the actual terms of any express agreement or declaration that gives rise to the obligation in question.

This has a significant bearing on our practical reasoning. As a legal subject, one has to act with regard to the prospect of legal remedies being brought to bear

---

[7] For full discussion, see N. MacCormick, *Institutions of Law*, ch 7.

through litigation or even the threat of it, and as a law-abiding citizen one has reason to respect legal obligations because that is what it takes to abide by law. As a moral agent one has to have regard to one's legal obligations and the duties to which they give rise, except if there is any conflict with a morally superior and overriding norm or principle.

Morally speaking, or in law, or in the ethics of good citizenship, one's obligations and duties are among the side constraints on one's action. The realm of moral liberty, or legal liberty, or civic liberty, is that in which one can act without violating any duty or obligation. Moreover, there are other forms of wrongdoing that are not themselves breaches of any obligation in the narrow sense. These may be sins or crimes or torts (delicts) or breaches of trust or civic misdemeanours of various kinds. All are exclusionary reasons. All place exclusionary side-constraints on one's conduct, restricting one's normative freedom within the relevant normative sphere of judgement. In practical reasoning, one's plans and projects aim at the realization of aims and objectives one perceives as good. Plans that are fully rational aim at, and when fulfilled achieve, some aspect of the good, whether animal or ideal, and whether in a self-regarding, in an other-regarding, or in a community-regarding way (normally some combination of all three, indeed all five). One's planning, and one's conduct in pursuit of a plan or project, exceed the bounds of one's normative freedom if they initially encompass or if they turn out to involve some wrongdoing, whether by breach of obligation or duty, or in some other way. Moral agents are free to act as they think best, within the constraints of moral duty. Legal subjects are legally at liberty to do whatever will not involve violating some legal duty or committing some crime or other form of legal wrong.

Obligations that are long-term relationships do not only feature in practical reasoning as side-constraints upon plans, projects, or activities. Someone may take up a job, or enter a contract with a publisher for a book to be written over two years, or may get married or form a civil partnership, or may become a parent of children. The relationships thus entered themselves shape major projects within a person's larger plan of life. To make a long-term success of one's job, or of writing one's book, or of one's marriage or partnership, or of one's parenting is an object of endeavour and of what we have called 'executive reasoning' from time to time. While it includes fulfilling positive duties and avoiding breach of negative duties, that never exhausts what such a relationship calls for. The kind of mutual consideration, love and support that go into successful relationships of this kind transcend the bounds of duty, without making the duties themselves in any way irrelevant. For the reasoning and reflection that go into playing one's part in such a relationship includes consideration of what is for the good, or the best, of those involved, not only what it is mandatory to do in their favour. There is also, however, a golden mean. One can put too much into one activity or relationship to the detriment of all others, or too little. Achieving balance in one's practical commitments is a great difficulty, but it is certainly desirable to achieve a kind of homeostasis over time.

5 Autonomous agents and institutional ethics

Chapter 3 drew attention to the contextual character of judgements about right and wrong. Contexts can be as varied as among the grammar of a language, or rules of games or sports, or of professional ethics, or of religious observance, or of the fundamentals of faith and morals in a specifically religious perspective, or of the law of a state or of some international organization, or some form of traditional law or traditional practice—traditional music might be a particularly fruitful example. Set against all these, the argument so far has assumed that there is also autonomous morality. There are standards of right and wrong that we are capable of applying as the fundamental moral judgement framed by each or any of us. Certainly, in such judging we seek and hope for (as the Smithian categorical imperative makes clear) a shared, common standard of appraisal that everyone can go along with. But that hopeful effort may be disappointed on occasion. Try as one may, one sometimes comes to a judgement that others find idiosyncratic or simply wrong, and yet there lies one's own honest conviction, at least for the time being, and after all opportunities to talk through the issues at stake have been temporarily exhausted. An explanation has been offered of the basis of such judgements.

That explanation does not directly apply to the other types of context mentioned, many of which have clearly an institutional character. They also, in many cases, have an element of commitment in them. To play chess or football, to speak a particular language, to take part in an orchestra, to be a communicant of a particular faith (at least in the context of a secular society with no compulsory establishment of religion) is to make a voluntary commitment. In effect, it is to enter willingly into a relationship of trust with the other players or participants or communicants. The trust includes trust that one will in a wide sense 'play fair' (in a game) or exhibit deep sincerity (in one's faith). More than that, however, there is in all these cases a more or less substantial body of more or less clearly established rules, often with some kind of official institutional recognition. To play the game is to play by these rules—and to play fairly in their context. To be a Roman Catholic or a member of the Church of Scotland or an orthodox Jew or a Sunni Muslim is to live and conduct one's worship by these rules or in these forms. No doubt there can be a certain laxity or latitudinarianism, more or less so in different times and circumstances. But it is true to say that with all allowances of that kind, the rules and established practices define the activity. Hence as a participant in it one has to have some sincerity in one's commitment to living by the rules. In games, to try to get away with less than faithful observation of the rules is to cheat. In religion, it is to be or become a hypocrite.

From the standpoint of an outsider to the activity or way of life in question, one's attitude to cheating or hypocrisy may be an equivocal one. One may think ridiculous the degree to which grown human beings, usually grown men, can become absorbed in the intense triviality and contrived glorification of organised games and leagues and knock-out competitions for cups. One may look upon cricket with a sad shake of the head at the antics of 'flannelled fools'.[8] Yet one cannot easily excuse those who abuse the trust of their co-participants, in whatever way they do this. To cheat at a game is much the same as breaking a promise or telling a lie, in a case where someone relies on you to do as you have undertaken or to say things how they really are.

This itself is, however, somewhat context-dependent. In a curious way, the most highly institutionalized instances of sports may be those in which the reality of personal trust is at its least. Where professional teams of players earning large salaries compete in strongly commercialized settings under the care of lavishly paid managers and coaches for victory in league or cup competitions, where every game is conducted under the governance of a professional referee with two or more professional assistants, a kind of displacement of the rules can take place. The rule that the referee's decision is final can have the effect of players 'playing to the whistle', rather than 'playing to the rules'. This means that whenever a player can get away with a piece of foul play undetected by the referee, it is 'fair game' to try this. Players should not handle the ball. But if, as in one famous case,[9] Diego Maradona cannot quite reach the ball with his head, he may artfully strike it with his fist outside the referee's range of sight, and be declared to have scored a goal. The award of the goal is valid notwithstanding a blatant foul that can be detected on a video replay of the game. The meta-rule that players must abide by the referee's decision overtrumps the necessity for strict loyalty to the primary rules of the game of association football. In circumstances of professional competitions this may be generally known and accepted, so that the institutionalized version of the game to that extent diverges from less formal variants of the same game played, for example, by young people on village pitches, with no professional referee.

One may seek again to know how it is morally appropriate to respond to the conduct of players in games. One may also ask how it is morally proper for players themselves to conduct themselves. The conclusion cannot be simply that the rules of a game have to be observed no matter what. Yet both the outsider to the activity and the insiders cannot but take seriously the mutual reliance between participants that alone makes possible a good play of the game. Allowing for the various ways in which variations of circumstances may alter cases, one has to conclude that participants in such activities voluntarily incur mutual obligations, with all sorts of attendant duties, by virtue of their in-principle voluntary decision to participate in the game or other like activity.

So far as concerns matters of religious observance or matters of religiously ordained norms of faith and morals, the perspectives of insiders and outsiders

---

[8] The reference is from Rudyard Kipling's poem 'The Islanders' in R. Kipling, *The Five Nations* (1903): "...ye contented your souls/With the flannelled fools at the wicket or the muddied oafs at the goals."

[9] See discussion of this case in F. Atria *On Law and Legal Reasoning* (Oxford : Hart, 2001) 6–8.

may be yet more sharply differentiated than in the case of mere games. An outsider may well think all or some of the doctrines of a certain religion to be pernicious falsehoods, and may view with serious dislike the psychological pressure which priest, minister, rabbi, pastor, or imam can bring to bear on individuals, especially when this is backed by the opinion of a congregation of the faithful. The autonomous moralist may see much here to be anxious about in respect of those who fall under the sway of religion. Yet, in principle, those who take part do so of their own free will out of their own conviction in the good news revealed through holy writ and inspired preaching. They are therefore subject to the same principle of commitment. One should stand by the commitments one has made, and few forms of moral weakness seem more contemptible than detected hypocrisy, when those who most firmly assert the doctrines of the faith are themselves detected in gross and knowing, but unacknowledged, breach thereof. From inside the faith, the condemnation of the backslider—and, possibly, of all infidels—is typically severe. The resentment of those who cheat on their faith is deep and genuine. How far this can really be assimilated to autonomous moral judgement depends on the facts of any given case, and the degree to which an individual is really a person who has made a free commitment to the faith she or he professes. From the outside, again, whatever one's opinion about the doctrines of a faith, one has to acknowledge the importance of freedom of opinion, freedom of worship, and freedom of association in any free society.

6 Non-voluntary obligations and institutional law

What about institutional obligations that are not dependent on the will of those subjected to them? In traditional societies (and all societies are to some extent traditional in their make-up) there are traditional standards of right and wrong by which members expect each other to live, and to some extent try to live themselves. There are decent and modest ways to dress, by contrast with more or less shocking and provocative forms of (un)dress. There is an understood gap of 'personal space' that we leave between each other to avoid seeming discourteous or threatening. There are registers of speech that are acceptable in polite discourse, other forms that are insulting to use or even allude to. Men and women approach each other in certain ways, but not others, likewise the old and the young, persons of high standing and persons of lower. Language itself, however much grammarians, educators and other public agencies have re-cast it in official forms of speech and writing, remains at bottom a traditional mode of communication. The measure of rightness in speech is the consciousness of the competent native speaker and the question who counts as competent is in turn determined by the attitudes of native speakers—and there are many registers and dialects and accents, and argots with their own traditions or sub-traditions that we know.

(When I was a boy and a teenager, I learned to play the Scottish bagpipes. I was not mainly taught through the now rather institutionalized system established by the Scottish Regiments of the British Army. I learned from two very old Great-Uncles who had themselves learned their music in the context of a Hebridean village in the fourth quarter of the nineteenth century, learning thorough the medium of their native Gaelic language, in the traditional setting of the *ceilidh* (an evening of song, instrumental music and conversation, and, sometimes, dancing as well) or the local highland games. My sense of how to play a tune, or to listen to one, comes out of that experience. I know what sounds right, what sounds not quite right and what sounds downright wrong. There is a tone and timbre, and above all a tempo, of play that captures the way my old teachers sung the melodies to me (they were too old to be able actually to blow the bagpipes or even the 'practice chanter'.) A piper's playing sounds just right to me to the extent that it matches a remembered pattern of sound that Uncles Neil and Dugald passed on as right because it sounded right to them. Difficult as it is to express this experience in words, because it speaks of an essentially non-verbal experience concerning a non-verbal skill, it seems to me to capture some of the points one needs to make in dealing with the difficult concept of tradition. It is difficult because one can only do so in the language of a philosophy that seeks to make discursive sense of all that it handles, and tradition is in an important way non-verbal and non-discursive, or only incompletely discursive.)

Traditional societies often include or included forms of traditional authority, based perhaps on clan or tribal chiefship or aristocratic status, or both. Penalties administered by such authorities could be arbitrary and barbaric with no recourse to effective higher authority. As Smith and others were astute to point out, this often amounted to extremely despotic rule and the condition of those ruled was often one of servile dependency or at any rate entailed a substantial absence of freedom of mind. Religion and other aspects of social order can be closely intermingled and the idea of a religion's being a matter of a person's free choice and personal commitment would be well wide of the mark in such a society. The idea of any clear line between 'law', 'religion', and 'morality' would be wholly lacking in application there. To the extent that all this is so, it may be difficult to pose, far less answer, the question whether an autonomous moral agent would owe an obligation of allegiance and fidelity to the traditions of the society in question. Yet to the extent that relationships of trust and reliance arise in that context, perhaps involving a very great intensity of trust and reliance, the same grounds for condemning violation of trust apply as in other settings.

Tradition or custom can never be absent from law, even with the highly differentiated law of the contemporary law state or constitutional state.[10] For at least the state's constitution has to be observed on the basis of a common custom

---

[10] cf. H. P. Glenn, *Legal Traditions of the World: sustainable diversity in law* 3rd edn (Oxford: Oxford University Press, 2007).

before any of the formal institutional arrangements it consecrates can take shape as working realities.[11] All law, it might be said, is traditional. But the tradition requires reference to authoritatively issued texts, statutes, precedents, delegated legislation and other law-making instruments as the main repositories of the norms of law only in one highly developed type of legal order.

In such a developed legal order, these are what the persons authorized by law are required to implement and what citizens are called upon to observe as law, however little they may be familiar with or even aware of the contents of the texts in question. Such law is Janus-faced. On the one hand, by setting limits on the powers of public officials, it can secure to citizens real civil liberty within the domains of normative freedom defined by law. On the other, by empowering public officials it creates scope for frightening abuses of power through selective enforcement even of laws that are on their face unobjectionable.[12] (What if only black people were ever prosecuted for speeding, or only Jewish people were ever subjected to serious scrutiny of their income tax returns?) On the one hand, by enabling the legislature to change or revise any existing law (while possibly imposing special constraints on constitutional amendment), the constitution makes the law responsive to citizens' moral and political opinions. On the other hand, the very same feature creates the danger of a 'tyranny of the majority'. On the one hand, laws may create conditions for the answerability of all power-holders before some appropriate judicial or democratic forum. On the other hand, laws may engender exemptions such that it becomes a refuge for irresponsibility in the face of glaring human need.[13]

Even when faced with law that expresses the preferable of these pairs, even in a state whose constitution and practice allow for a genuinely open and pluralistic democracy, it is possible that the contents of legal rules will on occasion outrage the consciences of some citizens. Consider these alternatives: to permit abortion or to prohibit it; to permit assisted suicide or to prohibit it; to permit insults to Jesus Christ or the prophet Mohammed, or to prohibit them; to allow the deployment of weapons of mass destruction or to ban them; to permit human/animal stem cell research or to ban it. All these and many others are issues on which persons of conscience differ deeply in contemporary societies, and on which religious leaders have spoken out on behalf of their communities, being answered both by secular humanists and by other religious spokespeople. Whatever the legislature resolves and enacts into law, or even if it simply refrains from enacting anything, somebody's conscience will be violated.

What then? Is there an obligation to accept the legislature's word as settling the moral issue? Surely not. The validity of enacted legislation does not entail, indeed cannot entail, its being morally justified. At most it gives evidence that

[11] N. MacCormick *Institutions of Law*, 45–9.

[12] See N. Simmonds, *Law as a Moral Idea* (Oxford: Oxford University Press, 2007).

[13] See S. Veitch, *Law and Irresponsibility: on the legitimation of human suffering* (London: Routledge-Cavendish, 2007).

in the opinion of the legislative majority, the law's contents are morally justified. Determining right and wrong is a matter of judgement framed, according to
the present work, by application of the Smithian categorical imperative. At any
rate, whatever is the method or mechanism of sound judgement, the autonomous
moral agent cannot be dethroned by the will of the legislature, however democratic the procedures and circumstances of its election. Acts of Parliament can
make legally wrong conduct that was previously legally permissible (e.g., smoking tobacco in enclosed public spaces). They cannot similarly change the moral
quality of conduct, in either direction. This seems obvious, yet one must at once
admit a qualification. For the fact that certain conduct is a criminal offence or a
civil wrong does make a moral difference.

The law (whether traditional or statutory or common law) that is in force or
at any rate generally observed in a territory has inevitable moral significance for
those who live there. I may wonder whether to light a cigarette here and now, and
to smoke it. But then I reflect that there has been a recent legislative change that
prohibits smoking here or in similar places. Or I learn that under the traditions
of the place, smoking in public is greatly frowned upon, especially on the sabbath
day. Whether or not I consider it to be in an abstract way right or wrong to indulge
in tobacco-smoking, or see it as simply a matter of normative liberty, and whatever my views about the morals of sabbath-observance, a serious question arises.
I do have to reflect now on what moral difference it makes that there is a law
against or a custom against what I propose to do. Do I propose to do it openly as a
public act of defiance of a law or custom I think unjust? Is this like the black lady
who refused to move out of the 'whites only' section of the bus in Montgomery,
Alabama, triggering the civil rights movement? Or do I simply think that the law
is impinging unreasonably on my moral freedom, and decline to change my ways,
taking the risk of exposure to punishment but far from actively seeking it? Or is
this a case like many people's attitude to violating speed limits? As far as I can see,
most drivers on Scottish roads, though they would concede that there have to be
some limits, nevertheless effectively treat legal prohibitions as only recommenda-
tions to keep one's speed down to a reasonable level in the light of traffic conditions, within a ten or fifteen percent margin above the posted speed limit.

Whether in a context of purely or largely traditional law or in the minimally
traditional law of the modern constitutional state, one may ask whether anyone else relies on one to observe the law, and whether they reasonably so rely. Is
there, moreover, an issue of trust here? Do I disappoint reliance or violate trust
if I break the law, even a law that I conscientiously think unfairly restricts my
moral liberty of action? There is certainly no equivalence here to persons who
voluntarily play a game of chess or a game of football, knowing that opponents
trust them to play fairly by the rules. Chess and football are voluntary activities.
Living in a certain territory within the jurisdiction of a state or a traditional
ruler is not the same. Opportunities for migration are few and one can only
migrate to somewhere else where some other state will be exercising jurisdiction.

States are non-voluntary associations—and they are coercive, asserting a monopoly on the use of force in a territory. This is precisely what gives them the ability to enforce laws against people who object to them, as also to apply coercion unfairly by using lawful force selectively or even occasionally using force outside of law altogether.

All this is enough to indicate that the moral theory developed in this book offers no one-size-fits-all answer to the question of 'political obligation'. To some extent all citizens (and non-citizen residents as well) rely on each other to respect the law, especially the basic rules of criminal law, that form the conditions of social peace. 'Mutuality of restrictions' is a fair argument to make among those who are similarly burdened and similarly benefited by the state's institutions as the necessary backdrop of a civil society that is genuinely civil, encouraging reasonable trust among strangers. Similar arguments extend to taxation law and the mutual obligation of citizens to bear their tax burden in a fair minded way, in parallel with their readiness to use the state's health and educational and other services—including the background benefit of adequate policing. To the extent that fair representative democracy functions in election to local and central authorities, so that over time minority opinions can come to prevail if the persuasive force of their arguments is properly heard through a free press and open media, participants may incur mutual obligations. Those who willingly participate in the democratic process of elections and other forms of political persuasion can fairly be called on to concede victory to those who win elections or whose persuasion has achieved greater success for the time being. There is at least an analogy between those who willingly participate in sport and those who participate actively in political processes.

Again, people who hold particular legal positions, such as police officers, judges, lawyers, and even law professors, owe a high degree of loyalty to the law that they are responsible for upholding in relation to other persons. There is a special hypocrisy in evading the rules you enforce on or teach to others. The same goes for ministers of state and senior executive civil servants.

The question whether it is morally obligatory to observe a particular requirement or prohibition on account of its being a legal requirement or prohibition is thus one which can only be answered in context. Who are you and where? Which law are you called on to obey? Does it require you actively to engage in doing a deed that you consider gravely wrong morally? In this last case you should certainly refuse, and consider carefully whether to do so with maximum publicity or maximum discretion. Whatever involves extreme injustice, such that no reasonable person could reasonably stand up in public and make a case for the rightness of what is required or prohibited, is not properly law at all.[14] So in the case of extreme injustice there is no true law to be obeyed anyway, but the likelihood of extreme and cruel force being in use by agencies of the state is high, and this also

---

[14] The case for this view is fully argued in N. MacCormick, *Institutions of Law*, ch 15.

affects the balance of rational deliberation. If it is in any way possible for a person to protect others effectively from such evil, it is morally incumbent to do so.

In general terms, however, in a reasonably democratic state with tolerable observance of the rule of law, there is normally a prima facie obligation on those who live a comfortable life under law. They ought to give considerable moral attention to the claims of the law, on the ground of the principle of mutuality of restrictions among those whom the law also serves well. For such persons, there is genuine virtue in striving to be a conscientiously law-abiding citizen. This clearly serves a common good, the prevalence of the rule of law by means other than police enforcement. But what of an underclass? What of the poor and dispossessed? Not everyone does in fact live a comfortable life under law, and indeed the law secures the comfort of the comfortable (at least partly) by enforcing their property rights, and protecting them from predatory thefts by the poor. That being so, perhaps the comfortable are only serving self-interest in upholding their relative wealth through the legal system whose morally binding character they therefore accept.

It must be said that the demands of distributive justice bear heavily on anyone who wishes us to take seriously the obligations of the comfortably off and to hope they will extend also to the poorer sections of a society. If there is a dispossessed underclass, it is morally imperative that something be done to bring about a fairer distribution of the assets a state's property system protects. Otherwise the claim of the law upon anyone's genuine moral obligation is a weak one or none at all.

These last reflections depend on an argument according to which property rights of all kinds fall to be included in the class of what Adam Smith called 'adventitious rights'. These are societally variable and depend upon presupposed dispositions of positive law, the law of the state or of the feudal kingdom or traditional society or whatever. People do not, so to say, bring property rights into society (as some variants of social contract theory suggest). People inherit and acquire property within a legal property regime, the point of which is that it enforces the protection of a person's property rights against all comers. This protection matters deeply to those whom it protects.

Smith points out that people resent being dispossessed of what they have more than they resent being disappointed of what ought to be given them. Thus, he says, they resent theft more than they resent breach of contract, and the law deals more severely with the former than the latter. In Smith's theory of justice, this gradation of severity is not merely presented as an actual sentiment of individuals, but as a justified one. In one way, he is obviously right. To take seriously the proposition that the rule of law and its enforcement are essential (though not sufficient) to sustaining the civility of civil society, one must include in it the enforcement of property rights and the effective control or limitation of theft. The justice of this is at least founded in the non-disappointment of expectations. Moreover, those who steal commonly seek to do so undetected and to enjoy the law's protection of what they themselves have, including what they have acquired dishonestly, until such time (if ever) as their dishonesty comes to light. Expropriation of the landlords or of the bourgeoisie during a revolution is a very different matter from ordinary theft, burglary, and robbery. Challenging a whole system is different from claiming special exceptions within a system that one wishes to leave in the large extent untouched. When, if ever, revolutions are justified is a quite separate question. The ousting of an unjust and tyrannical regime rarely takes place without the commission of countervailing injustices, and the establishment of a reasonable constitutional dispensation following a revolution is always difficult, to say the least. The strategy of patient reform, even in the face of apparently overwhelming odds, seems often to be the better course.

It remains to ask whether the repression of theft in an unequal society is really just. It seems to me that it is so only in a society that attends conscientiously to the issue of distributive justice among its members, so that those who bear the burden of respecting property norms also share in this benefit, within an acceptable degree of inequality of overall shares. These are matters to which we shall return in a later chapter.

5

Autonomy and Freedom

1 Transcending natural law

The idea of being in some way 'law unto oneself', whether expressed in terms of 'autonomy' or in the cognate but not identical terms of 'self-command', is fundamental to the view of practical reasoning advanced in this book. This point was already launched in Chapter 3, and will be continued here. Some historical reflections will be offered in this and the next two chapters in developing the idea, though this is by no means a work of historical scholarship. The aim is to establish truths for nowadays, not to explain the past, and reflecting on the past here serves the present-day purpose, which is to build a theory about practical reasoning that uses and perhaps develops ideas from two giants of western thought, in the light of one of their precursors.

It seems that both Smith and Kant were in their moral philosophy reacting against, and seeking to transcend, a part of the inheritance from the natural law thought that belonged among the common intellectual property of eighteenth century philosophers, jurists, and political thinkers. It was with Protestant versions of natural law thought that they were particularly engaged. This was part of their intellectual inheritance as citizens of nations whose dominant politico-religious groups had over the preceding century come to dismiss Roman Catholicism as a mass of superstitions and questionable traditions built upon but obscuring the basics of true and rational Christian faith. One strand of this idea of natural law portrayed it as a 'dictate of reason'.[1] By this it was meant that anyone acquainted with the general facts of human nature and aware of the relations of humans with God was able by the application of reason to understand the basic principles of right conduct among humans. Even heathens who had not received the divine revelation through the Bible knew the basics of this law 'written in their hearts' and to that extent had the law inside themselves.

Neither Smith nor Kant was morally innovative in suggesting new basic principles of practical conduct radically different from those that were considered

---

[1] The phrase comes from James Dalrymple, Viscount Stair, *Institutions of the Law of Scotland*, I. 1. 1; Thomas Hobbes, *Leviathan* (ch 15, 216 [80]) also uses it. In fact, this view owes as much to the older Thomistic tradition as to anything newly emerging with Protestantism, where there is a tendency to stress the inscrutable will of God.

as commonplace dictates of reason among natural lawyers and others of their period. What they did in their very different ways, but with surprisingly coinciding outputs, was to find a deeper explanation of how people could know the law rather than simply claiming that it stands to reason or indeed is dictated to us by our reason with some aid from revelation. Smith sought to develop a moral psychology that explained in an essentially empirical way how people come to judgements that they could also then represent as dictates of reason or divine commandments or whatever.[2] Kant applied transcendental rather than empirical reasoning to establish the fundamental principle according to which our will could bind itself to norms of right conduct. The element of ideal impartiality that enters Smith's account creates the bridge between these two otherwise opposed approaches, and it is upon that bridge that the ideas advanced in this book are built. The discussion in this chapter starts with some further reflections on autonomy, proceeds to consider how the natural law inheritance may help to understand the argument, and how it leads on to the quite radical ideas about human freedom that Smith and Kant advanced. Though they expressed them in strikingly different terms, they exhibit interesting similarity in content.

2 Autonomy and self-command[3]

Autonomy has a special place in accounting for morality itself, and in accounting for the special character of moral deliberation, and decision-making in questions concerning what is right and wrong, especially in an interpersonal setting. Each moral agent is the law unto herself or himself, that is, has to discern for herself or himself what is an acceptable ground of judgement at any moment of serious moral choice, and has to act accordingly. The moral law, as each moral agent confronts it, is something that she finds binding on her. It is binding because it expresses what she can will in universal terms as a rule for action by herself or anyone else, and thus also as a ground to judge her own acts and those of other people.

Though the judgement is always that of an individual agent, the law it expresses is not law for oneself only. Each judgement of what is right is implicitly universalizable. That is a point that Smith and Kant share, according to the reading

---

[2] Smith writes of 'those who in this [the eighteenth] and in the preceding century have treated of what is called natural jurisprudence', saying that they 'do not content themselves with characterizing in this general manner the tenor of conduct which they would recommend, but endeavour to lay down exact and precise rules for the direction of every circumstance of our behaviour.' He also remarks that they typically do so from the point of view of one to whom duties or obligations are owed and focus on the vindication of the rights thus arising. See *Theory of Moral Sentiments*, 329–30.

[3] This section of the present chapter largely replicates, and at points repeats, the message of ch 14.4 of *Institutions of Law*, where some issues were expressly left open for later resolution. The present chapter aims to tie up these loose ends.

proposed here. The Smithian categorical imperative as proposed above requires one to form a judgement about what is right from a ground that all affected in a choice-situation could accept if they were committed to maintaining mutual beliefs setting a common standard of approval and disapproval among themselves. To apply such a view: If it is all right for me to consume alcohol, it must be equally right for anyone else (in a similar situation) to do so; what is permissible for me has to be permissible universally. If abstaining from heroin use is obligatory for me, it must be so for everyone likewise situated. What is obligatory for you or me has to be obligatory universally. (But this applies in a way that depends on one's 'situation' in a wide sense. It is permissible or prohibited for me under what description in what circumstances? Is it for me as a human or for me as an adult human that alcohol is permissible? Is it true that even for me as an adult, heroin has to be considered absolutely prohibited, or only its non-medical use? And so on.)

It is necessary to draw a certain distinction between moral reasoning about what is universally permissible, obligatory, or prohibited, and more general practical reasoning about how to pursue a good life, that is, about what is of real value to humans (introduced already in Chapter 2 and brought to a conclusion in Chapter 9). The former, 'deontic' moral reasoning, as it may be called, generates reasons with exclusionary force in the manner discussed in Chapter 3. The latter questions are sometimes treated as 'ethical', concerning a person's ethos or way of life, in contradistinction to strictly moral questions about right *versus* wrong, obligatory *versus* permissible. This does not seem to me a very helpful terminology, since it cuts too sharp a divide between two essential parts of moral thought, and actually conflicts with common usages of the term 'ethics' such as those we find in the context of professional ethics. It is sufficient that we be aware of the difference between reasons that have exclusionary force and those that do not.

Anyway, even if I judge myself and others to be morally at liberty to take alcohol, or perhaps to indulge in some other 'soft' drugs, this would leave wide open the question what part I ascribe to them in a good life. Here, autonomy remains, but universality recedes. The good life for me according to my life plan is certainly something that I autonomously shape for myself, and which is my own responsibility.[4] Everyone has a life-story of her/his own, and each composes the story of that life according to choices made in response to reasons in the manner discussed in Chapters 1 and 2, and brought to a conclusion in Chapter 9. There could be no question of anyone legislating a personal conception of the good life as a recipe for anyone else. Certainly, however, parents, teachers, and other role-models have to exercise care in starting younger people off on the road to developing the capability to take responsibility for their own way of life, with some incipient or inchoate aspiration to some range of values and virtues. Their elders

---

[4] Compare, on 'public and private autonomy', J. Habermas 'On the Internal Relation between the Rule of Law and Democracy' *European Journal of Philosophy* 3 (1995) 12–20 at 17–18.

have a duty to help children and young persons to learn the art of autonomous living and of self-disciplined appreciation, and pursuit of the good within the framework of the moral law as they construct this over a lifetime.[5] At the stage of still being under tutelage and even a degree of compulsion by relevant adults, the child remains heteronomous. Autonomy supervenes upon heteronomy as full moral agency comes into being.

Heteronomy is autonomy negated. Heteronomy prevails where there is will, or decision-making capability, but where the compulsion to which the will submits is set by an extraneous or alien will, or where action is constrained in ways that do not involve the will at all. Where one person acts not on the basis of self-directed deliberation but on another's say-so about the rightness of an action, that person makes no autonomous decision. It is the other who judges and decides. Or events may lie outside of one's decision altogether. For example, I have reduced my weight not because of a decision to take my health more seriously and to eat, and drink in a better-controlled way, but because an illness prevents me from swallowing (much of) my food. It is in a sense good that I thus lose weight and get into better shape. But no moral credit belongs to me for this. My will was not engaged at all.

The conception of morality offered in this book proposes that deliberation and decision as moral deliberation, and decision have to be autonomous, involving the exercise of self-command. One must come to one's own conclusions about the right and the good, and act upon these. This is not an arbitrary matter.

The task of forming an impartial judgement in a situation of choice requires taking account of the feelings of all involved, oneself included. One test of impartiality concerns the question how the judgement to which one is inclined fits with prior similar judgements and even with the whole range of one's moral commitments and beliefs. One must be able to envisage these as amounting to a consistent and coherent set of practical principles on which anyone might act, without any fair objection from the person who has judged these principles to be satisfactory in his own case. Achieving this kind of overall coherence and consistency is not a task to be done in a spirit of heroic individualism. Nobody can do it without some help. Everyone has reason to compare notes and judgements with others when the context of deliberation makes this possible. Empathy enables us to feel along with others, but talking to them is pretty important as well.

It need scarcely be said that people's capability for moral judgement, like their capacity for speech and for learning whatever can only be learned through speech, is and can only be acquired in a social milieu. People develop the greater part of their moral beliefs out of an initially unreflective respect for taught and even inculcated moral rules laid down in families, at schools and by more diffuse forms of social pressure. This was not something either Smith or Kant doubted. Moral maturity comes about as a person comes to take individual responsibility

---

[5] Cf J. Nedelsky, 'Reconceiving Autonomy' *Yale Journal of Law and Feminism* 1 (1989) 7–36.

for a body of moral opinion, and tradition that she/he initially acquired heteronomously. As one develops autonomy and self-command, one engages in critical reflection on the moral tradition to which one has fallen heir. This involves seeking the reason behind seemingly flat injunctions and prohibitions, developing one's own conception of the deeper principles at stake, and in that light approaching situations of choice and judgement ready to take a fresh view where it seems right to do so.

One can be provoked to moral reflection and deliberation not only by immediate choices one faces oneself, but also by public debates on important issues, such as the reform of the law on abortion, or the development of the law on embryo research. (The question whether any form of human-animal cloning could ever be acceptable was hotly controversial in the UK in the Spring of 2008 on account of a Bill the Government had brought before Parliament. In the same Bill, the issue of the maximum period of gestation within which an abortion may be lawfully performed was also under question. Debates on both issues took place at a very high level of seriousness.) Questions of the legitimacy of recent wars, or of the moral acceptability of a state's reliance on weapons of mass destruction, such as nuclear-armed submarines, or of the requirement for action to prevent climate change or to alleviate third world poverty, and many others similar in kind, provoke both individual deliberation and much discussion among friends, colleagues, professional peers, even casual acquaintances.

The idea that everyone as a moral person has her or his own autonomy lends a particular character to discussions of this kind. No one may lay down the law to anyone else. Each is responsible for her or his own opinions and decisions. Hence moral discourses have to be mutually respectful and non-coercive. It is often possible to bully someone else into adopting your opinion. In legislatures, Party Whips have long practice in the black arts of heavy-handed persuasion. This may be instrumentally useful, and even necessary for such purposes as securing safe passage of a coherent body of Government-sponsored legislation. But only given special assumptions is it compatible with the moral independence of a member of the parliament in question. If you can't stand the heat, keep out of the kitchen. Do not stand for election as a party representative in a legislature without being aware that to some extent you surrender your right of independent decision. Yet the autonomous decision that one can achieve greater good by being elected to a parliament than by any other means has to be undertaken on the basis that the agreement to be an effective representative of the party curtails subsequent in-office exercises of autonomy. (This may be subject to exceptions in cases of deep conscientious disagreement with the party line. Whether this is enough to save contemporary legislatures from stunting the moral autonomy of their members can be left an open question.)

Anyway, the insight that one is oneself autonomous entails recognition of the like autonomy of every other, hence the equality of all moral agents as such. Truly moral co-ordination of moral opinions can only be achieved by those who reach common but independently endorsed conclusions, and this presupposes a readiness to engage in fully open and non-coercive co-deliberation with others. That is, moral deliberation morally ought to proceed through 'discourse' and should never proceed in a non-discursive way, by recourse to power-play, rhetorical tricks or the like.[6] An essentially discursive character, therefore, is crucial to moral thought since it is for each an expression of autonomy. Moral deliberation involves a discourse of equals, seeking some common answer to what is for all the same set of questions, to which, however, no one can lay down the answers with conclusive authority for any other consistently with sustaining the essential character of moral thought.

This leads to a third feature of moral thought that almost inevitably supervenes upon the other two. Moral opinions can be controversial. Since each of us confronts moral questions as an autonomous agent, nobody's answer is conclusive for anyone else. Given the complexity of practical life, perhaps an ever-increasing complexity, there is no *a priori* guarantee that all human beings, or even all human beings who come much into contact with each other, can come to identical conclusions in moral deliberation. In practice, as is obvious every day, conscientious and reasonable people thinking rationally and reasonably about moral issues do come to different and mutually incompatible, sometimes sharply opposed, conclusions. Issues about drugs, about euthanasia, and about abortion are no more than especially vivid illustrations of this. So we may conclude about morality: morality is both discursive and controversial because it presupposes the autonomy of all who take it seriously.

3 Is there moral truth?

The difficulty about the conclusion just reached is that it seems to undermine the possibility of any moral truths. *A* holds that abortion is always wrong, being a form of murder. *B* thinks it is sometimes justified, but only in particular cases and only in the early weeks of pregnancy. *C* thinks there are no justifiable limits on a woman's right to control her own fertility, hence no legitimate legal constraints on abortion at all. The three of them disagree, and as autonomous agents they must respect each other's right to come to a conscientiously held opinion on such a vital question. But what is the truth of the matter concerning abortion? Is it always wrong, sometimes wrong, or never wrong if carried out by the choice of the pregnant woman? If everyone is entitled to their own opinion and if the prospect of reaching agreement seems negligible, do we just have to say there is no truth of the matter or that each has an independent truth of his or her own— a sort of extremely relativized conception of truth?

---

[6] Cf R. Alexy, *Theory of Legal Argumentation* (trans. R. Adler and N. MacCormick) (Oxford: Clarendon Press, 1988) 114–35, 193–4.

This is not an acceptable conclusion. For it has to be observed that we start this argument from a common assumption about the right of each agent to moral autonomy. It is in the nature of our capacity for rational action that we must be treated as capable of acting for our own reasons, indeed we can hardly act for anything else than our own reasons, subject though such reasons may be to illegitimate manipulation by others, or to one's own bias. The apparent absence of moral truth on one question is generated by a conclusion that follows from a different moral truth, concerning the implications of autonomy. The proposition about autonomy has to be true before this version of the problem of moral truth arises at all. Moreover (reverting to the example above), the whole abortion debate proceeds under the common assumption that humans ought not to kill each other save in very exceptional cases. There is then an issue whether a foetus is relevantly a human being, and, even if it is, is this one of the very exceptional cases?

Underlying the conviction that there has to be a truth of the matter even where disagreement is inveterate and irresoluble there lies some kind of an appeal to the idea of human nature and what are the ways of life that best fit the nature of human beings. Here is the source of the perennial appeal of the idea that there is a law of nature, a law that matches the nature of humans and their relation to the rest of creation. It is interesting that Kant's first statement of the categorical imperative in its second formulation directs that we act only on the maxim that we 'can will as a universal law of nature'—'Why "of nature"?' one may ask. For persons of religious convictions, one possible answer will spring to mind. Nature is God's creation and if God has designed people to be the way they are, there are presumably laws of God that show how people should act in a manner fitting to their human nature.

The idea that there are 'laws of God' is picked up in Smith's discussion of the way in which we reason inductively from particular recurring judgements, based on impartial spectatorship, to establish general rules. Many such general rules belong in the commonplace beliefs of many people. They include the customary rules most people are taught in childhood. He says that it is quite proper to think of these long acknowledged moral rules as being 'the laws of God',[7] though truly our access to them is by induction from many judgements of many persons. One can make a quite subtle and interesting argument for this idea of Smith's. Scriptural sources represent moral rules like the Ten Commandments, or other parts of the Mosaic laws, as direct revelations by God to Man. But the biblical story of how this happened is surely myth rather than reality. Even those who accept the idea of direct revelation in some form are able to find other ways of accounting for it. If Smith is right, consideration of human moral psychology shows us how we are able to judge morally cases of (say) theft or adultery. His analysis shows how 'spectator' reasoning brings us to a certain conclusion in nearly all cases of a stealing or of an adulterous liaison. 'Thou shalt not steal' and

---

[7] A. Smith *Theory of Moral Sentiments* 163–172.

'thou shalt not commit adultery' are pretty reliable generalizations from many instances of judgement by many people, and are conventionally acknowledged as well as individually endorsed. Indeed, they are treated as more or less sacred rules of conduct.

Smith effectively tells us that this is a better explanation of them than that they were miraculously inscribed on stone slabs during a thunderstorm on Mount Sinai. Their grounding is actually in the common moral psychology of human beings, not in some divine revelation of the kind reported in Chapter 31 of the book of *Exodus* in the Christian Bible, Old Testament (also in *Deuteronomy*). This may seem an anti-religious or even militantly atheist usurpation of a text that belongs to scripture and indeed to God. But is it really so? At most, it seems to involve a mildly agnostic view.

If we suppose that humans are creatures of God, taking their place in a natural, evolved and still evolving universe, a universe which in its entirety is God's creation, then humans have the psychology they have because they acquired it through a divinely initiated evolutionary process. To discover laws of physics or laws of human psychology (or even reliable generalizations about it) is to unravel one or another element in the great divine scheme.[8] Hence the 'spectator' version of how we come by norms like those in the Commandments is actually a more persuasive account of God's way of giving laws to people than is the Old Testament story. That form of the story would certainly have seemed very much more plausible to the Israelites (and others later) at a certain stage in the evolution of human understanding of the world. So there are reasons why the 'divine revelation to Moses' account came to be believed, but they can now be seen as essentially mythical. On the assumption that there is a creating and designing God, this only amounts to giving a different account of the medium of divine revelation, not to a denial of the accessibility of moral truths.

The theistic assumptions, are not, however essential to the argument. Smith could have given, though he emphatically did not give, an account of all this in completely non-theological terms. The 'spectator' version of the story need not postulate the existence of God. To put the point in terms of twenty-first century cosmology, let us simply suppose that the universe started with a 'Big Bang'. If the Big Bang is simply an uncaused 'point zero' in some cosmic vacuum after which time commences and worlds eventually crystallize into distinct existence, it remains the case that all the subsequent events and phenomena that bear on human morality stand in need of explanation. They need it just as much in a scientistic account of what happened as they do in the theistic one.

If God is responsible for it all, then God breathed value into the world, and endowed us with a psychology that enables us to lock on to value, form value-conceptions, and live according to norms that seem fitting with the nature

---

[8] D. D. Raphael, *Adam Smith* (Oxford: OUP, 1985) gives a fascinating account of Smith's moral theology in relation to his general view of the philosophy of science.

we have as created beings. If no God is responsible, nevertheless it turns out that humans as they have evolved in a tiny corner of the universe possess a certain physical, physiological and psychological character passed from generation to generation through the 'DNA book' that is written in every cell of every human body. This includes a capacity for speech, as noted earlier. The capacity to speak presupposes a capacity to live according to norms and to set value on mutual trust—and that is not all. If the universe is god-free, then it was not God that put values there. But they turn out to be there anyway, and must have been present in potential from Big Bang onwards. You cannot evolve something out of nothing, but only through development of some pre-existing potential. God or no God, values are part of our nature, and norms geared to the values that are part of our nature can quite properly be considered as a kind of 'natural law' whether or not the God hypothesis is entertained. If it is, natural laws are indeed a kind of 'laws of God', but not in the sense that they were dictated and delivered through some kind of ethereal email.

This is why Kant's idea of universalizability of maxims that we can will as 'universal law of nature' bites home on the issue of the possible arbitrariness of the autonomous law-positing will of the moral agent. A law of nature in the sense of an evolved set of norms that set the framework for a satisfactory human life given the whole nature both of human beings (value-elements included) and of their terrestrial environment has to be a coherent set of norms that make sense together. It has to avoid contradiction in the sense of flat mutual opposition of norms, except to the extent that more general principles in some kind of ordering of relative importance according to context make possible the resolution of norm-conflicts by prioritizing one norm over the conflicting other. They have to deal with risks and threats to basic animal values and to specifically human values including common goods, and ideal goods. They have to take full account of the fleshly condition and vulnerability of people, and of their emotional make-up—that is, they must make sense in the light of the sentimental character of humans. Noumenally grasped laws regulate humans who inhabit phenomenal bodies and who feel phenomenal emotions,[9] and they must deal with the realities of this. Smith meets Kant again, after all. Those readings of Kant that write out of his script any attention to the contingent psychology and feelings of individual persons are radically unconvincing—the interpretation that brings Kantian and Smithian insights together is preferable, whether or not either of these Greats would have personally agreed with it. Stand fast by the Smithian categorical imperative!

'Enter as fully as you can into the feelings of everyone directly involved in or affected by an incident or relationship, and impartially form a maxim of judgement about what is

---

[9] Kant draws the celebrated but obscure contrast between the 'noumenal' or intelligible world, or aspect of the world, and its 'phenomenal' aspect. The latter is the domain that, from within the intelligible world, we grasp in terms of cause-effect relations. Moral discourse engages with the former only, in Kant's view.

right that all could accept if they were committed to maintaining mutual beliefs setting a common standard of approval and disapproval among themselves.'

And then:

'Act in accordance with that impartial judgement of what it is right to do in respect of the given incident or relationship.'

4 Natural law and natural freedom

There is nothing historically surprising in these reflections on the 'natural' character of the moral norms that Kant or Smith might derive respectively by the method of the categorical imperative or by that of impartial spectator reflections. Nor, therefore, would it be odd to say the same about results that we derive by the mixed method of the Smithian categorical imperative. Knud Haakonssen and other historians of ideas have traced in considerable detail the interactions of ideas of natural law with the moral philosophy of the Scottish Enlightenment and the links to similar intellectual currents in the German-speaking world.[10] Without descending to any sort of invidious sectarianism, one may nevertheless note how philosophies that ascribe importance to individual freedom of judgement, self-command and autonomy chime closely with Protestantism generally. The idea that Christians, indeed humans at large, are not confined to worshipping in accordance with an inherited and unquestionable tradition woven around the biblical texts entails a kind of autonomy in religious belief. It is a similar idea that they are to accept the word of God as they read it for themselves and not only as a hierarchically ordered priesthood has communicated and interpreted it to them. A revolution in thought was wrought by or around the doctrine that each Christian may and must read the Bible for him/herself, and receive the word of God directly by this means, and, all the more, by that of a 'priesthood of all believers'.[11] The denial of the need for specialized priestly mediation of the true faith makes all believers equal before God and equally responsible for achieving a good understanding of his word and his will, and living in accordance therewith. This is autonomy, this is the soil in which concepts like that of self-command find their roots.

Writers like Pufendorf stressed the rational character of the divine law as the basis for the law of nature and nations and thus as the ground and basis

---

[10] See K. Haakonssen, *Natural Law and Moral Philosophy: From Grotius to the Scottish Enlightenment* (Cambridge: Cambridge University Press, 1996); cf C. L. Griswold, *Adam Smith and the Virtues of Enlightenment* (Cambridge: Cambridge University Press, 1999).

[11] Here is a twenty-first century version of this view: 'Baptists believe that the scripture "There is one God, and one mediator also between God and men, the man Christ Jesus" (1 Tim 2:5) rules out the need for any other intermediary between the individual and God. They believe in the "priesthood of all believers" (cf. 1 Pet 2:5)'. See <http://www.newcastlebaptist.net/4.html>.

for positive municipal law in the Kingdoms of seventeenth century Europe. Pufendorf's main book was translated into English by Gershom Carmichael, Professor of Moral Philosophy at Glasgow University, the teacher of Francis Hutcheson, who, succeeding to the same chair, became teacher of Adam Smith as well as respected exemplar for David Hume. Even more than Pufendorf, Hugo de Groot (Grotius) had a half generation previously laid the greatest stress on the rationality of the divine law. He took this to the point of arguing that even if God were supposed not to exist (which it would be a great sin to suppose), the rational order of the universe would remain unshaken and unshakeable and available for discovery and analysis by the application of human intelligence. Both Smith and Kant were deeply familiar with Pufendorf and Grotius, and with many others like them. The law of nature concerned contemporary thinkers greatly both in itself and as the model for the emerging law of nations in the form of the new public international law that gradually came to be received following the Peace of Westphalia in 1648.

Kant's critical philosophy, aimed at grasping the foundations both of pure and of practical reason, therein including the metaphysics of morals, is nothing other than the product of critical reflection on the natural law theories of the place and period. This shows up in the reference to natural law in the second statement of the first version of the categorical imperative in *The Groundwork of the Metaphysics of Morals*. Smith's case is even more obvious. Both in his moral philosophy and in his never completed work on Jurisprudence, he interacts at all points with natural law thinking, and takes it for granted, for example, that some rights can be properly characterized as 'natural'.[12]

In considering the character of the natural law thinking with which Smith's and Kant's minds were engaged, it is useful to take a reasonably simple model. That course will be pursued here, and in this and the next few chapters considerable attention will be paid to the natural law theory used in the exposition of human positive law by James Dalrymple, Viscount Stair, in his *Institutions of the Law of Scotland*. Despite relative neglect of this work by historians of political and philosophical ideas, it is one of the greatest legal works in the English language. Smith frequently had unacknowledged recourse to it in his unpublished and never completed *Lectures on Jurisprudence*.[13] I present Stair's ideas here as illustrating a particularly clear and vivid exemplar of a Protestant natural law theory, and shall subsequently use it as supplying a particularly illuminating set of framework principles for practical reasoning.

Stair's summary definition of law is worth quoting again, this time in full: 'law is the dictate of reason determining every rational being to that which is congruous and convenient for the nature and condition thereof.'

---

[12] A. Smith *Lectures on Jurisprudence*, 399–400.
[13] To see how much Smith used Stair in relation to elucidating Scots law of his period, see A. Smith, *Lectures on Jurisprudence* 608 ('General Index'; entries under 'Stair').

No one should find this deeply rationalistic characterization of law in any way surprising. Stair was a firm Presbyterian and a trained philosopher (a philosophy teacher, indeed, for some years) as well as a lawyer. It almost goes without saying that he also had to be or become a rationalist natural lawyer of the school of thought of Grotius and, more immediately, of Pufendorf. The thinkers of that school, and certainly Stair himself,[14] were well read in, and quoted frequently from, Suarez and other Catholic writers, thus coming (albeit remotely) under Thomist influence. Nevertheless, they believed that humans can derive what needs to be known about right and wrong either directly from reason and through reasoning or from straightforward reading of the scriptures without the interposition of the corrupting accretions of the Roman ecclesiastical tradition.

Bearing this in mind, let us review the introductory ideas that Stair put forward about the sources of natural law and of our awareness of it. Critically important is the thought that first principles are known to all humankind without learning or experience. But only first principles are known immediately—once it comes to working out subordinate principles and judging well about their concrete application in particular cases, learning and experience and a good understanding are required. What then does reason dictate? What is it that we are capable of knowing without reasoning or experience? Here is a brief and summary account.

It belongs to God always to act and judge in accordance with goodness, righteousness, and truth. He is quite capable of doing otherwise, being all-powerful, but, as an absolutely good being, God never does so. Men and angels, being creatures of God, have the duties of adoration of Him and obedience to His commandments, this being implicit in the nature of created beings. Further points are specifically appropriate to human nature and the human condition, in contrast to that of angels. We humans ought to be humble and penitent, careful, and diligent for the preservation of ourselves and our kind. Therefore also we ought to be sociable and mutually helpful, and act only in ways that would be acceptable to human beings were everyone considered free to act in the same way in the same circumstances. Stair quotes the New Testament version of what is often called the 'golden rule', from Matthew vii 12: 'Do to all as you would have them do to you'. He considers this an excellent formulation, though with the rider that it applies only 'if you were in their case and they in yours'. This he considers preferable to the merely negative version found in heathen classical writers 'Do not do that to another which you would not wish to have done to yourself.'

To summarize, Stair considers it to be fitting and in accordance with the very nature of human beings that they should seek to live peaceably and sociably with their fellow humans, working to secure the subsistence of themselves and their families, while observing the golden rule towards others. That means treating them only as one would wish to be treated by them, assuming roles to be reversed.

---

[14] A. H. Campbell *The Structure of Stair's Institutions* (Glasgow: Jackson, 1954) gives a thorough account of Stair's use of his sources.

Scriptural revelation conveys the finest understanding of this, but it is not essential either to its being true or to its being understood—perhaps a little imperfectly—by every human being. The laws and customs observed even by pagans and heathens demonstrate that even without revealed law, people can have the law within themselves (or 'be a law unto themselves'). Stair pointedly cites Paul's *Letter to the Romans*, discussed earlier in Chapter 3, as giving scriptural authority concerning this possibility of knowledge without scriptural revelation. It is also worth noting that 'goodness, righteousness and truth' as part of the divine nature do not depend upon the divine will, but are rather the values to which the divine will freely orients itself. Hence, for Stair as for Grotius but not Pufendorf, the whole intellectual edifice is intelligible (not that Stair expressly entertains the point) even without God.[15]

So let us ask again whether God could be dropped, even in principle, from this scheme of things? We may ask again what a Richard Dawkins, an evolutionist believer in the 'big bang' theory, might make of this.[16] Obviously, it would be necessary for such a thinker to have some other account for the way values and the teleological conception of nature that encapsulates them could have a foothold in the universe as he characterizes it. As credible as any other answer, it seems, is that the evolution of such a species as ourselves, whose self-understanding cannot be without some assumptions about value, shows that in some way values are part of the stuff of the universe. Our apprehension of them is tied up also with an apparently strong propensity to some kind of faith, some personification of the evolutionary process through which we have emerged. This belief in God may, however (as Dawkins and others contend), be a result of our apprehensions of value rather than their cause. If everything that there is did indeed emerge from nothing or from a void, values turn out to be among what emerged and they remain a part of our being.

Emphatically and in contrast to such speculation, one must affirm that Stair's conception, even more than Smith's or Kant's, is essentially a theistic one, and specifically a protestant Christian one. But even without theistic premises the same picture of what is fitting for human nature could be credibly sustained. Indeed it would be difficult to frame a credible conception of humanity that denies our propensity to the preservation of our own lives and that of our nearest and dearest in the context of some kind of larger society. Such a larger society seems in turn inconceivable save if we envisage its members living at least under reciprocal constraints on unacceptable behaviour, the unacceptable being susceptible to judgement by reference to the golden rule. The golden rule bears

---

[15] In this point, it might be remarked that Grotius and Stair stand a little apart from the Protestant mainstream, where there is a tendency to voluntarism and to resting everything finally on the inscrutable will of God. They are perhaps closer to St Thomas Aquinas than most of their school.

[16] See R. Dawkins, *The Blind Watchmaker* (Repr. with an appendix) (London : Penguin, 1991); *The God Delusion* (London: Black Swan, 2007).

an obvious resemblance to Kant's categorical imperative, but he firmly rejects any identification of the two, calling the golden rule 'merely derivative from our principle'.[17] One might surmise that it was the very formula that he designed the categorical imperative to transcend. The categorical imperative is a grander conceptualization of much the same thing, grander in that it transforms a rule about case-by-case reciprocity into a general methodological prescription for the forming of any moral judgement.

The line of development running through the Protestant natural law theory of which Stair's is a strikingly lucid exemplar thus runs straight on to the Kantian metaphysics of morals. It can also cast similar light on the background assumptions to Smith's theory of moral sentiments. For Smith's theory seeks to provide an empirically testable moral psychology that enables us to see how humans form the judgements that Stair is content to treat as the dictates of reason or some more elaborate derivation from such basic principles.

Stair presents justice as a human virtue in the typical civilian version derived from classical sources. It is a virtue exhibited in the exercise of the will, what Justinian called the steady and unvarying will to give everyone that which is rightfully due to them. So far as we can exercise self-command and behave justly, peace can be secure among us. But we are sometimes weak-willed—or strong-willed in the wrong direction—and fall into mutual injustice, which upsets the conditions of social peace. Without some kind of impartial judgement, peace is almost impossible to uphold—and, in fact, human societies everywhere have found ways of institutionalizing, albeit often with serious imperfections, practices of impartial judgement among persons who have fallen at odds with each other in ways that threaten civil peace. From such institutionalization, human law emerges as an additional security for natural law and natural right, not in complete substitution for it.

Clearly, this kind of natural law theorizing contains much that Smith—and also Kant—would recognize. The ideas that they refined, through a 'critical' philosophy in Kant's case, are all to be found here already. But they remove the need for simply asserted 'reason' and its deliverances, and they do not rely on scriptural revelation. Truth in moral matters does not depend on some kind of correspondence with a pre-existing rational order of things in the world. It depends on the correct forming of a judgement. This can be conceptualized through impartial spectator reasoning, or through application of the categorical imperative, or through the combination of the two that has been suggested here as the 'Smithian categorical imperative'. In the context of a moral discourse of equals, it may be impossible to establish convincingly which among reasonably arguable rival positions or judgements is the correct one, that which the relevant reasoning most convincingly supports. But often it will be obvious that one position is not even reasonably arguable against any rival. That we cannot always agree what

[17] See H. J. Paton, *The Moral Law* (London: Hutchinson, 1958) 92, footnote.

is true does not mean that nothing is. And the test to which we should look for resolution of disagreements ought to be an articulated understanding of human nature as a value-laden concept.

5 'Laws of freedom' and 'natural liberty'

The Kantian stress on autonomy as essential to moral agency coupled with the stress on the good will acting for duty's sake as the only unqualified human good[18] gives rise to a difficulty about the role of positive law in a kingdom or republic or other form of state. State law uses coercion, in the form of enforced criminal penalties and also enforced civil remedies. But coerced action is not good action. He who refrains from murder or assault because afraid of paying the penalty for murder does not act virtuously. He who pays his debts only for fear of being named on the trade association's blacklist is not an honest trader. Yet surely it is better in some sense that the murder to which one was tempted was not after all committed, and that the creditor did receive the due payment in a timely way. Looking at it the other way round, we should note that the person from whom the threat of murder is lifted is thereby the more free to go about her/his ordinary business and to live in accordance with her/his own plan of life. Likewise the satisfied creditor is not deprived of expected resources to go on with his/her business and plan of life. Violence and injustice among persons deprive of proper freedom the weaker or disadvantaged party in a relationship of threatened violence or injustice. That party cannot act freely in accordance with the prompting of duty because of coercion applied by someone else. In Kant's view, it is the task of the state to protect every person's capability for free action. The law's hindrances should be applied only to hinder those kinds of act that are themselves hindrances to freedom. Such 'laws of freedom' are the only positive laws to which an ideal society would give force and validity.[19]

This is only partly comparable, yet it is also strikingly comparable, with Smith's idea of 'the system of natural liberty' as the foundation for political economy. Smith's *Wealth of Nations* is an extended argument in support of the value of free market economies. Humans have a natural propensity to truck, barter, and exchange, yet all too often there are artificial—state-imposed—restraints on people's ability to trade freely with each other. The merchant and trade guilds of eighteenth century cities gave their members exclusive privileges in the conduct of their business and the law banned new entrants from coming into the relevant market. In other instances, certain businesses could receive active financial assistance from public sources that were denied to their rivals. These practices

---

[18] H. J. Paton, *The Moral Law*, 66–88, 95–8.
[19] See J. Ladd (trans), *Kant: The Metaphysical Elements of Justice* (Indianapolis, IN: Bobbs-Merrill, 1965) 36–7.

injured consumers of goods and services, who had to pay too much for them, and they were unfair to those potential competitors who were willing to attempt entry into the market place to offer terms more favourable than those offered by persons already established in it. As consumers and as potential workers, people are impoverished through state favouritism towards a privileged few. This should cease. 'All systems either of preference or restraint, therefore, being thus completely taken away, the system of natural liberty establishes itself of its own accord. Every man, as long as he does not violate the laws of justice, is left perfectly free to pursue his own interest his own way, and to bring both his industry and capital into competition with those of any other man, or order of men.'[20] Of course, the state is not a mere bystander in respect of the establishment of a market, for markets depend on peaceful interaction, with repression of violence and rapine. They depend on the background maintenance of an effective system of civil and criminal justice and on the provision of important public goods like an adequate road network and a system of elementary education, and, generally, on satisfactory 'police'.

Despite that, and despite the difference in their dialectical origin and specific philosophical context, the 'system of natural liberty' and the 'laws of freedom' propose as political ideals rather similar frameworks of positive law. The next chapters will show to what an extent Stair's legal exposition had prefigured this.

---

[20] A. Smith, *Wealth of Nations*, 687 (book IV.ix.51).

6

Obedience, Freedom, and Engagement—or Utility?

1 Obedience, freedom, and engagement

The earlier parts of the book suggested that justifying reasons for action, looked at in a critical-rational way, include self-regarding, other-regarding, and community-regarding reasons that may have either animal or ideal goods as their content and that may or may not have exclusionary force in deliberation. Reasoning in the context of a relevant normative order may introduce considerations of what is right and wrong. Where some act or conduct is wrong in the given context, that is a ground for eliminating such a course of conduct from practical deliberation in that context regardless of other reasons there are in favour of doing it. This is of particular salience in the context of moral reasoning, where obligations and duties to others (and possibly on occasion to or in respect of oneself) make some act or omission wrong in respect of certain other persons, or other people in general. The point about moral reasoning is that it is universal in its reference, and is applicable to all domains of human activity. Hence, unlike institutional reasoning, it is not domain-specific. In principle, therefore, moral obligations constitute positive reasons for doing whatever is obligatory and they ought to override or exclude reasons, however strong, originating in any specific institutional domain.

One doctrine of seventeenth century natural law theory suggested that there were three basic practical principles, 'obedience, freedom and engagement'. This meant: You must fulfil all your basic duties; beyond that you are morally free to do as you think best; but you can limit your freedom by making engagements (promises, contracts etc) with others. It is a three-step argument, and I shall here dub it 'Stair's Three Steps', for it is in his *Institutions* that this idea is advanced.

The first principle 'obedience' holds good on condition that there are basic interpersonal duties (which have as their correlatives certain basic interpersonal rights,[1] or fundamental common law rights, we might say) that we must observe.

---

[1] These are not the human rights one can vindicate against states or governments, as in the Universal Declaration on Human Rights of 1948, but yet more basic rights that avail against fellow human beings in abstraction from any particular governmental arrangements.

It is not hard to specify some such duties: we must not kill or injure others, nor violate their family relationships, nor defame nor deceive them, nor otherwise damage them by lying to or about them (bearing false witness). Perhaps there are others, but these are enough to be going on with. Stair regarded them as duties to which we were bound by the will of God, hence his use of the term 'obedience' here. They deal with topics in respect of which it is not difficult to set up basic moral precepts of the kind Smith thought we could establish inductively from the fruits of 'spectator reasoning' based on frequently occurring cases. Kantian universalization tested by the possibility of willing the maxims of our actions as a 'universal law of nature' seems likewise to yield a pretty easy answer for these basic topics. Assuming it is possible to modify Smith's sentimentalism and adapt it along the lines of the Smithian categorical imperative, the picture is all the clearer about these basic duties we owe each other, as will be argued later in this chapter. The principle of obedience is simply the principle that we must always fulfil all the basic duties that we find binding on us. We must exclude from deliberation any otherwise attractive course of action that presents itself as a rival whenever it would involve violating such a duty.

Conversely, in a way we have already noted, we have freedom in the sense of normative liberty wherever no duty exists or applies. We are free to deliberate among whatever seem to us desirable courses of action, and in a large way we are morally free to construct and periodically revise our own plan of life, just so long as we do not plan to infringe the basic duties. We are free to go ahead and carry out our decisions in fulfilment of plans and projects. As rational moral agents, we of course act for reasons, and we act in a fully rational way to the extent that we consider well all the reasons or motives that bear upon our situation and succeed in doing what is best on the whole. But since we are outside of the realm of duty it is necessarily the case that we are not accountable to anybody for the correctness or incorrectness of our judgements about what it is best to do. We may hope to have friends and colleagues whose advice we can seek and can ponder in our deliberations. We may hope to have good friends who will warn us when we appear to be embarking on a foolish and perhaps dangerous course of conduct. But advice and warnings are not binding directives. We are in the end free to do as we think best, though foolish if we ignore advice and warnings, or weigh them lightly.

This freedom can be self-limiting, however. For it includes freedom to enter into all sorts of commitments with other people—promises, contracts, partnerships, marriages, trustee relationships and so on. For reasons already discussed, these in turn generate mutual (or sometimes unilateral) obligations. Contract (or its cognates) is a device whereby we may freely fetter our freedom, but as between any contracting pair the constraints are (or would be in circumstances of reasonable distributive justice) fully reciprocal or even mutual constraints, well-balanced on either side. Assuming people enter these after reasonable deliberation, they can be presumed to express judgements about courses of action that are in principle preferable to the alternatives. In this restricted sense, voluntary and contractual obligations are burdens undertaken for what is (or may be judged to be) on balance the greatest available advantage (or least unavoidable disadvantage) of the person(s) undertaking the burdens. The principle of engagement delineates a way of exercising moral freedom, notwithstanding the specific limitations of freedom that follow from the undertaking of promissory or contractual obligations.

Apart therefore from basic duties, and from obligations incurred under the principle of engagement, the principle of freedom leaves moral agents free to live their own lives as they think best. They have to construct their own view of a good life, or their own plan of life. It is open to them to deliberate as and when necessary concerning the most desirable course of action open to them (always assuming they have fulfilled and will fulfil their duties and obligations). Putting it simply, we have to do what is right, keep our engagements, and act for the best within the sphere of discretion bestowed on us by the principle of freedom. That is how a good human being lives.

2 Utilitarian objections

Put simply and summarily, Stair's Three Steps seem to give a rather good and clear picture of how a person ought to live. The picture presented has not, however, been without its critics. Utilitarians from Jeremy Bentham onwards have ridiculed all such ideas for overcomplicating the basic moral truth that can be said yet more simply, and better.

Utilitarianism is the doctrine that we should always act so as to maximize the good (whatever 'good' may be, or whatever may be good). It necessarily denies that there is any difference between deliberating in the so-called domain of freedom and deliberating in the domain of either 'obedience' or 'engagement'. If we ought always to act for the best in the supposed sphere of freedom, our actions are no more free here than anywhere else. We have to realize the greatest possible net good by all our actions. This may call for the exercise of discretion in judgement, but only in the sense that we have to reason our way through to a difficult and sometimes disputable view about what is best on the whole. Once it is determined (however tentatively or confidently) what it is best to do, that alone is what it is right to do. So there is no true liberty in the end, but a single right answer to the question what one must do.

Conversely, utilitarians hold that the supposed principles of obedience and of engagement are themselves subordinate elements of the principle of utility, since they depend also on a judgement about what is best all things considered. Even if we derive the basic duties via a Kantian argument or some modified Smithian universalizability argument through the 'categorical imperative', we end up asking 'What can a person rationally will as a universal law?' Since unrestrained violence and unrestrained lying, cheating and breach of promise would cause widespread social breakdown and general misery, one can safely say that rules prohibiting such conduct ought to be observed—for utilitarian reasons. The greatest good of human beings requires common observation of such rules. They do not contradict the principle of utility but are mandated by it. The same goes for the rule that promises and contracts seriously made must be kept. To have such a rule obviously serves the general good of a community. To the extent that it does not, there should be exceptions to the rule that promises and contracts are binding. So everything boils down to the proposition that one ought always to act for the best. Sometimes, perhaps, this may best be achieved by observing certain strict rules and applying them to everyone impartially and rigorously, but sometimes it is achieved by directly working out what it is best for a person to do in the whole circumstances of a given dilemma.

Jeremy Bentham was certainly the father of English utilitarianism, in the advocacy of which he so thoroughly excoriated all forms of natural law thought as to become (without knowing or intending it) also the father of English legal positivism.[2] For sure, Bentham did oppose in a conscious and deliberate way the leading appeals to the 'law of nature' that he found in his contemporaries' and his elders' writing about law. From the start, he adhered unswervingly to a voluntaristic conception of law. Laws exist because intelligent beings will that they shall, and manifest this by addressing imperative mandates to those whose conduct they have power to influence by this means. Except in a highly metaphorical sense, nature issues no such mandates. As for nature's God, Bentham observed in the main a studious silence concerning divine existence or divine concern for human affairs. (This opacity was not emulated by his disciple John Austin, who was, without apology, deistic or even theistic in his beliefs, and unhesitatingly acknowledged the existence of divine laws as perfectly genuine laws because perfectly genuine commands. Indeed, Austin took the principle of utility to be the central commandment of the divine law.[3])

Bentham also believed in this single great practical principle, that of utility. He therefore rejected the claim that there are laws (stressing the plural) of nature. This claim had the unacceptable implication that there is a plurality of fundamental practical principles. These are supposed to be certified to us by divine revelation, or some kind of 'common sense', or through the appeal to supposedly

---

[2] The term and perhaps the concept 'legal positivism' had not yet emerged in scholarly usage at the time when Bentham was writing. He certainly believed that the only real law was positive law laid down by the authorities of a state. He also believed that the only good law was explicitly enacted legislation, not law snared in all the ambiguities of precedent and capriciously supported by appeals to 'natural law'. See in particular J. Bentham, *Of Laws in General* (ed. H. L. A. Hart) (London: Athlone Press, 1970); *An Introduction to the Principles of Morals and Legislation* (ed. J. H. Burns and H. L. A. Hart) (London: Athlone Press, 1970); *A Comment on the Commentaries* and *A Fragment on Government* (ed. J. H. Burns and H. L. A. Hart) (London: Athlone Press, 1977); see generally R. Harrison, *Bentham* (London: Routledge and Kegan Paul, 1983).

[3] See J. Austin, *The Province of Jurisprudence Determined* (ed. W. E. Rumble) (Cambridge: Cambridge University Press, 1995), lectures 2 and 3.

uniform moral sentiments, hence the 'principle of sympathy and antipathy' (an unambiguous side-swipe at Adam Smith), or, in a word, the principle of 'caprice'.[4] All this amounted to a licence for arbitrariness in legislative action or in moral judgement and conduct. In legal life it amounted, in yet more sinister and dele-terious fashion, to a cloak for sectional or class interest masquerading as natural right. Bentham had a sharp eye for what later thinkers would recognize as dis-tinctively 'ideological'. It seemed to him obvious that theories about natural law in effect extracted a set of principles out of the legal order found in contemporary kingdoms, certified these as 'natural law', and then read the self-same principles of natural law back into the positive law. In a quite fallacious way the 'natural law' could thus be appealed to as something that guaranteed the legitimacy of the positive law after all—and set an obstacle to any change in it. It needs scarcely be said that Sir William Blackstone's *Commentaries on the Laws of England* consti-tuted for Bentham the grand exemplar of this fallacy.[5]

Against Blackstone, Bentham's ideology-critique took the form of a blis-tering attack on the use of natural law as a cloak for a conservative defence of established dispositions of wealth, power, and privilege. In revolutionary times, he pilloried with equal vituperation the anarchical fallacies[6] of revolutionary thought, using much the same critique. For here again was an appeal to natural law, this time expressed in subjectivist style as manifesting itself in natural rights, given the false dignity of the objective under claims to 'inalienable and impre-scriptible' natural rights whose neglect by governments demanded their violent overthrow.

At all times, Bentham saw in any unreflective resort to fictional ways of thinking the error that certain twentieth century thinkers were later to damn as 'reification'.[7] This occurs when essentially modal or verbal elements in our thought get captured in nouns, as when 'it is right that you pay me £10' becomes 'I have a right to be paid £10 by you'. Folk-grammar then licenses us to think of 'rights' and such like as names of things, so we ascribe independent existence to non-physical entities that we then claim as independent objects to be protected or secured by human arrangements. The truth is that the only origin of these feigned things is the very human arrangements that are supposed to be justified by the role they play in protecting the things, the rights, the property in land and moveable objects.

Some obvious questions arise. What is the general character of the arrange-ments in question? Whence emerges the apparent naturalness of our belief in

---

[4] J. Bentham, An *Introduction to Principles*, 21–5.

[5] See *A Comment on the Commentaries* and *A Fragment on Government* passim.

[6] See B. Parekh (ed) *Bentham's Political Thought* (London: Croom Helm, 1973), excerpt on *Anarchical Fallacies*. Cf J. Waldron, *Nonsense upon Stilts: Bentham, Burke and Marx on the Rights of Man* (London: Methuen, 1987).

[7] See C. K. Ogden *Bentham's Theory of Fictions* (London : Kegan Paul, Trench, Trubner & Co., 1932) and compare on 'reification' W. Twining and D. Miers, *How to Do Things with Rules* (London: Butterworths, 4th edn. 1999) 143–6, 372.

feigned or fictional entities like rights, and how are they truly to be accounted for? Further, how can such arrangements be justified if not by reference to natural rights, natural law, and perhaps a social contract thrown in for good measure?

Bentham's account of the social arrangements was radically voluntaristic. Habitual patterns of obedience by the many to some person or agency that issues directives is constitutive of political society; and appropriately issued directives ('mandates', in Bentham's preferred terminology,[8] 'commands' in Austin's) constitute laws. To have the required compulsory effect, such directives require the backing of sanctions that can be enforced when necessary. The power-structures constituted by patterns of habitual obedience in turn make possible such enforcement processes in organized form, as against the diffuse social pressure of moral opinion.

The idea that some ways of acting are wrong or are 'offences' depends on this. Offences are acts that infringe sovereign directives, and our duties are the converse of the offences. (Wilful killing is prohibited under severe penalties; that is, murder is a crime; that is, we have a duty not to murder anyone.) Thus 'duties' are no more than the negative and positive actions that legally we must perform in response to sovereign directives. Where duties are rationally imposed, that is to say, where directives are rationally issued, there must be some valued end in view. If this valued end is the wellbeing of some person or persons, that or those persons are beneficiaries of the duty as regards whatever abstention or performance the law requires, in relation to whatever material objects may be involved. What we call 'having a right' is being in the position of a beneficiary of the legal duty imposed on another person, or perhaps on every other person. Where such duties require leaving a person in undisturbed possession of a thing, and where they are imposed on other persons at large, the right is what we call a right of property.[9] Being the only person not required to refrain from driving my car without my own permission, I am uniquely at liberty to drive it and use it otherwise just as I choose. This liberty, this absence of any binding mandate, is another way of 'having a right', but this remains truly a negative modality of duty-bearing, not a 'natural' thing that exists in the world apart from structures of human command and non-command.

Property is thus neither a mysterious quiddity of natural law nor a pre-political natural right. It is, in relation to any given thing, a complex congeries of rights to use the thing and to exclude others from it or to grant them access to it. This is coupled with a power to divest oneself of and invest another in the same congeries of rights. All of this depends in one way or the other on the mandates or directives that constitute offences by imposing duties.

So much, in sketch, for Bentham's view about what are the required social arrangements. So far as concerns justification, the test is the principle of utility. Do these arrangements tend to secure the greatest happiness of the greatest

---

[8] J. Bentham, *Laws in General*, 13.   [9] J. Bentham, *Laws in General*, 176–183.

number, that is, treating all persons as equals, does the totality of pleasures experienced exceed the totality of pains suffered attributably to the arrangements? Could any adjustment improve the balance of pleasure over pain? In short, any body of laws should have its costs and benefits calculated by reference to the 'hedonistic calculus', and judged for achieving or failing to achieve a practicable maximization of net overall happiness.[10] On this, I need not go into detail here. But it is important to stress that the principle of utility coupled with the principle of equality ('each to count for one, none for more than one') led Bentham in his later years to a belief in democracy on the basis of universal adult franchise.[11] For this was in his opinion the only electoral system that would create a coincidence of interest between the members of the legislature and the whole population. Amartya Sen argues convincingly that there is empirical evidence in favour of this view of Bentham's.[12] Anyway, it is scarcely surprising, given his premises, that Bentham found much to censure in the contemporary law and contemporary legislative politics of the United Kingdom, and the other states to which he directed his intention. He did, however, retain the view that the reformer's proper course of action, while censuring freely, was nevertheless to obey punctually. He was no revolutionary.

A little-noticed further corollary of Bentham's overall stance is that there is built into the very idea of law a utilitarian aspiration. It implies that whoever undertakes the role of a legislator faces in that capacity the demand that power be used to further human felicity. The pretension to have made law successfully and satisfactorily exposes the law-maker to the demand that success be proved in the coin of utility. Robert Alexy's idea of an implicit 'claim to correctness' in all legal and especially lawmaking activity[13] fully applies here. Not all that is done in the name of law is useful (or, therefore, just) by the utilitarian test. But given that law is in the business of threatening and imposing pain, those in charge of it have a very special responsibility to see that there is no unnecessary, no useless pain. In this sense, an aspiration to justice is built into the very concept of law; but this aspiration is often neglected. The duty of the utilitarian as censor is to campaign for reform, not to agitate for revolution, since revolutions usually cause as much evil as they set out to cure.

The time has come to pause and summarize the tenets of Bentham's anti-naturalism as we have skimmed over them here. They include both theoretical and practical points:

1 **Voluntarism:** Law is grounded in will so far as concerns its existence: this was not a new view in itself, but what was new was the dropping of any assumption

---

[10] J. Bentham, *Intro to Principles* 38–72.
[11] See O. Ben Dor *Constitutional Limits and the Public Sphere* (Oxford: Hart, 2000) 95–135.
[12] See A. K. Sen, *Inequality Reexamined* (Oxford: Clarendon Press, 1992).
[13] R. Alexy, *The Argument from Injustice: a reply to legal positivism* (trans. B. Litschewski Paulson and S. Paulson) (Oxford: Clarendon Press, 2002) ch 4.3.3.

that human law-giving wills operated simply to concretize or make determinate broader principles of natural law.

2 **Non-contractarianism:** Law-giving power depends on no social contract but on the availability of coercive force and on habits and attitudes of deference to persons or institutions (noting that law-making institutions could be democratic in composition); the social contract is a pointless fiction.

3 **Priority of duty over right:** Duty is a concept intelligible to us through reflection on the mandates of legislators or legislatures that are sanctioned by the threat of punishment in case of breach; given utilitarian reasons for imposing duties, namely in the interests of others, this makes intelligible the notion of right. Those for whose benefit a duty is imposed have a right that it be performed.

4 **Critique of natural rights:** So-called 'natural rights' are therefore a needless theoretical postulate. Even if there were a social contract, the idea that it would contain terms securing natural rights is accordingly false and ideological.

5 **Critique of reification:** The theory of fictions is an extended warning against becoming bamboozled by noun-forms, as well as an exposition of the use of such forms with proper caution.

6 **Critique of caprice:** All natural law thinkers of Bentham's period had included some version of the principle of utility along with other fundamental moral principles implicit in law. Bentham threw out the pluralistic bath-water, but kept the utilitarian baby and transformed it towards being an empirically applicable yardstick for a science of legislation.

7 **Critique of oligarchy:** Unrepresentative legislatures typically fail to weigh equally the pains and pleasures of all affected by their laws. Democratic institutions are therefore preferable, and thought should be given to the arrangements for an effectively democratic constitution.

8 **Critique of common law:** Blackstone and other natural lawyers had portrayed the common law as a pinnacle of reason quite faithfully embodying the natural law, though capable of incremental development toward perfection. Bentham saw it as a largely sinister product of oligarchy, deficient in the character that law should have as a body of explicit mandates from the sovereign aimed at the utility of the subjects.

9 **Preference for codification:** As a corollary of (8), (6) and (1), legislatures should take the initiative in law-making in order to promote the happiness of the people. This requires clear and well-articulated laws, ideally cast in the form of a coherent code, sufficiently detailed to prevent mischievous and sectionally interested law-making by the judges under cover of interpretation.

Taken as a whole, Bentham's was an intrinsically and intensely practical, action-oriented programme. It emerged from a critique of certain principles of 'natural law'. That is, it emerged from a critique of the arguments of certain powerful representatives of established social order and positive law who found the rhetoric of natural law comfortable for accomplishing their ideological ends. Tom Campbell's recent and powerful *The Legal Theory of Ethical Positivism*[14] has restated positivism in this practical tradition, not as an essentially descriptive or conceptual account of how law happens to be, but an ethically grounded vision of how it should be. Duncan Kennedy has made an eloquent plea for the merits of the United States' tradition of assigning large-scale ideological debate and decision to Courts.[15] Writing from another federal system, Australia, Campbell argues passionately that the best form for law is legislation, with a very diminished law-creative role for courts, lawyers, and the legal academy. How far one goes along the line with Campbell may perhaps depend to a considerable extent on the degree to which one accepts Bentham's other theses as summarized above.

On this, there are two critical lines of division, that concerning voluntarism and that concerning utilitarianism, to be considered in that order. As for voluntarism, it need not be doubted that in empires, feudal monarchies, benevolent-despotic governments, or liberal states there have always been and still are law-making arrangements. These involve the formation and the implementation of a will, individual or collective, concerning the rules people are to observe, and the definitions the law-applying agencies are to apply of the wrongs they are to sanction and the rights they are to uphold. The efficacy of the body of rules backed by the sovereign will is to be judged in the first place by the regularity of compliance by the subjects or citizens, not by inquiry into their motives. If you wonder whether there is an effective legal system in a certain territory, information on the 'habit of obedience' will suffice for this purpose.

But if you wonder about the very idea of 'rules' among people, that is, about the way in which our social interactions and our individual moral commitments can exhibit a normative, judgment-guiding, quality, the voluntarist theses do not yield the answer. Indeed, they presuppose it. One can lay down the rules that are to be observed only if the population in question is capable of rule-oriented, rule-interpreting, normative awareness. Inquiry into that dimension of the human mind, into this aspect of mind's active powers, reveals the necessity but insufficiency of the 'habit of obedience'. It yields much more fruitful conceptions of conventions and customs, some of which directly guide judgement and action, others of which effectively clothe with authority legal sources that can articulate rules in a much clearer form than custom in its nature can achieve.[16] Voluntarism as a basic explanation of law is a dead end.

---

[14] Aldershot: Dartmouth, 1996.

[15] D. Kennedy, *A Critique of Adjudication* (Cambridge, MA: Harvard University Press, 1997) 33–79.

[16] This line of response to Bentham's project owes a great deal to the seminal work of H. L. A. Hart (and he in turn stood on the shoulders of other sociological and philosophical giants). My own version of this has recently been fully stated in N. MacCormick, *Institutions of Law* (Oxford: Oxford University Press, 2007) chs 1 and 2.

So far as concerns utilitarianism, its single-principle character has certain attractions, all the more when it is yoked to a single-scale value theory,
whether in terms of the pleasure/pain calculus advanced by Bentham, or in
terms suggested by successor utilitarians such as preference-satisfaction,[17]
or wealth-maximization.[18] For this promises the possibility of objective and
interpersonally checkable calculations of rightness in action, including legislative and other governmental action. The most powerful current jurispruden-
tial defence of this general position emanates from the so-called 'economic
analysis of law'.[19] Even though this advances a methodology for judicial
reasoning, there is a case for the view that the kind of calculations involved
are even better performed by the bureaucracy than the judiciary, and fed into
law through legislation rather than adjudication. So the arguments of Bentham
and Campbell in favour of a relatively passive, law-applying, neutral judiciary
can make a strong appeal if these premises hold good, quite regardless of the
failure of voluntarism. Respect for each human person as such is not necessarily neglected by this approach. It is satisfied by the methodological injunction
that decision makers must always count each human being for one and none for
more than one. Provided that is done, the rights of individuals are best interpreted as derivative from the actual set of duties that the law does lay down, or
from the ideal set that the law would lay down if it fully satisfied the demand for
value-maximization on the relevant scale of value.

This stance would not itself preclude the inclusion of a Charter of Rights in
a constitution. It would, however, militate against the view that such a charter
merely confirms people in the possession of what is in any event theirs by right. For
it would hold that the rights have to be justified by reference to some cost-benefit
analysis, and that the act of specially entrenching them would require a further
application of the same sort of analysis. Still, the case for doing this would be
harder to establish than it would be for somebody who considers justice to comprise a plurality of principles, or to call for recognition of a Stair-like set of basic
duties. For, in that case, a person to whose detriment any such principle or duty is
infringed thereby suffers serious wrong.

3 The economics of everything

Bentham's present day followers ought to be recognized as including those economists who contend that decision-making guided by cost-benefit reasoning is a
completely comprehensive account of human practical rationality. The key point
in Bentham's utilitarianism lies in the claim that what is good for humans is

---

[17] For example, by A. K. Sen in *Choice, Welfare, and Measurement* (Oxford: Blackwell, 1982).
[18] cf R. A. Posner, *Economic Analysis Of Law* (Boston: Little, Brown, 1972).
[19] R. A. Posner, *Economic Analysis Of Law*.

always and completely commensurable both as concerns a single individual and interpersonally. His calculus of pleasures and pains was the method he proposed for calculating utility. The action that promotes most pleasure at least cost in pain is that which is most useful (has greatest utility) towards the maximization of human happiness. Happiness is the only ultimate end for humans; the best action is that which produces greatest happiness. Happiness is defined in terms of pleasure and pain. The greatest number of units of pleasure you can produce at the least cost in units of pain defines the maximum of happiness that you can realize in acting now. Your act ought to maximize happiness. Every other principle of action that theorists suggest involves some kind of caprice, not simple rational motivation.

Preferences supplant pleasures in contemporary economic thought. Each subject has her/his own preferences. Preferences are comparable, and have to be. Do I prefer a visit to the theatre to an evening of writing at my desk? Do I prefer a grand dinner party to either? That depends on me, and depends on the occasion. Some day I prefer one another day another. But at any time I can rank my preferences among all options open to me. If I could not, I would face an agony of indecision, and decide nothing. All this is subjective, and every subject has her/his own subjective preferences. There can however be objective measuring of differences among preferences. In money economies, people typically (and necessarily) express their valuations in terms of benefit and cost. Whatever gives a greater surplus of the one over the other is to that extent preferable. If I would pay more for one thing than for another of essentially the same kind, then I prefer this to that, and the cash difference gives a scale of preference. Similarly as between individuals, differences of valuation are expressible in terms of what people do, or hypothetically would, pay to have more of one thing and less of another (or none at all, in case of things we actively desire not to have).

On this view, rational decision-making is easy to explain. That decision is, for a given decision-maker, most rational if it yields greatest benefits at lowest costs. Individuals do this in terms of their own preferences. Collective decision-makers like Ministers, Cabinets, and Parliaments have a more complex task, but it is in principle the same one. How to maximize benefits at lowest costs overall, taking account of everyone's positive and negative preferences. There may also be problems of time-scale—over what period must the balance be struck? But that again can be incorporated into the same basic method by seeking to find how far people discount preferences in terms of their immediacy or postponement to the future. (Bentham already foresaw this in his 'hedonistic calculus'.)

Psychologists and economists have disputed over the question whether this analysis of reasoning is essentially descriptive or prescriptive. Perhaps people are natural cost-benefit calculators—not infallibly good at such calculation, of course, but naturally inclined to seek greatest benefits at lowest costs. Or perhaps this is a skill they ought to learn, or be taught. There has been recent literature to the effect that people can be taught to become better at such calculation than, in

an untutored way, they normally are.[20] Such a controversy is not of great importance for present purposes, however. Either way, economic analysis suggests a
simplified schema of practical reasoning that combines the merits of Bentham's
original proposal with more perspicuous means for putting it to practical use.
This involves subjecting the choices we face to some kind of rational analysis such
that there is an in-principle straightforward calculation concerning what is best
to do. Moreover, it builds in interpersonal comparability where decisions bear
upon the preferences of more than one subject.

If this is so, then the pleasing simplicity with which we started, relying on
Stair's Three Steps of 'obedience, freedom and engagement' turns out to be illu-
sory. Matters are yet more simple. Or are they?

4 Smith's sentiments, Kant's Universal Will, and Stair's Three Steps

At an early stage, we took note of the idea that where there are duties to be done,
or where some course of conduct is (by relevant standards) wrong, there is a
corollary. The corollary is that people can demand performance of the duty, or
demand abstinence from what is wrong. If there is a person who suffers the wrong
or who suffers the breach of duty, that person has ground for protest, and for
self-protection, even in acute cases, self-defence. In the context of the state and
civil society, it is to be expected that there will be some available form of public
intervention, some public sanctioning of the wrong or breach of duty. In a moral
community the wrongdoer suffers opprobrium and blame from fellow members
of the community. This can itself be distressing, even painful, and may lead to
adverse consequences in loss of trust and good will from others. What, then, can
warrant such demands?

It is a matter of mere common observation that no similar blaming and opprobrium attaches to people who act merely foolishly. You may try to act for the
best but often fail and sometimes fail badly and in a laughable way. You may
be Icarus trying to fly too close to the sun with waxen wings. Your downfall
may provoke cruel laughter. But no one complains about violation of rights or
breaches of duty. In the sphere of freedom of action we ought all indeed to act for
the best. But the point about freedom is that no particular act can be demanded
of us however much it may be right to advise taking that course. If utilitarianism
or cost-benefit analysis cannot account for this, they are oversimplifications, not
benign clarifications.

Bentham was too quick to dismiss Smith's 'principle of sympathy and antipathy'. Smith certainly did not say that right and wrong are determined simply by

---

[20] See e.g. Richard E. Nisbett (ed), *Rules for Reasoning* (New Jersey Hove and London: Lawrence
Erlbaum Associates, 1993).

a person's momentary sentiments of sympathy or antipathy that have been aroused by the actions of others. If he had done, he would have issued no more than a recipe for arbitrariness and caprice—which is exactly the complaint Bentham made. This complaint, however, completely ignores the elaborate apparatus of the ideal impartial spectator that is at the heart of Smith's moral theory. This theory has been adapted in the present work to try to establish a rapprochement between Smith's and Kant's moral theories, or at least an adaptation of Smith's ideas to the kernel of what is best in Kant's.

Smith starts with what he takes to be an undeniable fact of experience. This is the fact that what human beings do can have effects, or even (metaphorically or literally) impacts, on them. These effects or impacts can be either painful or beneficial. Sometimes a painful impact appears to have been intended by the actor, sometimes a beneficial impact seems likewise intentional. Sometimes it is a side-effect of what the actor was primarily intending to do, and again sometimes a foreseen side-effect, sometimes not foreseen but foreseeable, sometimes a pure accident, neither foreseen nor foreseeable. A second no less deniable fact of experience is that people respond to the impact of others' actions in characteristic ways, starting with immediate pain or pleasure and then involving secondary sentiments depending on the deliberate or negligent or accidental quality they impute to the actions of their neighbour. A third fact is that bystanders and more distant but still involved parties can enter into or share in similar reactions to those of the persons directly affected.

The more harmful and more malevolent (intentionally harmful) a person's act toward another is (or is perceived to be), the stronger is the reciprocal complex of sentiments felt by the sufferer—pain, anger, and finally resentment. People are not inclined to suffer this in silence nor do bystanders expect them to (though sufferers and spectators may on occasion be terrorized into silence, which may well exacerbate their sense of a wrong done at the same time as inhibiting any effectual response). In any human community such events heighten tension and threaten communal peace. To say nothing of 'natural law', it seems entirely natural that people react adversely to harmful conduct especially when and to the extent that it appears to be actuated by malevolence or to express contempt for another person. It is equally unsurprising that the language of 'wrong' and its cognates is used in the expression of this reaction. It is a short step from the raw reaction to the identifying of that which is wrong as one person's acting harmfully and with ill will towards another. So to identify it is implicitly to universalize it as a ground of judgement. Further, the attempt (however prompted) to take a reasonably impartial view predisposes at least the spectators toward this or some such universalized statement of the ground of judgement of wrongdoing.

At this point it seems not inappropriate to switch to a style of reasoning inspired by Kant but avoiding anything like Kant's too sharp dichotomy between rational will and animal feelings. Humans with the emotional or sentimental characteristics that Smith has identified are also rational and speaking animals. They thus have to live in quite close communities, and in some wider congeries of communities in some kind of society. Do they then have to acknowledge any basic mutual observances if this is to be possible? It seems that they do. To will the end is to will the necessary means for its realization, or, rather the necessary conditions of its realization. Whoever will live in a community must will the conditions of viable community. That means willing the norms that define basic mutual duties as a foundation of possible reciprocal actions and abstentions based on mutuality of beliefs and (indeed) 'mutuality of restrictions'.[21] This 'rational will' modification of Smith goes beyond what he himself allowed for. He saw this as a matter of people deriving moral rules from inductive reflection on recurring particular judgements. The Kantian revision allows for a way of confirming and re-issuing in a fully universal-normative form the merely inductive generalization. This revision also expresses a form of reasoning that calls upon one to think articulately about the interaction between any one such universalized rule of conduct and an overall moral view. Such a view, if it is to be rational, has both to be self-consistent internally and to express an overall coherence. Only by being rational in that way could it be an element in a reasonable plan of life. The extremely elastic concept of 'natural law' has certainly one legitimate understanding according to which the minimum requirements to make possible a reasonable plan of life for any and every human being is a natural law for all, needing no formal enactment by any state or government or international body or agency. In this sense, we identify here a fundamental element of natural law.

We thereby confirm the first of Stair's Three Steps. We affirm the necessity of certain basic mutual duties among human beings, and the principle that these must be observed and used in reasoning with the 'exclusionary force' so lucidly explained by Joseph Raz.[22]

Is there then a distinct principle of freedom which nevertheless commends the rational use of freedom as expressed in the proposition that one should act for the best all things considered? In favour of an affirmative answer to this question is a fact of common experience parallel to the facts of pain, anger, and resentment discussed in relation to the principle of obedience. People respond well and warmly to acts of kindness and good will, just as they respond with resentment to malevolent acts. They regard benevolent people well and are ready to praise them and their works. But there is no common predisposition to demand kindness and generosity. Why so?

---

[21] The phrase 'mutuality of restrictions' is one I derive from H. L. A. Hart. See his 'Are there Any Natural Rights?' (1955) 64 *Philosophical Review*, 175–91; also published in *Political Philosophy*, ed. A. Quinton (Oxford, OUP, 1967), 53–66; see at 184 and 61–2 respectively. See also discussion in N. MacCormick, *H. L. A. Hart* (2nd edn; Stanford Ca: Stanford University Press, 2008) ch 13.

[22] J. Raz, *Practical Reason and Norms* (Princeton, N.J.: Princeton University Press, 1990) 193–9. For reasons of no importance to the present argument Raz now speaks mainly of 'protected reasons', not to qualify their exclusionary aspect, but to clarify that exclusionary character is only one aspect of such reasons as he accounts for them.

This seems to me to be in a way a corollary of the 'resentment' argument. Demands by one person on another are themselves burdensome. They divert the recipient from the ordinary run of life to focus on something apparently imperative. I do not welcome demands made upon me if I do not consider them justified. Yet if what I am trying to do is to build into my whole set of activities elements that are beneficial to you, I wish this to be a matter of my own uncoerced good will. I shall not take kindly to a demand for it. The Scots legal proverb says that unkindness cannot be a ground for legal enforcement ('we cannot poind for unkindness') and this surely has an analogue in common human attitudes. If one person threatens another with some ill-deed, the spectators' sympathy goes with the victim, including sympathy with the attitude expressed in her/his demand that the assailant desist. If one person is in a position to give another significant help, and the needy one demands the help (as distinct, perhaps, from politely asking for some assistance), spectators do not seem to go along with this in the same way. Moving from spectator-sympathy arguments to a universalistic formulation, we derive something like this: people must be free to act for the best, helping each other as they think best to do, but not being subject to imperative demands for kindly acts. To will this as a universal principle is not merely not adverse to the conditions for sustaining a viable community, it is probably an essential one among them.

To confirm that proposition, we might reflect on what are frequently considered to be instances of positive duties that are covered by the principle of obedience, not left to discretion under the principle of freedom. These include parental duties towards children and duties of mutual support among spouses, or (where the institution of civil partnership exists) civil partners. These have certain particular features. First, there is a specific and special relationship between the bearers of such duties and their beneficiaries. Second, there are natural emotions and attitudes of concern that typically though not universally engage persons in these relationships as between duty-bearer and beneficiary. Third, these relations and common emotions exempt the demand for favourable treatment from being a resented burden (at least when children are under the age of being able to look after themselves.) Fourth, parents who neglect their children, or who cause neglect by ill-treating a spouse, effectively impose a burden on the community at large. Hence a universal norm treating neglect of other parties in such a relationship as wrongful and asserting a duty of care and nurture, or of mutual support, is one that can be willed consistently with a general restriction of basic duties to negative ones calling for refraining from harmful conduct. There is also an overall coherence of view. For there is apparently no limit to the persons anyone might seek to help, and no obvious basis for making any one person the proper and inevitable target of anyone else's special benevolence. This does not, however, apply in the case of parents and children, or spouses, or indeed relatives in broader degrees. Each can be detailed off, as it were, to take special responsibility for her/his own, without any kind of 'benevolence overload' resulting.

There is a very good argument, however, for certain 'good Samaritan' duties over and above those it may be rational to prescribe in the context of family relationships. People can suffer unforeseen and overwhelming misfortune in a wholly innocent way or even in circumstances where they perhaps partly brought misfortune on themselves. Either way, they may be in a dire predicament facing death or absolute destitution after some natural catastrophe like an earthquake or tsunami, or some act of human wrongdoing as happened to the Samaritan who fell among thieves and was beaten and robbed and left for dead or dying. It seems that there is a strong human instinct that makes 'neighbours' in such situations feel a compulsion to help, and makes demands for help to the afflicted seem proportionate and reasonable. The depth of misfortune identifies the target of obligatory assistance, and the proximity of possible helpers marks them out as those of whom some demand may be made. It is a topic of ongoing controversy how systems of state-law should deal with 'Samaritan' situations, and I for one opine that the law should not intervene to enforce good Samaritan duties. Morally speaking, the converse holds. We ought to recognize positive 'good Samaritan' duties as among the moral basics, without accepting any excessively wide drawing of the perimeter of neighbour relations that trigger the moral demand.

Another argument in favour of this concerns the moral virtues. Certainly, there is virtue in doing one's duty and being a conscientious person. But one even more admires and values people who, not neglecting duties, go the 'second mile' in one direction or another. People can be brave beyond the call of duty, kind and considerate beyond the call of duty, generous beyond the call of duty, dedicated to truth and advancement of knowledge beyond the call of duty, and (whatever be the truth in matters of theology) exceptional in religious self-dedication. Such virtues do not tend to flourish on their own, but to be reciprocally intertwining—it takes courage to find out the cause of malaria by having yourself in cold blood bitten by what you think (indeed, hope) is a disease-bearing mosquito. Those who go beyond the call of duty frequently (and even sometimes as a direct corollary) endure self-sacrifice in receiving or enjoying less than they would otherwise enjoy, and often less than they are entitled to did they but demand all they might demand.

The quality of mercy is not constrained—a forced remission is not a merciful one. In general, the virtues have the quality of being unconstrained, and this is a conceptual truth. It is also a matter of moral significance. A community, a society, a state, a world in which there are good people, people dedicated to the pursuit of human good in one or another of its dimensions is, relatively speaking, a place of light and joy. It is in contrast with a grim but viable community of those who observe basic duties, mind their own business, and follow their own life plans with a narrow concentration. Either, however, is preferable to a community or a world of wrongful cruelty and exploitation. The real world of the early twenty first century has all too much about it of the last-named. Its being the case that virtues are not constrained or capable of being inculcated by compulsory demand makes invaluable the principle of freedom.

People who live as contemporary human beings do, in the heart of or under the shadow of global capitalism, face many more compelling demands on their time and efforts than the principle of obedience accounts for. They are not very often at leisure for eager cultivation of the higher virtues. They are bound up in the cogs of the principle of engagement. Morally speaking, this is a matter of promises freely made and relationships of various kinds freely entered. Legally speaking, we operate in the capitalist world of work in one or other of the various roles this economic system yields, as employer or employee, independent professional sequentially engaged in contracts for services, public employee, elected public representative, unemployed person, full-time parent, pensioner, or carer for elderly relatives. Almost all these roles are defined or established by wholly or partly voluntary 'institution-arrangements'[23] enshrined in some branch or another of private or public law. In many ways also in contemporary legal systems they can be backed up by legislation protecting consumers or employees or travellers by rail, air or sea and in myriad other ways. As owners of property in land and moveable goods, whether being rich or poor, people have a multiplicity of other relationships including tenancies, mortgages, and mortgage debts.

Already in Chapter 4 we discussed institutional reasoning and morality. Here, it is sufficient to remark only that, whatever be the bare bones of the principle of engagement considered as an abstract matter of moral philosophy, the real life of every person remotely likely to read this book is inevitably deeply bound up in many engagements of the kind mentioned. Whatever may be their binding force in a purely moral perspective, these are typically both legally binding and (much more salient most of the time) practically essential gateways to participation in the economy with any prospect of self-sufficiency through earnings, dividends, pensions or the like. They are a precondition of any kind of a life plan, and may often put the sharpest of constraints on the real scope persons have for independence in planning the further course of their lives.

It remains the case, however, that the principle of engagement endorses as binding arrangements which, as sources of obligation, do differ from basic duties under the principle of obedience. Being voluntary and usually consensual, they can be varied by further agreement, and they can be defeasible under changing circumstances, rather than being absolute for all purposes. Engagements are in principle freely made and thus can be freely renegotiated, though only in circumstances of relative distributive justice (see Chapter 8) is this as rosy a prospect as it sounds. Bentham was wrong to think that the idea of imprescriptible rights was 'nonsense on stilts'.[24] The basic duties that Smith's or Kant's natural law

---

[23] On 'institution-arrangements', see N. MacCormick, *Institutions of Law*, 35.
[24] J. Waldron, *Nonsense upon Stilts: Bentham, Burke and Marx on the Rights of Man* (London: Methuen, 1987).

endorses are neither alienable nor cancellable (though rights can be forfeited, as when one person attacks another and suffers death as a result of a reasonable act of self-defence). The duties and obligations under the principle of engagement, being freely negotiable are also freely renegotiable.

We may conclude that a theory of practical reasoning that adopts Stair's Three Steps gives a good account of the place of moral duty and consensual obligations in a more general view of the human condition. It also provides a convenient sketch map on which to plot the interactions there may be between the various kinds of reason for action that moral agents may confront.

7

Society, Property, and Commerce

1 Positive law

The theoretical approach typified by Stair's Three Steps has further implications if one envisages embedding the three principles in an established polity with law-making and law-enforcing institutions. Surveying life in contemporary cities, one cannot but regretfully conclude that not all persons seem willing to exercise such self-command as is necessary in order to keep them from breaching the basic duties of mutual coexistence. Assaults, rapes, and murders are distressingly frequently reported, as are shocking cases of child-neglect by parents. Some would say that this is simply an inevitable feature of the duality of human nature. We may understand what is right, but we are capable of aggressively embracing what is wrong. This might be a pure matter of original sin, or it might be a kind of corruption of humans' better nature that is exacerbated by current social and economic systems (as Adam Smith supposed), and might be less salient in other conditions.[1]

However that may be, for persons such as contemporary residents or citizens of 'western' states, it seems undeniable that we do not and cannot simply rely on people's moral self-command or self-restraint to achieve controls on and protection from violent acts violating the basic duties as we have identified these. This is obvious. We rely on laws and institutions of law such as police forces, criminal prosecutors, courts of criminal jurisdiction and prison, and probation services. However ineffectual these may sometimes seem against tidal waves of crime and bad behaviour, it is a political commonplace, whether or not it is true, that things would be very much worse without these institutions and the hard work of those who serve in them.

In these circumstances, it is of course not only the basic duties that the criminal law enforces. We have road traffic law, health and safety law, data protection law, and all the rest of it in rich profusion, appropriately backed with criminal sanctions. But, in an important way, upholding the basic duties constitutes the criminal law's core, as a glance at the place of 'crimes against the person' in any

---

[1] Cf C. L. Griswold, Jr, *Adam Smith and the Virtues of Enlightenment* (Cambridge, Cambridge University Press, 1999) 128–9.

standard criminal text book, or at the contents of the crime pages of popular newspapers, will testify.

From several points of view, this capability of the organized polity—in the case primarily under consideration, the democratic law-state—to enforce basic duties can be considered to be an important factor in what justifies the state's possession of, and exercise of, physical coercion in the context of law-enforcement. For this is not only a matter of trying to enforce people's duties and to encourage voluntary observance of them. It amounts also to a way of, or an attempt at, protecting the reciprocal rights of those who are exposed to the risk of violence and other wrongdoing. Moreover, it may thereby discourage vigilantism and self-help, so that for a substantial number of people, possibly a majority, the condition may be one of relative civil peace and of largely 'voluntary co-operation in a coercive system'.[2]

This is an issue of civility. Whatever else might need saying in order to elucidate the very slippery idea of 'civil society', at any rate one must surely acknowledge that a degree of mutual civility, with willing abstention from interpersonal violence and other unwelcome intrusions into each others' lives, is essential. In this sense, the state with its coercive powers, at least when these are exercised with restraint and under the rule of law (or largely so), is surely a necessary guarantor of civil society. States can, though they do not always, create and uphold the essential conditions for the civility of civil society. This will certainly be so where large numbers of people are brought together, most of them complete strangers, and all but a few relative strangers, to each other. Civil society implies some degree of impersonal trust, such that people do not feel the need to go out and about armed and ready to defend themselves against casual attack. They encounter others as peaceful fellow-users of social space, ready for such interaction with each other as occasion may prompt.

Stair's principle of freedom, indeed, could hardly be made a reality without some such institutional arrangements in place. Normatively, no doubt, a person is always free to do anything that it is not wrong for her/him to do. But that normative freedom adds up to very little, and can be said to be worthless,[3] if one is afraid to go out of doors or to go about one's business without a pervasive and debilitating fear of violence. The principle of freedom as a matter of pure moral principle or pure 'natural law'—the normative order that would obtain even where no organized social or legal institutions existed—is an ideal only. To make a reality of it calls for established legal and social institutions (which of

---

[2] The phrase is H. L. A. Hart's—see *The Concept of Law* (2nd edn, Oxford: Clarendon Press, 1994) 198.

[3] On value or worth of liberty, as distinct from its existence, see N. MacCormick, *H. L. A. Hart* (2nd edn) (Stanford CA: Stanford University Press, 2008) 189, and cf J. Rawls, *A Theory of Justice* (Oxford: Clarendon Press, 1972) 204–5; H. L. A. Hart, 'Rawls on Liberty and its Priority' Univ of Chicago Law Rev 40 (1973) 534–55; but see also N. Daniels, 'Equal Liberty and Unequal Worth of: Liberty', in N. Daniels (ed) *Reading Rawls* (Oxford: Basil Blackwell, 1975) 253–81.

course come also with great risks, for they create huge opportunities for abuse and for crushing the very freedom it is hoped they can defend). Responding to this thought, Stair asserts a 'principle of positive law', the principle of 'society' as a *doppelgänger* with his 'equitable' principle of obedience. In upholding established legal institutions and improving them if possible, people sustain the conditions of viable society.

Kant's conception of the 'laws of freedom' is not very far removed from this idea about the principle of 'society'. Kant, we saw, believes that the good will, the will of a person doing duty for duty's sake, is the only unalloyed good known to humans.[4] But this will can be exercised at all only if it can be exercised freely. This entails, of course, that it would be absurd to use positive law to make people virtuous. People doing what is right merely out of apprehension of some sanction do not exhibit good will, but self-protection. So what use is positive law towards human good? The answer is that it can hinder hindrances to freedom. The brutal coercion of person by person is the antithesis of a situation where virtue can flourish. A body of criminal law is well justified if it prevents you from abusing your freedom by inhibiting mine. Law can create the conditions of liberty by securing people in their enjoyment of those rights that are correlative to the basic duties. For Kant's ideal moral order to flourish among humans there will need to be some form of state or other polity that secures what we have called the basic conditions of civility.

2 Freedom and property

How are people to exercise their liberty? Nearly everything a person might want to do, or think it good and worthwhile to do, will involve some use of the earth's resources. One will have to be at some place on the earth's surface, or suspended above it or out at sea, perhaps even under water. There will often be some things, some moveable objects that are essential to pursuing some project—perhaps no more than a pencil and paper for the writer of a book. But for most contemporary authors, nothing short of a personal computer will do. That in turn will be attached to the internet and to a printer and paper will be required for the printer and a power supply is necessary and so on. Planting a crop for next year's harvest calls for a great deal more. We use the earth's resources in living a life and, above all, in making and pursuing plans of life. Twenty-first century humans are coming to realize, indeed, that they are collectively using resources past the limits of sustainability, and will have to do something about it.

Natural lawyers in the protestant tradition like Stair had strong views about the use of resources. The earth and all its contents had been given to humans for their use, and they were to make the best use of it that they could. To make this

---

[4] See H. J. Paton, *The Moral Law* (London: Hutchinson, 1958) 66–88, 95–8.

feasible, however, required the institution of property. There has to be an appor-
tionment of rights of use, and this is an essential task of positive law, whether
in the form of customary law, statutory law or some amalgam of the two (like
the common law). Without positive law, there is no concept of property, without effectively enforced positive law, there is no secure property, and without
secure property there can be no creative use of resources. Material resources
can be developed and improved for the greatest good of human beings only in
conditions of secure property rights. Facilitating the use of property is therefore,
in the context of positive law, the corollary of the principle of freedom in ideal
natural law.[5]

The full possibilities of maximizing the valuable use of property depend on
everybody's being able to have some access to it. Given inherited and accidental
inequalities to be found in all human societies, this presents a difficulty. But out
of the principle of engagement comes a possible solution. This calls for a positiv-
ized version of the principle of engagement. Legally recognized and enforceable
contracts of various kinds can facilitate the exchange of assets and the employment of people to work on them and improve them. *Commerce* opens the advantages of property to everybody, though not in an equally advantageous way to
all. So the three principles of positive law that mirror the three of natural law are
'society, property, and commerce'.

Like Stair, Smith conceives of property as an 'adventitious right', indeed
all rights of and akin to property are 'adventitious' in the sense that they are
acquired under, and presuppose institutions of, established positive law.[6] These
institutions are, moreover, variable according to socio-economic context. In the
economically simplest form of human community, that of nations of hunters
and fishermen ('hunters and gatherers' in more recent usage), people have few
assets—spears and fishing canoes, perhaps. What is caught or gathered is con-
sumed where it is caught on a communal basis—there is no storing up for the
future. Once animals come to be domesticated, herds, eventually great herds
of sheep or cattle, can be accumulated and driven to fresh pastures, or round
a circuit of pastures, as the seasons dictate. Wealth is then in cattle (or sheep),
and the able and lucky increase their holdings while those less able or less lucky
are thrown into being dependent on the luckier ones. Social hierarchy emerges,
with powerful clan chiefs and their henchmen controlling wealth and access to
it under pretty despotic conditions of governance. With the establishment of
settled agriculture and the planting and improving of crops, immovable property emerges for the first time. People as individuals or in groups assert and
vindicate private rights over tracts of land. The population grows, as cultivated
land can feed more people than unimproved prairie or hill pasture. Again, those

---

[5] Stair, *Institutions* I. 1. 18, 22.

[6] Smith, *Lectures on Jurisprudence* (R. Meek, P.G. Stein and D. D. Raphael eds) (Oxford: Oxford
University Press, 1978), 400.

who have no land become beholden to those who have, and become toilers on the land of those who have large holdings. Marriage and primogeniture tend to concentrate larger holdings in fewer hands and to create a large class of dependent tenants and agricultural labourers. Military aristocracies can acquire and exercise the powers of territorial landlords.

The commercial society that Smith observed in the Netherlands and the cities of Northern Italy in the eighteenth century, and that he saw emerging in much of England and the lowland parts of Scotland, differed yet again. Commerce created conditions for free labour and fostered the manufacturing industries in which labourers found work, with much greater productivity achieved through division of labour than can be achieved in simple workshops. Commercial societies focused to a greater extent than other societies on markets, and free markets created the best possibility for producing the greatest number of valued goods at the lowest prices. Markets operating under what Smith called the 'system of natural liberty' were the best guarantors of fair buying and selling, and fair reward for ingenuity and labour in the case of those with only their labour to sell.

Especially in this condition of economic and social development, the principles of 'property and commerce', indeed also of 'freedom and engagement', come into their own. Notwithstanding inherited or acquired inequality of fortunes and resources, each has a chance to better his or her lot in the circumstances of free commerce. In this context, the proper function of the state is (almost as with Kant) to free people from hindrances to their freedom and let markets work, as they do best, under 'the system of natural liberty'. Aside from matters like defence of the realm, or the provision of courts of justice, or provision of education (in near-universal schooling at least to elementary level, eighteenth century Scotland was a precocious example), the state should stand back from interference in the economy. It should dissolve existing monopolies and resist cries for establishment of new ones.

3 Property, government, and justice

Whoever may take a one-sided, rosy, view of the virtues of commercial society, Adam Smith did not. He was well aware of the impact of inequality on people's moral character and life-chances. He saw that interpersonal violence and strife were not so much proofs of original sin as the consequence of envy and resentment concerning unmerited differences in wealth. It would be wrong to suppose that Smith envisaged a succession such that a simple society that enforces only the basic interpersonal duties is followed by a more complex one that has to enforce both these duties and the duties of respect for property, under whatever property regime has evolved. The property regime that can be upheld only if it is effectively enforced may itself be the cause of the ill-will between people that makes necessary also the enforcement of basic moral duties that people might otherwise have respected voluntarily.

'Till there be property there can be no government, the very end of which is to secure wealth and to defend the rich from the poor.[7]

Wherever there is great property there is great inequality. For one very rich man there must be at least five hundred poor, and the affluence of the few supposes the indigence of the many. The affluence of the rich excites the indignation of the poor, who are often driven by want and prompted by envy to invade his possessions. It is only under the shelter of the civil magistrate that the owner of that valuable property, which is acquired by labour of many years or perhaps of many successive generations, can sleep a single night in security.... The acquisition of valuable and extensive property, therefore, necessarily requires the establishment of civil government. Where there is no property, or at least none that exceeds the value of two or three days labour, civil government is not so necessary.'[8]

This is not to say that Smith was egalitarian in outlook. He considered inequality to be both inevitable and desirable, since it resulted from the greater providence or industry of some, and created incentives to industriousness and providence for all, hence tending to improve the general condition of people.

Much of what Smith had to say about justice is said in this context. Government exhibits proper care for justice in establishing courts that are fully independent of the executive, and leaving them to carry out fair and rigorous application of the law to all cases disputed before them. Justice effectively means due application of established law.[9] That law contains provisions protecting basic rights (as we have called them) and also property rights. The latter are fully dependent on provisions of positive law, and the former might not need so strong enforcement but for the inequalities attendant on a property regime.

As a personal virtue, justice between individuals requires mutual respect for rights of all kinds. Justice need not be accompanied by benevolence. It is sufficient that each person strictly respect what the law requires in favour of others, keeping their contracts and other engagements, and leaving them undisturbed in their person and their family relations and in peaceful enjoyment of their property, movable and immovable. David Hume regarded justice as an 'artificial virtue' (not a 'natural' one) since it depended on human conventions about distribution of property rights.[10] Smith does not share this terminology, but in substance agrees.[11] Although they did not believe in any 'natural right' of property, neither

---

[7] A. Smith, *Lectures on Jurisprudence* 404.

[8] A. Smith, *Wealth of Nations* 709–10 (Book V ch 1 part II).

[9] See the discussion of 'the expenses of justice' in A. Smith, *Wealth of Nations* 708–23.

[10] On justice as an artificial virtue, see D. Hume *A Treatise of Human Nature* (ed. L. A. Selby-Bigge; 2nd edn revised by P. H. Nidditch) (Oxford: Clarendon Press, 1978) pp 477–525, esp at 477–83 (Bk III Part II sections i–v, esp sec. i).

[11] On justice in Smith, see: *Theory of Moral Sentiments* 86–91 (punishment and justice, justice and utility) also 269–70 and 496–7 and compare the editors' introduction by A. L. MacFie and

of them considered property law to be a purely arbitrary matter. For both considered that human flourishing depended on a good form of government, including a system of property ownership within which there were strong incentives on owners to make improvements and exploit assets to the full. Smith in particular made clear that he saw the development of commercial society as creating considerable overall gains, notwithstanding the deficiencies that were manifest in the lives of the labouring poor, especially labourers in cities. In commercial societies, legislators and governments could establish and uphold the principles of natural liberty that would let people improve their lot to the greatest extent possible. The task of philosophers and political economists was to teach them how to sustain or develop a legal regime that would be maximally effective to this end, a task wholeheartedly undertaken in the *Wealth of Nations*.

There is not a wide gap between this and, from the end of the seventeenth century, Stair's summary of the point of it all:

'[T]he first principles of right are obedience, freedom, and engagement.

There are also three prime principles of positive law; whose aim and interest is the profit and utility of man.... [T]he three principles of positive law [are] society, property and commerce. The principles of equity are the efficient cause of rights and laws: the principles of positive law are the final causes or ends for which laws are made, and rights constitute and ordered. And all of them may aim at the maintenance, flourishing, and peace of society, the security of property, and the freedom of commerce.'[12]

From this, one can see that Bentham may have had something of a point after all. If the 'aim and interest' is the 'profit and utility of man', why do we not just base our whole practical philosophy on that proposition? Then we could work out what rights it would be good to establish and assert by considering what rules of positive law—or rules of common morality—would conduce most to our 'profit and utility'.

That is, however, too swift a way to dismiss a subtly established position. But for our apprehension of the basic duties, the freedom that exists when they are satisfied, and, beyond that, the possibility to enter engagements, we would lack a concept of rights and duties. The principles of equity are the 'efficient cause' of our apprehending these concepts. Within a framework of institutional normative order, that is, of positive law, we can seek so to order and design our institutions that they maximize the prospect of human good. But we are able to do this because we are already norm-using creatures. We do not become norm-users by establishing positive laws. The case has already been made for the view that a modification of Smithian sentimentalism to adapt to the Kantian categorical

D. D. Raphael at pp 13–14; see also *Lectures on Jurisprudence*, 399 'The end of justice is to secure men from injury'; compare the section in the *Wealth of Nations* 708–22 'On the expenses of Justice'.

[12] Stair, *Institutions of the Law of Scotland*, I.1.18 (p. 91).

imperative gives a theoretical underpinning to something very like Stair's three principles of equity. That case still stands.

4 Justice? A byway in history

Stair was a predecessor of Smith in his advocacy of 'the security of property and the freedom of commerce' as the proper ends to pursue through positive law (its 'final cause'). Whether or not he was himself influential in relation to political economy (as Smith so obviously was), there can be no doubt of the prophetic quality of what he wrote. Throughout the islands of Great Britain and Ireland, the seventeenth century was a century of conflict about religion, law and the proper forms of government. One thing is plain about Stair. At the end of the long conflicts of his century, he fetched up on the winning side. He died before the Anglo-Scottish Union of 1707, but his son and successor, the Master of Stair and subsequently the first Earl of Stair, was one of the principal architects of that Union, which was effectively the consummation of the revolutions of 1688–89 in the three British Kingdoms, securing their relative unity as a protestant-dominated polity embattled with the nearest continental neighbour, France, and thus, as a side-effect, creating the conditions for the building of a great empire.

The polity the Stairs and their allies envisaged in the new united kingdom of Great Britain was one that was to be safe for 'society, property and commerce', as any reading of the Union debates in the Scottish Parliament makes clear.[13] Well before 1707, it had become clear that they and their allies were ready to use the most ferociously coercive of means to bring a new order into being. An infamous government-inspired massacre led by government troops took place in Glencoe in the Scottish West Highlands in 1691. The Master of Stair was the minister responsible, and the warrant for the action bore his signature and that of King William. This way of making an example of the MacDonalds of Glencoe in 1691 was specifically grounded (and, the government considered, justified) on the issue of enforcing loyalty to the new parliamentary monarchy, and punishing stubborn loyalty to the ousted King James VII. But the deeper issue was about the kind of polity Scotland was to become.[14]

It is scarcely too much to say that what was started at Glencoe was finished, or at any rate reached its apogee elsewhere in the Scottish Highlands during the following two centuries, starting mainly from the early nineteenth century. A notorious example is provided by the 'clearances' of native people in their traditional settlements from the fertile parts of the Highlands to make way for sheep-farming there. This reached a peak of notoriety in Sutherland during the

---

[13] See C. A. Whatley with D. J. Patrick *The Scots and the Union* (Edinburgh: Edinburgh University Press, 2006).

[14] J. Buchan, *The massacre of Glencoe* (London: P. Davies, 1933).

clearances overseen by Patrick Sellar in the first half of the nineteenth century. The 1816 trial of Patrick Sellar[15] on the charge of culpable homicide, oppression, and real injury, relating to cruel evictions and the death of an elderly woman during the process, notwithstanding the acquittal he eventually obtained, reminds us of the continuing ruthlessness of the proselytes of the new commercial society. What was begun in Sutherland during the Napoleonic wars continued throughout most of the Highlands for most of the nineteenth century, frequently amidst scenes of violence.

Eric Richards presents in his *Patrick Sellar and the Highland Clearances*[16] a remarkable study of the life and times of this most infamous clearer of them all, factor to and tenant of the first Duke and Duchess of Sutherland. He rightly stresses to what an extent Sellar was a child of the Edinburgh Enlightenment. He sat at the feet of Dugald Stewart in Edinburgh University, becoming a devout disciple of Adam Smith's disciple, and a bearer of the message that Stewart took from Smith, which both, with or without recognition or acknowledgement, inherited also from Stair.[17] The Highlands according to the 'enlightened' view of Sellar and his like had to be brought out of backwardness and superstition and ushered into the world of commerce and gainful employment.

The old way of life was in fact, as is now known, a relatively sustainable one. It was a cattle-based agricultural economy in which small hardy animals spent the summer months in high mountain pastures tended by the young women of the townships at summer shielings while the men cultivated the 'in-bye' land by their main dwellings for the slender crops suitable to terrain and climate. In winter, the animals returned with their herds to the lower land. But the improvers considered that these ancient traditions of pasturage and transhumation, farming for subsistence rather than for the market, needed to be set aside. The 'barbarous' language of the people would have to be suppressed. Shifting the people to small seaside crofts on very poor and stony ground would give people a basis for bare subsistence such as would have to be supplemented by work at commercial fishing or other available employment, for example, in quarries. The full advantages of a progressive division of labour should begin to spread over the landscape and with it an ever more sharpened propensity to what Smith had called 'truck, barter and exchange'. This might call for ruthlessness to get it started, but the improvers considered it to be ruthlessness in the best of good causes. (Or so it seemed to the clearers—in fact, over time, sheep-grazing damaged the pastures in a way the old cattle-grazing did not, with long-term environmental degradation as a result.)

It would be absurd to say that nineteenth-century industrious and industrial Scotland with its lowland ironworks and its sheep-producing straths and hillsides resulted simply from publication of a book about law by a judge, even an eminent Lord President, in the closing years of the seventeenth century. We should,

[15] I. Grimble, *The Trial of Patrick Sellar* (Edinburgh: Saltire Society, 1993).
[16] Edinburgh: Polygon/Edinburgh University Press, 1999. [17] Op. cit. at 18–24.

however, turn that thought the other way round and see how closely compatible is Stair's idea of 'society, property and commerce' with subsequent developments in the world of ideas and in the worlds of farming, manufacturing and 'improvement' generally in the following two hundred years. In passing, we may remember that one key figure was another judge of the generation following Stair's own, Henry Home Lord Kames.[18] He, in addition to playing both the role of speculative historian and philosopher, and that of advocate and then judge, was also a leading agricultural improver on the Blair Drummond Estate he acquired through his wife. Lord Kames, in turn, was a patron of Adam Smith, giving him help and encouragement in the early period of his ascent up the academic ladder.

Agricultural, industrial, and commercial developments were not principally brought about by political action but they required a political framework. The politics of the Stair clan—their successful politics—were about making the framework for the kind of law in which they believed. This was in turn the necessary framework for the kind of economy and society in which they also believed. The model of a successfully improving society and economy was there for all to see in the Netherlands. Some saw it from the standpoint of political exile (like Stair) in the 1680s, others from that of a law student in Utrecht or Leiden, others (like Smith) as travelling tutor of a young nobleman doing the Grand Tour. It was a much visited attraction until eventually closed off by the wars of the French Revolution, and subsequently the Napoleonic War, which ruptured the close intellectual, social, and political ties that the previous two centuries had built up.

Perhaps everyone will find it difficult, and certainly I find it impossible, to view all this with unmixed satisfaction and admiration. The policies that were supposed to be justified by the principles of 'society, property and commerce' did not triumph without a heavy cost in human lives and human culture. I for one descend from those who suffered, sometimes grievously, through these transformations. The culture of Gaelic Scotland, to which I would ascribe myself, has been more or less extinguished except for memories and relics. This is a sad loss. Still, it does not absolve us from asking whether the intellectual framework shared by Stair, Smith, and Sellar ever did make sense and to what extent if any it still makes sense for understanding morality and law. Surely it has to be acknowledged as strikingly apt and prophetic.

If all private property were effectively suppressed, there would remain a necessity for some 'administration of things' for each human being needs some access to natural resources in order to survive, or, preferably, to thrive. Experiments in state-socialism attempted in many countries in the twentieth century effectively tried to shift the management of the economy and the control of access to necessary resources out of traditional private law, which was permitted substantially

---

[18] See W. C. Lehmann, *Henry Home, Lord Kames, and the Scottish Enlightenment: a study in national character and in the history of ideas* (The Hague : Martinus Nijhoff, 1971).

to wither away. A new expanded model of public law was called into being to supplant the bourgeois institutions of private law. To date, all these attempts have ended in failure, though conceivably with the exception of Cuba. They may perhaps one day succeed in different circumstances than when first tried. I rather doubt it. Until they do, it seems to me that what Stair summarized under his three principles of positive law is alive and well. Such principles retain a kind of grand-scale explanatory value when we contemplate contemporary legal systems. Of course, we have to supplement them with appropriate reflection on public law, which has grown beyond all recognition in the intervening centuries, and the specialist forms of criminal law are also of relatively recent provenance.

One should avoid reaching such a conclusion too blandly. Does Stair's account of natural law and positive law seem convincing because it matches in a rough way liberal capitalism and foreshadows the political economy of Adam Smith and his successors? In which case, should we not perhaps look with a little suspicion at the premises. Are these really independent truths that allow us to work out the sustainability of such principles as those of 'society, property, and commerce'? Or is this more like what the Marxists (and also Bentham, as remarked in Chapter 6) tell us about ideology? Here we see class interest expressed in a somewhat refined way by the principles in question, hence the credibility of the alleged premises depends on the interests that are legitimated by their supposedly independent truth. We do not need to go into that in the present context, but we do need to acknowledge it as a serious question, to which no answer has yet won general acceptance.

I spoke of the Highland clearances and the spirit of commerce. Those who resisted clearance there, or in other places, as did the Plains Indians of the American mid west and west, or the aboriginal people in Australia, or the tribal peoples of southern Africa, and all those dispossessed anywhere by the forward march of commercial society, were simply pushed aside. Much of what they said about their traditions and usages and their reverence for ancestral lands was dismissed by clearers and settlers as mere superstition and obstinate adherence to blind tradition in the face of inevitable and desirable progress. The notion of a single landowner with absolute dominion to use or abuse a tract of land was foreign to the people who were being cleared. Land was tied up with family and tribal or clan tradition, linked with the names of generations of ancestors whose genealogy could be meticulously recited even by illiterate peasants.[19]

The triumph of 'society, property and commerce' indeed crushed out the old communities that saw the world in different terms. History has brought us, however, to doubt the sustainability of the view that all nature may be exploited totally freely by human beings clothed with legal ownership. The sight of environmental

---

[19] As a boy, I myself experienced the tail end of this kind of self-understanding in stories my great uncles told me about the Ross of Mull, to which my ancestors over many generations had belonged.

degradation and a newly awakened concern for sustainability make many think there is some cause to re-cultivate a sense of reverence for the earth and its many inhabitants of multitudinous different species. Whatever maybe said of the 'principles of positive law' for their time and place and for successor generations, there can be no doubt that they now at least need to be very substantially supplemented to seem still credible for the present and, all the more, the future. Reason dictates more concerning nature and humans than Stair thought. It also requires deeper reflection about justice.

5 Observations on justice

The conception of justice with which Smith and his contemporaries worked was one that applied inside systems of moral and (most particularly) legal thought. Largely, it was justice according to law. One element fits closely with Smith's ideas about resentment and the impartial spectator. His conception of retributive justice, the justice of a just punishment, concerns that degree of harm inflicted on the perpetrator of an offence that matches the extent of the impartial spectator's sympathy with resentment on the part of the victim. But his broader conception of justice tends to equate it mainly with justice according to law.[20] Whether we look at the judges who purport to administer the law with an even hand to all manner of people who bring suit in their courts or contemplate our own dealings as moral persons interacting with each other, Smithian justice is primarily about respect for the law as it is. It is a matter of 'giving to each his or her due' (*suum cuique tribuere* in Justinian's *Digest*), where what is due to a person is determined by reference to the established normative order. Above all, it calls for respecting property rights and keeping one's contracts, promises and other engagements, not cheating nor overreaching those with whom one has business to do. Justice does not call for generosity, merely for punctilio in respect for rights and observance of duties owed to others.

Times change, and concepts evolve with them. This cannot but seem a very partial and incomplete (though not totally erroneous) conception of justice now. On 31 March 2008 it was reported in the UK daily press that Adam Applegarth, the chief executive of the Northern Rock Bank, which had collapsed under the weight of its debts, having borrowed short but lent long, was to receive a payment on his resignation of £760,000. He would also enjoy access to a pension pot of £2.5 million. Two thousand ordinary employees of the bank would be made redundant, with a tiny or no pay-off, and the 86% of employees who had opted in to the company's 'share save scheme' would, like all the company's ordinary shareholders, find their investment almost completely worthless.

---

[20] See sources cited in fn. 11 above.

By the justice of contract-enforcement and property-respect, this was perfectly just. Mr Applegarth's contract of employment as CEO gave him those very entitlements of which he took advantage on leaving the bank, for whose collapse he was the ultimately answerable officer. The collapse was a result of policies deliberately pursued under his guidance. Yet he was due his contractual pay and his pension. Shareholders (Applegarth no doubt included) were not deprived of their shares, but in the ordinary working of the market they found them to be practically unsaleable. The dismissed employees had less favourable contracts than their CEO, but that can scarcely occasion surprise.

All this misses the point. The structure of contracts now typical of high-ranking executives in great companies insulates them very substantially from risks of business error on their part. They can run their company on to the rocks and still walk away with a good reward. There are many instances of this. Simply to say that it is just, because their contracts entitle people to this, will not do. Nor can one make any headway with the argument that companies can only obtain the most skilled and creative bosses if they pay enormous sums and make huge provision for termination of employment. For in a case like that of which we are taking note, the point is that the vastly paid executive has made a catastrophic botch of his job. In any junior employee, incompetence to remotely the same degree would result—quite lawfully—in instantaneous dismissal without compensation. There is a grotesque lack of proportionality about the whole business. At the very minimum, we are entitled to raise the question whether such a set up is itself just, and therefore to ask whether justice truly does require honouring of the CEO's contract in this case, even if the legal right happens to be unchallengeable.

Simply put, we can ask about the justice of the law, not only about justice in its administration and its observance by citizens. More generally, one can ask about social justice or distributive justice, not so much by way of querying a particular entitlement like that of Mr Applegarth's, but by way of criticizing the structure of rewards that advanced corporate capitalism facilitates. In the contemporary market order, with overlapping directorships in different companies, non-executive directors may be involved in arranging salaries for executive directors of one company, while holding executive office in some other company themselves and benefiting from a similarly high estimation of their worth in the eye of their own company's remuneration committee. The whole contemporary property regime and the distribution of fortune that it entails may thus be brought somewhat into question. 'Justice is the first virtue of social systems as truth is of systems of thought' said John Rawls,[21] and rightly. In fact, once one concedes the thesis of Hume and Smith that property rights are essentially conventional, not natural, we can at once start to raise questions about the expediency and justice of the scheme that exists at a particular place and time. When Smith (for example)

---

[21] J. Rawls, *A Theory of Justice* (Oxford: Clarendon Press, 1972) 3.

criticized entailments of property on the ground that they imposed an unreasonable fetter on its free use, he in effect made the same point.[22]

Environmental justice and (thus implicitly) justice between generations is already on the table. The natural lawyers are open to criticism in an environmentalist perspective. Likewise, their conception of justice is too narrow; it is important not only to have justice in accordance with law, one also demands law in accordance with justice. The lens must be opened out to consider distributive justice at large. There is much useful insight in the theory of 'society, property, and commerce', but it does not take us quite far enough.

This chapter and its predecessor have reviewed the thought of Smith and Kant against one particularly interesting version of the protestant conception of natural law that was part of their shared intellectual background, and to which their work marked a partial reaction. Yet there is more of continuity than of outright rejection. A summary of morality and law that describes equity (or 'natural law') in terms of the principles of 'obedience, freedom, and engagement' and that organizes positive law around the principles of 'society, property, and commerce' has strong intrinsic plausibility. One may account for what are our basic duties to each other by means other than appeal to a timeless or divinely granted natural law, and one can also account for the reasons why engagements have to be treated as binding and worthy of respect. This was done in Chapters 2–4, making considerable use of intellectual resources derived from Smith and Kant. What remains in the generous normative space between these is the domain of moral and legal freedom, though freedom under law is both facilitated and at the same time sharply constrained by the norms of property law. For a person in the capacity of an owner, these define freedom, but in respect of that of which one is a non-owner, they amount to restriction and constraint. It is certainly in the nature of humans to pursue what they consider to be valuable, but, in doing so, to acknowledge the necessity of mutual restrictions on their behaviour. In that sense, it is perfectly acceptable to ascribe to 'natural law' whatever one takes to be the morally necessary mutual restrictions. On the other hand, there is no codebook of such restrictions awaiting discovery or revelation, so if this makes the use of the concept 'law' misleading, there is certainly no necessity for it.

What is important is not to linger on this point of terminology, but to turn our attention to the so-far unanswered questions. These are questions about distributive justice, including justice between generations. Justice between generations may capture all that needs to be said about environmental justice—but, in case it does not, that is a further necessary subject for consideration.

---

[22] See A. Smith, *Lectures on Jurisprudence* 70 'Upon the whole nothing can be more absurd than perpetual entails.'

8

On Justice

1 The problem of the greedy guests

There was recently a wedding party. Mary and Joe (not their real names) were young professionals who had been living together for some time, but they were thinking of starting a family and decided that being married would be good for that. The young couple's parents were elderly and poor, but they themselves were beginning to make their way successfully in their work, so felt they could afford to have a nice but not indecently lavish party for friends and relations to celebrate the nuptials. After a quiet ceremony at the local registrar's office, they arranged a buffet supper with dance to follow in a pleasant local hotel, and asked about one hundred and fifty guests. They provided enough wine for two or three toasts, apart from which the hotel bar was open to slake the continuing thirst of their guests, at their (the guests') own expense.

Being ecologically conscious, J and M had a horror of parties that leave large quantities of uneaten food to be thrown out, especially since the recent panicky banning of pig-swill following an outbreak of foot-and-mouth disease traceable to a swill-farm. So they made a reasonable estimate of what their guests could reasonably expect to eat and did not over-provide beyond that. Unfortunately, however, some of their guests behaved rather badly. Those who had passed earliest along the receiving line and went first to the buffet turned out to include rather many greedy people who piled their plates high and demanded frequent refills of their wine glasses. In the result, those who, perhaps being less pushy by nature, came later along the receiving line and into the supper room found the buffet tables seriously denuded. Worse still, those at the end of the line—the last dozen or so—got practically nothing except some rather unappetizing ends of salad and bread.

Despite this, the speeches were amusing and the dance was a success, so the wedding party was not a total failure, but the episode at the supper buffet left (in a manner of speaking) a bad taste in the mouth. M and J felt that they had come out of the affair looking a bit mean when they had really tried to run a sensible, ecologically acceptable party that would have worked had all their guests, or even most of them, behaved a bit more considerately and less greedily. The guests who got little or no supper did not, of course, starve to death, but were left with a partly unhappy memory of an essentially happy occasion. Those who had travelled some distance to be present were genuinely aggrieved, and thought quite badly of the greedy guests.

Not for the first time, the story of a wedding party introduces a serious moral point. There is involved in it a kind of injustice, yet in a context that falls short of any violation of anybody's rights in a strict sense, even moral rights, far less legal ones. You do not attend a wedding party thinking you have a right to be fed, though you have a happy expectation of a pleasant meal. You do not regard yourself as having a right that your hosts feed you. Nor do you think you have a right to regulate the quantity or rate of consumption of other guests. Nor do the hosts regard themselves as having a right to good behaviour by their guests. We do not litigate over impoliteness. At a social occasion of this kind, by contrast with any background contract with the hotel proprietor, issues concerning rights one might enforce or demands one might make are, as a matter of courtesy and even as a matter of autonomous morality, set aside. Mutual expectations and mutual goodwill are all that one relies on here.

Even so, there seems something obviously and reprehensibly unfair as well as ill-mannered about the conduct of the greedy guest, and when there are rather many greedy guests the problem becomes obvious. For other guests end up getting little or nothing and the hosts can be seriously embarrassed by this (they are not rich, and had to work to a fixed budget for the occasion, and everyone should have realized this). If all the guests had taken a fair share, everyone would have had enough and all could have equally enjoyed the party. A 'fair share' is in this context a reasonably modest portion off each serving-dish, with considerable minor variation admissible around the 'reasonable' and the 'modest'.

No particular greedy guest wronged any particular hungry guest. This is a typical 'free rider' problem with many riders, where the cumulative effect of the excessive behaviour of several people to the detriment of other people exceeds any effect that a single case of excessive behaviour would bring about. Any party can cope with one greedy person, or two,…but not thirty out of one hundred and fifty. The greedy people are not acting in concert with each other to do other guests down or to make the hosts feel wretched. Each is just being greedy for himself or herself without much thought for anyone else (that is indeed the problem). The upshot is unfair treatment for some of their fellow guests. Alternatively, if you want to shift the blame, you can say the hosts should have known some of their guests would over-indulge. So they were themselves being unfair in asking people to an evening party without making absolutely sure there was enough food for everyone, even if that would have meant some food going to waste at the end of the evening. (Yet is it not somehow shameful when well-fed people throw out good food when so many others are starving?)[1]

---

[1] Cf. O. O'Neill *Faces of Hunger: an essay on poverty, justice and development* (London: Allen & Unwin, 1986).

This is not an urgent case of crying injustice, of course. But it draws attention to some interesting points. Here we are dealing with a situation where people have reasonable mutual expectations, partly of a conventional kind, to do with relations of guests and hosts, and of guests among themselves, in the context of a social occasion that is generically recognizable, even if its particular instances all have some kind of personal particularity. People can in this situation behave badly without meaning harm to anyone, and yet in a way that has unfair effects on someone else whom they cannot identify in advance. People can suffer unfair treatment just because of the thoughtlessness of others. We may therefore wish to ask, 'What is it that the thoughtless people fail to think?' The answer seems to be that they fail to consider (in this case) how much it would be right and reasonable to take from the common table, and what may become of others if they go over the reasonable limit. This amounts therefore to a failure of consideration both towards the hosts and towards the other guests.

Always, it is incumbent on humans as moral beings to treat each other with consideration and respect. Disrespect, or even failure of respect, is at the bottom of most kinds of interpersonal wrongdoing. Here, we need not impute active disrespect to anyone; but we can certainly identify a failure to think about what respect calls for, and a failure to act on that thought. 'Spectator' reasoning seems even more obviously to fit the case than straightforward Kantian reflection via Kant's categorical imperative (in any of its versions, even that which directly concerns respect for rational agency[2]). Failing to think about other people shows want of concern for them, and indeed there is good authority for the view that the foundations of morality and of justice between persons lie in the requirement that we treat everybody with adequate and equal respect and concern.[3] Equal concern is certainly missing from the thoughts of the greedy guests (or, if present, its demands are ignored).

The present story of a wedding party can also be taken as a parable concerning humanity in its contemporary global predicament. Like the guests, we confront limited resources, but they are globally limited. They are not limited because of a cautious, parsimonious provision by a party-giver. They are limited, and we are pressing up to the limit, because of the growth of human populations and their ever-increasing demands for material goods and economic growth, set against the physical capacity of the planet Earth. We cannot in this case suggest that the host should have provided more—though sometimes we behave much as if we thought we could. To respond to oil shortages by asking oil producers to deplete yet more speedily the remaining reserves they have,[4] rather than by responding

---

[2] See H. J. Paton, *The Moral Law*, 91.

[3] See Ronald Dworkin's discussion of 'concern and respect', R. Dworkin, *Taking Rights Seriously* (New impression, with a reply to critics, London: Duckworth, 1978) 277–8; cf S. Guest *Ronald Dworkin* (Edinburgh: Edinburgh University Press, 1992) 225–53 (ch 9).

[4] Compare the visit by UK Prime Minister Gordon Brown to Saudi Arabia, reported in *The Times* (London) 23 June 2008.

to price rises by restricting current consumption, is a bit like blaming the host for the greed of some guests.

There is a problem, certainly, about simply letting fuel prices rise. For this can exacerbate the impact of existing inequalities that may hitherto have seemed acceptable. Rising prices hit fastest those who live on the narrowest financial margins. Rising oil prices kick on into rising food prices, and those who are already at the limit of their capability to meet food bills feel the pinch at once. Others may only have to tone down their indulgence in luxury travel and exotic holidays. This applies within countries that are already rather affluent. The whole populations of these countries have collectively an uneasy resemblance to the greedy guests when judged against the majority populations of the starving countries, in which, however, the self-preference of quite wealthy members of politico-military-economic élites is even more visibly scandalous.

This also has a bearing on intergenerational issues. If the human beings now alive continue to deplete resources at current rates of depletion, the next generation or generations will face severe shortages (though we cannot foresee by what turns of human ingenuity they may be able to alleviate the situation). If the human beings now alive continue to tolerate the levels and kinds of environmental degradation that became common during industrialization and after it, this will in other ways impoverish future generations. 'We' who live in the affluent 'west' and others in other countries who seek to live like us can then be seen to be playing the role of the greedy guests. By eating too much we starve others both in the future and now, or condemn them to a needlessly dull diet by comparison with our own.

Yet, as John Rawls pointed out, any change in the present way of life is likely to hurt most the poorest in the target population.[5] If Europe or the USA were voluntarily to undertake a phase of economic shrinkage in order to diminish their overall impact on resources (a barely thinkable suggestion), or were even to forego rates of growth hitherto considered normal, then it would be the poorest Europeans and the poorest Americans, some already desperately poor, who would suffer the greatest burden. The challenge of securing environmental common goods and of dealing with intergenerational justice calls for more than simply tinkering with reducing average consumption among those who already consume too much, taken in gross as states or societies. This calls for more reflection on the idea of what is due to each of us. What kind of shares of economic goods are fair? What can we in good conscience take, regardless of the question whether there is anyone who is giving it to us?

---

[5] See J. Rawls, *A Theory of Justice*, 284–93; cf H. P. Visser 't Hooft *Justice to Future Generations and the Environment* (Dordrecht: Kluwer Academic Publishers, 1999) esp at 55–7.

2 *Suum cuique* and the rule of law

Let us therefore take another look at the wedding parable, in terms of the ancient idea that justice is a matter of securing 'to each her (or his) own'—*suum cuique*. There was in principle and by design a fair share of the buffet available for every-body to have a pleasant meal, and perhaps a second helping for the very hungry. But too many greedy guests took far more than their share, so others did not get what they should have had. It is already established that 'what they should have had' in this context does not equate to a positive right. Even so, it comes within the scope of the *'suum'* generously interpreted. Injustice always presupposes some prior conception of what a person should have; that is, of what is due to her, for injustice is the state of affairs in which for some reason a person is denied, or any-way fails to get, what is due.

This is a concept with wide application. There is unjust criticism where a writer is criticized for faults her work does not actually exhibit, and unjust blame when someone is blamed for what he did not do. There is injustice in an appointment when a less well-qualified candidate succeeds against a better qualified one. There can be unjust favouritism by a parent between different children. Players can be unjustly penalized in some game or another. There can be unjust acquittals and unjust convictions in criminal trials, where somebody is let off for a crime he obviously did commit or somebody else is convicted of a crime she did not com-mit. There can be unjust awards of damages, and unjust failures to award dam-ages, when errors occur in civil litigation.

Not all such cases in which persons suffer injustice through failing to get their due are cases in which someone else can be blamed for having acted unjustly. To act unjustly is to act in knowing or careless disregard of the merits of the case, whether as book-critic, moral complainant, member of an appointing commit-tee, parent in relation to children, referee in a game or jury or judge in some form of legal process. To disregard the merits of a case in a matter touching what is due to another person is to show serious want of respect and concern. (In the unjust acquittal, it is often considered to be the victim of the crime who suffers the worse disrespect.) Whoever is charged in any context with making decisions that relate to what is due to another or others therefore ought to dis-play what the classical Roman jurist called a 'steady and unvarying will to give to each his (or her) due' (*constans et perpetua voluntas ius suum cuique tribuendi*). Failing to exercise your will in this spirit when making decisions that affect others is unjust. The just person by contrast cultivates such a will. This indeed calls for self-command and engages one's commitment to an 'impartial specta-tor' approach to such matters.

Clearly, injustices can occur by way of some persons' failure to receive what was due to them, even though nobody tried to bring this about or was care-less about it. There can be erroneous acquittals and convictions even in trials conducted by fair and honest prosecutors before good and conscientious judges and jurors. For the evidence may turn out to have been inadequate or misleading in ways none of them could have detected at the time. Parallel instances can easily be envisaged in other contexts. Nevertheless, it shows there is real need for care and vigilance in situations where fairness to others is a salient matter of concern.

How does this apply to us in our ordinary way of life, when we are not exercising some office or position that calls for some sort of authoritative decision-making? In the eighteenth century, thinkers like Hume and Smith took it plainly for granted that justice is paradigmatically displayed in the conduct of those persons who attend carefully to fulfilling (and, of course, to not trespassing against) rights of others.[6] In this sense, to be just is to be law-abiding, that is law-abiding in matters touching any other person's rights. Conversely, one who acts unjustly lays himself open to suffering the enforcement of the law against him either through some civil process of litigation or via criminal indictment, trial and, eventually, punishment. Justice is the virtue we can be compelled to observe, by coercive legal means when necessary. Obviously, this further depends on the existence of legal institutions whose agents act honestly and justly and who are put as far as possible beyond corruption, and who avoid even the appearance of improper involvement on one side of a case or the other.

This last requirement concerning public justice is often encapsulated in two time-hallowed juristic maxims, to hear both sides in any dispute, and to abstain from judging in any matter in which as judge one has a personal interest likely to be favoured or disfavoured by the decision one has to take. '*Audiatur et altera pars*' and '*Nemo judex in causa sua*', let both sides be heard, and let no person be judge in her own cause. Among common lawyers and Scots lawyers, these have come to be known as the 'principles of natural justice'. Respect for them in relation to the conduct of public administration was an important element in the development of mature systems of public law, especially administrative law, in the legal systems of the United Kingdom since a landmark decision by the House of Lords in 1964.[7] They have also had an impact in the development of European Union law,[8] alongside of the initially Germanic principle of proportionality, according to which any public act may not exceed in content or form what matches the objective that justifies carrying out the act in question. Applied in domestic criminal law, such a principle, for example, precludes over-punishment even of a serious criminal whose crimes have aroused public resentment, a case to which Smithian spectator reasoning is also relevant and yields similar results.

Some might observe that this so-called 'natural justice' is nothing more than the rule of law in fancy dress. To the extent that we live in states under

---

[6] D. Hume *A Treatise of Human Nature* (ed. L. A. Selby-Bigge; 2nd edn revised by P. H. Nidditch) (Oxford: Clarendon Press, 1978) 477–525; A. Smith, *Lectures on Justice* 399.

[7] *Ridge v Baldwin* [1964] AC 65.

[8] See, e.g., P. Craig, *EU Administrative Law* (Oxford: Oxford University Press, 2006) 270–3.

state-enforced systems of positive law, it is an obviously legitimate demand that the state and its agencies properly uphold the laws they have enacted or developed by other means, e.g., through a system of judicial precedents. The judge who is personally biased or who unfairly hears one side to the exclusion of the other in a dispute violates procedural rules that are no more than what is essential in ensuring that the laws announced by the state are the actually governing rules of official conduct. This is true, but does not undermine an important truth about the quality of life under genuine law that Nigel Simmonds has expounded forcefully in *Law as a Moral Idea*.[9] His argument is that one cannot accept any depiction of the 'rule of law' as a purely formal feature of legal systems, though it certainly has significant formal aspects, revealed in requirements for prospectivity and generality of rules, publication of them, absence of conflict among them, and so forth. For the additional essential demand that the officials of the system must act faithfully to the rules bears heavy moral traffic.

A legal system might in its published form contain nothing but the most formally elegant rules stating on their face completely acceptable rules of civil, criminal, and public law. But the officials might enforce these rules in a highly selective way, deliberately picking on women or Jews or blacks or some other racial or ethnic group, or members of one or another religious sect, pursuing only members of the target group among all those detected in wrongdoing. This might also include an element of corruption by way of demands for protection-money from the richer members of the target group. It would not even have to be the case that people who suffered from being picked on were not in fact guilty of infringements with which they were charged, though in corrupted regimes such scrupulousness might be pretty unlikely. The difference between them and members of a majority community whose infractions were disregarded would still be morally intolerable. The point is that a law that on its face promises equality of treatment and even handed justice to all can in practice become an instrument of cruelty, injustice and oppression. Whoever demands that the rule of law be respected demands something which has moral worth, because governance of a state or other polity under genuinely universalistic laws is of profound moral value, expressing the value of treating people as equal citizens and equal human beings. Only under the rule of law so understood can systems of positive law approximate to being laws of freedom, and only then would it be possible for an economy to be genuinely structured around Smith's 'system of natural liberty'. So the principles of natural justice are indeed more than merely technical legal requirements, but express sound moral demands and belong quite centrally in the internal morality of legal order.[10]

---

[9] N. Simmonds, *Law as a Moral Idea* (Oxford: Oxford University Press, 2007).
[10] This argument accepts and confirms that of L. L. Fuller, *The Morality of Law* (revised edn) (New Haven, CT; Yale University Press, 1969); cf R. S. Summers, *L. L. Fuller* (London: Edward Arnold, 1985).

3 But what is due?

So far, we have pursued the idea that justice and injustice focus on what is due to people, even beyond the reach of their positive legal or even moral rights. This will not get us far towards enlightenment unless we can lay hands on a credible conception of what is due. Can this be done?

It will be of value to consider in outline two powerful contemporary theories concerning what is 'due' to people beyond the confines of any particular state system of positive law and outside any particular current economy. These are theories that aim to establish a basis for appraising critically the present distribution of social goods in any polity or society, and the present constitutional and institutional framework for upholding and or rectifying any undue shares. John Rawls[11] proposes the so-called 'difference principle' laying down what is sometimes called a 'maximin' method of calculation. 'Maximin' favours maximizing the minimum in any relevant situation, thus, in the context of reviewing the distribution of incomes in a society, this principle says we should maximize the minimum income and wealth of the worst off citizens. The wellbeing of the least well-off members of society should be at the maximal level that can be achieved through redistribution from wealthier to poorer citizens. Redistributive systems of taxation should tax the wealthiest citizens up to the point at which any increase of the tax-burden would reduce the tax take, diminishing what could be redistributed to the poorer citizens, and making them worse off than they would be according to maximin. According to Rawls, such over-redistribution would be undesirable, even if the resultant gap between richest and poorest were narrower than it would be under maximin. For this further narrowing of the gap would be imputable to envy rather than to a regard for justice. Justice, in this view requires a scheme in which everyone is as well off as they can be, in circumstances in which the least well-off are better off than under any alternative possibility.

Ronald Dworkin offers a rival theory based on equality of resources rather than equality of welfare. He postulates an ideal initial equality of resources shared out among all members of society, or, perhaps, those who will become citizens and residents of a given state.[12] Since each is entitled to adequate and equal concern and respect, there is no plausible reason why anyone should start out with any more or any less than anyone else, in the way of an initial endowment of resources from the total assets available in what is to become the territory of the state. There is also no reason why there should not be maximal opportunity for all persons to develop their resources and talents as they think best to do, in the context of a fair and free market economy—Smithian 'natural liberty' in effect. Given differential

[11] J. Rawls, *A Theory of Justice* 152–7.

[12] R. Dworkin, *Sovereign Virtue: The Theory and Practice of Equality* (Cambridge, MA: Harvard University Press, 2000); cf A. Ripstein 'Liberty and Equality', in A. Ripstein (ed) *Ronald Dworkin* (Cambridge: Cambridge University Press, 2007) 82–108.

luck, industry and talent, different people will make more of their resources than others, partly also because of different preferences and inclinations. Some people prefer a fair amount of leisure along with some hard work, while others are more driven souls, workaholics, even. There is no reason of justice why the initial equality of resources should not over time give rise to considerable differences in people's holdings of assets, at any given time, far less over the whole course of their lives.

What this does not yet take into account, however, are the risks of disability, sickness, and accidents of many kinds that can stunt a person's possibility of development even from a starting point of equal resources. Also, it makes no allowance yet for the fact that in real societies people start out with considerable differentials of resources available to them or for their care, nurture, and education. The solution to this offered by Dworkin refers us to a hypothetical insurance market. Suppose that people knew they were starting out in a society that would be based on initial equality of resources but did not (yet) know their own genetic, familial, and environmental luck as of the time of decision about the basis of social co-operation. Such people would find it rational to insure against risks of various kinds of misfortune that would disable them from playing effectively in the market, or at least hamper them in making a start in the market order. In societies as they really are, therefore, if we seek social justice by reference to this model, the answer will be to have a socio-economic system with a modified market economy. It will be modified by adoption of a comprehensive scheme of social insurance against various forms of innocent misfortune, calculated in a way that can also take into account the actual inequality of initial endowments accessible to infants of parents in different income groups.

Whereas Dworkin works from a hypothetical insurance market, Rawls (as is well known) asks us to envisage a hypothetical social contract. He asks us to imagine what terms of mutual association would be acceptable to people coming together from a state of nature aiming to establish a polity on terms acceptable to all. The key point is that he asks us to envisage the potential co-contractants deliberating behind a veil of ignorance—none knows his or her own particular characteristics, though each is aware of the general facts of human psychology. Crudely to express a conclusion reached after a long and subtle argument, we may say that the 'maximin' solution is in Rawls' opinion, the basic principle of justice to which people would agree, subject to a qualification concerning the priority of liberty. In a slightly simplified summary, there are two principles the first of which has priority over the second:

Each person is to have an equal right to the most extensive basic liberty compatible with a similar system of liberty for all; liberty can be restricted only for the sake of liberty;

Social and economic inequalities are to be arranged so that they are both (a) to the greatest benefit of the least advantaged and (b) attached to offices and positions open to all under conditions of fair equality of opportunity.[13]

---

[13] J. Rawls, *A Theory of Justice*, 60.

Whether or not one finds plausible the hypothetical derivation of the principles from an artificially conceptualized 'original position', they have a certain attractiveness. This derives from the way they insist on securing first certain basic liberties, and then excluding any social and economic inequalities that emerge otherwise than from schemes that maximize benefits for those who get least from them. There is an upper limit to the admissible gap between richest and poorest in anything Rawls could acknowledge as a just society. This is material to concerns that were expressed in the latter part of Chapter 7 above. For Dworkin, by contrast, there does not appear to be an upper limit to what a person may make of her resources. But this holds good only as long as the situation at any time is compatible with each having notionally started with the same resources as everyone else, and with everyone having been properly compensated according to accepted principles of insurance for any of the insured risks that have materialized in her case.

Both approaches, that of Rawls and that of Dworkin, like others in similar vein, do address a problem concerning any enforced public scheme of social justice. The problem arises from the claim of autonomy in moral reasoning. What makes it right for a state to tax everybody under a regime of progressive income tax together with flat rate taxes on consumption (such as Value Added Tax)? Why should people be forced to give up some of their income from their own free activity? Why should a top slice be added to the cost of any goods or services they buy, and be appropriated by the state? Why should this money then be redistributed in the form of various free or subsidized services to people who cannot pay the market price for the services in question? How can this be compatible with 'laws of freedom' or have any part in a 'system of natural liberty'? A possible answer depends not on what actual self-interested people do say once they know what they stand to gain and to lose from a given overall pattern of taxation and public expenditure. It depends rather on what they would say as fully rational and autonomous agents at a point in time when they did not know how the future would work out.

There can be fair betting on a race only if bets are all placed before it starts and if no runner has been nobbled, so that everyone bets in ignorance of the actual outcome of the race. So likewise, it may be argued, there can be a fair system of social co-operation among people who agree the terms of its establishment only at a time before they know exactly how they will fetch up themselves. 'Did you agree to this?' is not the question. We should rather ask, 'Would you have agreed to this before you knew exactly how things would turn out?' If so, we might claim, it is quite legitimate to insist that you accept the proposed system, since as an autonomous agent you would have had to accept it if voting before all the facts were known. Or, perhaps better, one can point out that if you applied impartial spectator reasoning carefully, you would concede that there was no justification for resentment about redistributive taxation in this case. By analogy, a person who is justly punished for a violent assault may not in fact accept of his own free will that there must be such a law and that breakers of it must be punished in the very way in which he is being punished. But surely if such a person were to reflect about the possibilities for human society of a general permission to use extreme violence whenever one chooses, he would see the point. As he languishes in jail, his will is overwhelmed by the coercive infliction of punishment, but in a sense his rational will has to go along with the rule against violence and the enforcement of appropriate penalties for assaults. Why is it not the same with the putative tax-dodger?[14]

The argument is persuasive up to a point. Yet, in the case of any such hypothetical scenario for the reaching of rational agreement, the plausibility depends on that of all the assumptions made in setting up the hypothetical negotiation, whether by way of social contract or insurance deal. If you disagree with the output, you can challenge the input. Since the input is defensible mainly by reference to the output it generates according to the hypothetical negotiation, this process risks begging the question. For, in the end, the argument has to focus essentially on the principles generated rather than on the process that generated them.

From the point of view of a concern about justice, that is, a concern about everybody having what is due to them, inequality of possessions between individuals is problematic. Certainly, one cannot have any kind of free society and free economy without some inequality arising through the working of the various sectors of the market for goods, services, land and labour. Not all inequality is unjust. But extremes of inequality militate against any kind of equal citizenship and any sense of sharing in a common good. Vast fortunes can hedge their possessors against all or practically all of the contingencies that can have a severely adverse or even ruinous impact on poorer people. Something like Rawls's 'difference principle' has a real attractiveness. There would be a real sense that even the richest and the poorest had a shared interest in each other's welfare if a society could secure the maximization of the minimum and thus limit the acceptable differential between those at the bottom and those at the top of the economic pile.

But how is one to go about achieving an approximation to this kind of distribution of social primary goods?[15] We may recall that 'Social and economic inequalities are to be arranged so that they are both (a) to the greatest benefit of the least advantaged and (b) attached to offices and positions open to all under conditions of fair equality of opportunity'. Who is to 'arrange' this? By what means? F. A. Hayek objects to all schemes of 'social justice'[16] on the ground that in the 'great society', where the 'system of natural liberty' prevails, no one

---

[14] Compare on all this also T. Scanlon, *What we Owe to Each Other* (Cambridge, MA and London: Harvard University Press, 1998.

[15] Identified by Rawls as 'income and wealth and the bases of self-respect', *A Theory of Justice*, 61–2.

[16] F. A. Hayek, *Law, Legislation and Liberty* (London: Routledge, 1993) vol 2 *The Mirage of Social Justice*.

'arranges' inequalities at all. They emerge from the free activity of many people interacting through the market, which is itself best considered as a kind of information system. Moreover, there is no stopping point at which you can say who has got most and who has got least out of it, for its inputs and outputs are always in flux. Trying to 'arrange' that the least advantaged get the greatest possible benefit would require you to identify the least advantaged and then to pay them sums of money that would bring them up to a new level of wellbeing while meantime others slipped back in the race, and so on. Such considerations led Hayek to conclude that 'social justice' was a wholly empty concept—a meaningless phrase, compared with the justice of securing to everyone their due within the legal order that a working market economy requires.

Such considerations might drive one back to something like Dworkin's theory. Markets include insurance markets, and people really do insure themselves against many risks. But there are some risks that lie outside of what the insurance market can handle. Still, it is not too hard to envisage and grant credibility to the kind of hypotheses in the light of which we would agree to collectively insure against such risks. Indeed, in many states, systems of social and health insurance funded out of tax revenues exist to ensure that people have access to medical care when they need it[17] and are covered against risks of unemployment, at least temporary unemployment, and disability. A public education system secures to all children and young people an adequate start in life to develop the talents they have. These, suggests Dworkin, indicate the kind of arrangements that might be improved or even perfected to bring about some fair approximation to his ideal of a free economy in which everyone has in effect had an initial endowment of resources (or of access to resources) equal to that of everyone else. Then inequalities will indeed emerge, but they will not be 'arranged' in any sense, nor will they be open to criticism as unjust or imposed inequalities.

4 Justice in the 'real world'

There may be another way to press home a similar point, in a way that makes no appeal to hypothetical social contracts or insurance markets, but sticks to the real world. Let us take up again Adam Smith's idea that property causes government rather than vice versa. That is, in some forms of human society, such as hunting and gathering communities, nobody has any substantial or permanent property. They may have hunting equipment and simple tools, and of course food that has been caught or gathered belongs to the catcher(s) and their associates. But there are no permanent assets. It is only with the growth of different forms of economy and society that any durable property comes into being. Those who have no

---

[17] N. Daniels, *Just Health: Meeting health needs fairly* (Cambridge: Cambridge University Press, 2008) 29–102.

property, or very little, have grounds at least to envy those who have some, especially those who have a lot. There is a standing temptation to the use of subterfuge or violence to reallocate assets. A crucial function of emerging institutions of government is thus the protection of those who have some property against those who have none.

In contemporary democratic states, in circumstances of postindustrial society, with purely capitalist economies or more likely mixed economies, where capitalism is modified by some degree of social democratic redistribution, this remains true. The great wealth generated in such economies, and held moment-by-moment by individuals with fluctuating but wildly contrasting personal wealth, is manipulated through elaborate institutional arrangements. Public Limited Companies, Trusts, Private Equity Firms, Partnerships limited or unlimited, as well as individuals acting for themselves, hold property in land and in moveable and immoveable property (not least, intellectual property rights). Stock exchanges and the banking system trade in all sorts of strange assets dependent on some mixture of contract law and securities law. The assets of the population, and especially of its wealthiest citizens, are not just protected by laws against trespass, theft and the like. They have no existence at all apart from the law and the legal regimes in which they are encapsulated (or, as we might say, institutionalized).

It is sometimes said that the poor get much more out of the welfare state than the rich do—they use the public health service and the public school system. They may rely from time to time on social security payments of one kind or another. They may end up living on a state old age pension and receiving state support in a retirement home. The rich pay for all these things themselves and for their own children and elderly parents. And they pay taxes on top of that. So rich people subsidize the state and poor people draw down the subsidy. But to claim on this ground that the burdens are all on one side and the benefits on the other ignores the credit side of the balance sheet altogether. Whose assets primarily do the defence forces defend and the police forces protect against intrusion? Whose assets depend on the existence of a relatively efficient and un-corrupt judicial system and legal profession? Whose assets depend for their very definition and security on the well-ordered working of the system of commercial law and property law? Who would lose disproportionately if the existing political order collapsed under some form of political revolution? These questions are virtually self-answering. The institutions of government protect the rich in their possession of a vastly disproportionate share of assets, judged on any kind of *per capita* basis. It is as true now as in the days of Adam Smith that government exists to protect the rich from the poor. Surely it follows that the costs of government ought justly to be borne by the rich in great preponderance over the burdens it would be fair or reasonable to place upon the poor.

Smith even acknowledged that the poor typically resent (not merely envy) the riches of the rich, while at the same time looking up in admiration to great (and rich) personages, much as still occurs, perhaps even more meretriciously, in the 'celebrity' culture of the twenty-first century. Is this, perhaps a targetless resentment, or simply one with which the impartial spectator cannot go along? Is it that, on reflection, one must realize that the rich have themselves taken nothing from the poor, so there is no invasion or attack of any kind to ground the resentment or to suggest a proportionate remedy?

These questions should be answered in the negative. We may at this stage, look again at the parable of the wedding party. There are finite resources available to the whole of humanity now, and even in wealthy and thinly populated states there are limits to the resources available. Real people as they are now started out with very different endowments (both natural and adventitious). Those who were born into or have forged their way up into the ranks of the super-rich, or even the very rich, have some resemblance to the greedy guests at the party.

The resemblance is certainly far from perfect. There is not a table filled with a specific and calculated amount of life's goods, such that those who take more than their share make it inevitable that others will get less, or even get none. It is arguable that some who are highly successful in business or industry, and become rich thereby, create opportunities of employment for many people and open up possible market niches for more entrepreneurial others. Market economies are not zero-sum games, and it is possible for nearly everyone else to grow somewhat better off by way of 'trickle down' from the activities and expenditures of the rich. All this is true. Nevertheless, we remind ourselves that the assets in which wealth is measured are not like the nuts and berries and fresh-caught fish of the hunter-gatherer. They are not objects given by unimproved nature. They are assets of a kind that depend through and through on the state, and the state depends through and through on the relative civility of the society its citizens constitute. The state indeed guarantees through its coercive mechanisms the civil peace on which civil society depends. But it does so through the agency of citizens employed to that end, and they cannot succeed except with at least the tacit support of the majority of people around. Especially in a democracy, the state depends on the consent, perhaps tacit perhaps sometimes grudging of nearly all its citizens, and the government of the state is ultimately subject to the will of the people filtered through very imperfect systems of voting and representation. Undoubtedly, everyone whose earnings and capital exceed the average for all citizens at any moment in time is a net beneficiary of the systems of civil protection and property protection that the state establishes, and the more they exceed the average the more is this so.

To demand this continuing advantage is not necessarily in itself to demand more than is one's due. But to demand it and at the same time deny any liability to make a suitably proportional contribution to the common public revenues of the state does cross the line of seeking more than one's due. It is entirely right that people in this relatively fortunate position should make a proportionate, and perhaps even at the highest levels a progressively graded, contribution through taxation. This is not merely a matter of contributing pro rata to common costs like those of external defence, internal policing and civil and criminal justice and internal roads and transport. It also must include contributing through the institutions of a welfare state to meeting the needs of the young, the sick and the indigent. We are all insured, but some of us pay a higher rate of premium, for we have more to lose.

It seems that we can get further than Smith got if we apply Smithian principles of moral judgement to economic systems structured mainly according to the principles of his 'system of natural liberty'. At least, such an argument may apply a real-world supplement to the hypothetical-contractual or hypothetical social insurance schemata deployed by Rawls and Dworkin in their arguments for social justice in a liberal state. The Smithian categorical imperative applied in the circumstances of the societies under consideration mandates that we seek rules for redistribution of excess goods from the rich and reallocate these among the poor. Either way round, we come to a conclusion that favours upholding the claims of distributive justice (or social justice) along side of corrective and retributive justice. In other work I have showed how these three aspects of justice are material to the shaping of, respectively, public law, private law, and criminal law in contemporary legal systems.[18]

In terms of practical possibilities as things currently stand, the balance of advantage in trying to match public arrangements to ideal theory seems to favour the Dworkininan approach, that looks to social insurance as the effective means of securing to all citizens a decent share in the overall wellbeing of the citizen body. The tendency of a tax system with some element of progressiveness built into it, and with a bar upon confiscatory top rates of taxation that are self-defeating, is bound to be towards a 'maximin' effect that would to a degree mimic Rawls's difference principle. This would certainly be so if the levels of social insurance were calculated so as to ensure that measures were developed in favour of environmental common goods an a planetary as well as a local scale and in favour of intergenerational and trans-statal distributive justice, and that these measures did not erode the level of poorer persons below their postulated 'decent share'. There are clear and compelling reasons[19] why the states of the world should enhance their still rather threadbare efforts towards concerted action both on environmental concerns, with their strong intergenerational impact, and on international distributive justice. One's entitlement to a decent share of the resources necessary for life and for some basic comfort and opportunity of self-development cannot be restricted according to one's citizenship or one's date of birth. Justice apart, mere self-interest in the wealthier states should let their citizens see the necessity to stem the causes of the ever-growing flood

---

[18] N. MacCormick, *Institutions of Law*, chs 10–13.

[19] Brilliantly stated, albeit within a utilitarian frame of reasoning, by Peter Singer, in *One World: The Ethics of Globalization* (New Haven, CT: Yale University Press, 2002).

of 'economic migrants' from poor countries to richer ones where mass immigration creates grave social pressures.

It does not follow that everything desirable to be achieved can be achieved through the compulsory mechanisms of state justice, with the inevitable bureaucracy of public law and its necessarily attendant audit-culture to control against corruption and inefficiency. We inhabit a world that has to wait seemingly indefinitely for agreement on the Kyoto Climate Change Treaty or on the Doha Round of the World Trade Organization's talks to secure fairness in international trade between developing and developed countries. There is much that can best be done by appealing to the higher virtues and by developing a proper sense of shame concerning the many vices that have selfishness at their core. Law will never abolish the greed of the greedy guests, but a widespread sense of shame and disgrace just might inhibit grosser exhibitions of it.

It is true that no ideal scheme of distributive justice can be even approximately realized without state agencies designed to realize it, in accordance with political decisions emerging from some more or less democratic political process. It is therefore also true that imperfections inevitably arise through the complexities of bureaucracy. All this is further compounded in international arenas through which the states, urged on by the opinion of (some of) their citizens seek to diminish trans-national injustices in favour of very poor people, for example, in sub-Saharan Africa. This can lead to a paralysis of despair, or to a kind of helpless cynicism, among ordinary private citizens. Even those who wish to live in a more just society and a more just and environmentally prudent world order may see no prospect of being able to bring this about in any co-ordinated fashion.

Still, cynicism is not inevitable. To pursue justice and to guard against injustice is not only a duty of states and their public officials. Whoever does injustice or knowingly tolerates an injustice is morally at fault. Justice is a virtue all people can cultivate and should. It includes, as Smith and Kant insisted, a scrupulous respect for the legally established rights of others. Indeed, it starts from this, and can proceed no further till this is satisfied. But, as we have seen, it also goes beyond that. It extends to looking with proper concern to the question whether I myself in some context have acquired and am holding on to more than is my due in a context where (inevitably) other people near to or remote from me have less than their due. If so I should take such inevitably imperfect steps as are available to me to rectify this situation. And I should dedicate myself to some involvement in political or voluntary 'third sector' processes capable of achieving better co-ordination of individual efforts to this end. Surely it is good to have 'steady and unvarying will to give to each his (or her) due', and this is not a virtue whose cultivation we can safely delegate entirely to the state.

This chapter has not established, nor attempted to establish, a comprehensive theory of distributive justice. That would require a whole book to itself. What has been done is to show why and where considerations of distributive justice as well as those of corrective justice belong within practical thought. Duties toward distributive justice, however these are in the end most satisfactorily determined, belong along side of the 'basic duties' in delimiting the scope of the 'principle of freedom'. Stair's principles of 'society, property and commerce' have to be strongly supplemented with principles of public law dealing with the agencies of distributive or social justice as well as with the infrastructure needed for a Smithian order of natural liberty (indeed, they should be seen as part of that infrastructure). We must bear this in mind as we proceed in the next chapter to ponder what are good and wise uses of the substantial sphere remaining to the principle of freedom.

9

Using Freedom Well

1 Trying to act for the best

The difficulty with deontic moral reasoning comes after we have done the reasoning that identifies our duties. Doing the duties is difficult. But it is a problem more of will than of reason. Practical reasoning about the good use of moral freedom is difficult in a different way. Being motivated to do the best one can is not too hard. But figuring out what it is best to do can be very hard. The aim of this chapter is to see if it can be made any easier.

Since the domain under consideration is that of freedom—clear of basic duties and duties of justice (distributive justice included) on the one hand, and of binding engagements on the other, there necessarily are no pre-existing rules, nor is the task one of identifying rules. We are trying to think about what is good beyond the confines of any binding rules about what we must do. The utilitarian mistake is to think of an injunction like 'you should always do the best you can' as though it were a rule rather than an exhortation, a binding norm not a rule of thumb or a practical truism. Here, the universal and law-like character of moral norms is missing. All human beings have their own path to pursue, their own life to lead, making the best of it they can.

There are many human beings for whom the struggle to stay alive and keep their dependants alive in dire circumstances exhausts the whole of their energy and ingenuity. Planning for anything beyond personal and familial survival is totally impractical. Even survival grows problematic or impossible under conditions of drought, flood, failure of harvests, natural disasters, or economic collapse in industrialized countries. Those who live in circumstances of relative plenty owe, but seldom adequately fulfil, duties not only of benevolence but also of distributive justice to such profoundly unfortunate fellow humans. The institutional means for fulfilling these duties remain woefully inadequate in the early twenty-first century, but this only partly excuses non-fulfilment of duties that cannot be fulfilled perfectly in an uncoordinated way. Any discussion of practical reasoning in the domain of moral liberty nevertheless proceeds in the shadow of this at best imperfectly fulfilled duty of those who participate in the discussion.

In Chapter 2, it was suggested that when a person tries to decide about what is best to do, the most useful guideline may be one concerning the virtues that are expressed in the tasks and activities the person undertakes. Do the kind of thing that would be done by the kind of person you seek to become. The time has come to pursue this suggestion further, reminding ourselves first concerning the context of the reasoning.

Our established hypothesis is that there are states of being and states of affairs that it is good for human beings to realize or to sustain, and others that it is good to eliminate or ward off so far as possible. Those that we should eliminate or ward off are evils. We always have reason to pursue good and shun evil. The most basic goods concern sustenance of our basic animal existence, and this also requires sustenance of a communal existence in which, for each member, it is an aspect of one's own good that the community is collectively flourishing. Some aspects at least of communal goods are such that they can be realized only by community-oriented action that also contributes to individual good, but that cannot be realized simply as a side-effect of individualistic self-interested action. We also have reason to act in other-directed ways in respect of the basic goods, at least in favour of friends and family and also as a matter of more general benevolence. To be capable of exercising general benevolence is conditional on already having secured the most basic goods for oneself and one's narrower circle.[1]

Also in play, beyond the press of dire necessity, there are ideal goods that humans have reason to cultivate and pursue, while trying to ward off any threats to their realization or persistence. All this we take for granted following on the conclusions of Chapter 2.

How then can a person go about building a reasonable life that seeks to make the best of the opportunities and possibilities that she perceives to be open to her? What kind of a person should she strive to be or become in order to make the best of her life?

2 How to act well: the auxiliary virtues

There are at least some characteristics that are always required if one is to achieve anything good, whatever one's particular bent of character and particular opportunities may turn out to be. They are not ends in themselves, but dispositions of character that incline one towards worthwhile objectives, and help to make them attainable. Those for treatment in what follows are: integrity and independence of mind, self-knowledge, courage, reasonableness (or prudence), technological competence, considerateness for others, politeness, self-respect without selfishness, diligence and a will to hard work, along with patience in the face of adversity and ill-luck.

---

[1] Peter Singer rightly insists that the justification for favouring most those nearest to us is quite tightly restricted. See P. Singer, *One World: the Ethics of Globalization* (New Haven and London: Yale University Press, 2002) 160–163. Cf, on 'selective care and concern', O. O'Neill, *Towards Justice and Virtue* (Cambridge: Cambridge University Press, 1996) 195–200.

Integrity of character and independence of mind are the first prerequisites for any self-managed life. One has to have a capacity for taking decisions that determine one's short-, mid-, and longer-term aims and objectives, and one needs to be resolute in sticking to these even in the face of some discouragement. The decisions must be one's own, though (as often repeated already) they are usually best taken in discussion with friendly others and after attending to advice from wise counsellors. Over the longer run, they need to exhibit an overall coherence of approach and an intrinsic mutual compatibility in the aims and objectives they delineate. Complementarity of different aims, and variety in one's life-style are valuable, but self-defeat is the fate of those who pursue flatly incompatible aims at the same time, or who flit from one project to another without ever finishing anything.

Integrity is not the same as obstinate inflexibility. The physical universe and the human context continually throw up events relevant to our activities that disrupt our plans, making them impossible of fulfilment as originally conceived and sometimes forcing a complete reconsideration. The contingency of facts and circumstances is of course a permanent feature of our lives, and, whatever a person is doing, some adverse changes are to some extent foreseeable and may even be open to some kind of insurance protection in some cases. Brilliant but unforeseen opportunities also occasionally turn up. Either way, everyone has to stand ready to expect the unexpected and react with sensible flexibility in the light of changing possibilities, threats and opportunities.

Typically, as in all discussions of the virtues since Aristotle's time, we find ourselves aiming here at a mean between dangerous extremes. Integrity is essential, but it can shade over into the arrogant inflexibility and obstinacy of a character like Shakespeare's Coriolanus. Or think of the British General Staff during the Battle of the Somme in 1916. Their obstinacy in pursuit of an evidently unattainable objective resulted in the pointless slaughter of many thousands of troops on both sides of the conflict, even more on their own side than on that of the enemy. Such resoluteness is not admirable. Yet on the other side, there are risks of excessive flexibility. One who does not test out the strength of resistance to the pursuit of an objective may often withdraw unnecessarily, being too readily discouraged by initial failures in a tricky task. Timidity can be as destructive of one's enterprises as want of reasonable caution. Those statesmen, like UK Prime Minister Neville Chamberlain, who sought to appease Hitler in the late nineteen thirties in effect missed the last opportunity to have stopped the advance of Nazi Germany when this could have been achieved at a relatively low cost in lives and resources. They were over-impressed with the risks they faced and made the situation worse by backing down in face of the (ultimately self-defeating) arrogance of Hitler and his Nazi Government. Integrity and firmness of purpose stand at the mean between reckless arrogance and self-mistrustful timidity.

Self-knowledge as well as self-command is a further essential component of one's capacity for sound reasoning in practical matters. Most people have a greater tendency on one side or the other of a given median line that defines a virtue. If you see in yourself tinges of a Napoleon-like character, you should suspect yourself of tending to over-confidence and should seek advice that will (as it were) sober you up in your assessment of risks and difficulties. If your tendency seems normally to be more towards a Chamberlain-like readiness to bow before risks rather than face up to them, you should take advice from persons who are in your view somewhat more tough-minded.

Generally, there is a balance to be struck so far as concerns listening and sometimes deferring to others' advice. One can be over-confident and too ready to ignore advice, or one can be too diffident and too ready to listen to others rather than use one's own judgement. Respect for others' opinions can degenerate into mere sycophancy, independence of mind can degenerate into megalomaniac disregard for the good sense of others. A haughty spirit can indeed lead one to self-destruction, while excessive humility can destroy one's independence of character. Between these lies a proper and decent pride in one's own standing as an autonomous and self-commanding moral agent.

An over-enthusiasm for independence can also lead to failures of co-operation where co-operative effort is either essential, or preferable to individual effort. Faced with a threat of flooding from a river, if each riparian occupier seeks only to build up the river-bank adjacent to her or his own ground, nobody is likely to succeed. A collaborative scheme of flood defence is likely to work better, and ought to include some element of mutual insurance so that the burdens of (partly) unprevented flooding are shared rather than left to lie where they fall. Readiness to engage freely in co-operative pursuit of communal goals is not a failure of independence or integrity in the presently intended sense. Again, one seeks a mean between selfish individualism and crushing collectivism. One is reminded that freedom in the trio of 'obedience, freedom and engagement' essentially includes freedom to enter into engagements, with willing commitment to carrying out the obligations that one's engagements generate.

Courage is another essential character trait that one has to cultivate as far as one can. It is difficult to sustain independence and do what one honestly considers to be for the best in circumstances where others may not agree and where one has to face down risks while avoiding the perils of obstinate inflexibility. One has to be brave to assert independence of mind in moments of crisis or difficulty, where one has really tried to work out the right course of action in the light of all advice but on the basis of one's own final decision. This again implies treading the line between being foolhardy and being too scared to do what one really believes needs doing. For many people these considerations enhance the motives toward communal rather than individual action, since it can be less daunting to try and be brave in company than when one is alone. Yet again, too often the mutual support the members of a group give each other can lead to a threatening arrogance towards outsiders. In extreme cases this can even erupt into forms of gang violence.

Reasonableness (or *Prudence* in one usage of the term) is another general virtue needed in all practical contexts. It is always good to act reasonably, whatever one's specific aims and objectives. This means several things. It calls, first of all, for as full as practicable an awareness of the context of one's action, and an exploration of what are the realistic possibilities open for one. What can one bring about by taking one or another available course of action? What are the likely side-effects or remoter consequences? Is there a risk or threat of damage to oneself or others in one's neighbourhood? (This point will become salient in the second part of the next chapter.) Nobody acts in a practically reasonable way who fails to give as much attention as is practicable in a choice situation to the actual state of affairs and its probable future evolution in response to whatever acts or omissions one decides upon. Prudence as a virtue has much to do with timely foresight, for one should avoid getting boxed into a situation of choice without time for due reflection, where earlier deliberation at greater leisure might have made the pressures of decision-making less urgent and given more time to explore all avenues.

Reasonableness also calls for reflection about values themselves, that is, about goods one seeks to bring about and evils one seeks to avert. This is especially so when this reflection bears also on the greater contours of one's plan of life or on one's sense of the story one hopes to be able to tell of one's life. For it is necessary in our reasoning to identify what really is good and how important one aspect of the good is in relation to others, and how far there can be proper trade-offs between some elements of good with some of evil unavoidably intermixed. There is a degree of reflexivity in all this, according to the thesis advanced in Chapter 2. For it is figuring out the virtues one hopes to cultivate that enables one to make a reasonable comparative evaluation of different, but not co-achievable, goods relatively to each other, and in relation to possible evils risked.

Technological knowledge and expertise, or prudently obtained advice from those who have it, are essential to nearly all pursuit of any aim beyond the very simplest of situations. Humans' capacity to wreak changes in the physical world and its components has reached awesome proportions, division of labour having made its own large contribution to this. Achieving good outcomes often requires considerable skill and technological know-how, both to bring about desired states of affairs and to guard against undesirable and unintended side-effects. To make sure by one means or another of technological adequacy up to the current level of knowledge is an essential component of reasonableness—for it is unreasonable to neglect effective means to the achievement of intended ends, or to overlook the risk of bad unintended consequences.

Respect for others is always incumbent on us as a fundamental principle of moral duty. The accompanying virtue, also a very general one, is *considerateness* for the feelings of others and toward their interests and their hopes and plans. This covers both what was known as '*caritas*' or 'charity' and what was known as '*humanitas*' or 'kindness' among the classical Christian virtues. One cannot please everybody all the time, and should not even try to do so. But that does not make it in any way good to ride roughshod over the hopes and aspirations of others. One should approach one's own activities in a way that shows consideration for others and seeks wherever possible to avoid avoidable confrontation. Where necessarily others may operate within rather limited horizons, a person able to afford a broader view should not exhibit disrespect far less disparagement or contempt for others' more restricted ambitions, where these are an unavoidable feature of the limitations within which they have to live.

Politeness and good manners enter the picture here. Clearly, one can easily err in the direction of stiffness and over-formality even to the point of thinly veiled snobbery. But on the other side, an excessively casual or off hand approach to people can be or seem disrespectful. Here one is very much in the realm of shifting and contextually variable conventions, and there are those who think that autonomy and authenticity require a revolt against all hidebound conventions. There may be occasions and situations when protest against stifling proprieties is necessary for the sake of directness and honesty in communication, but there is a risk of mere boorishness in more ordinary circumstances. In such matters, one returns to an aspect of integrity, and independence of mind and action, noting the risk of a slide over into arrogance, with the countervailing opposite extreme of the slide into sycophancy.

Unselfishness is a key virtue, just as selfishness is a besetting sin and a potential trap for everyone. Naturally and rightly each acts for her or his own motives and responds to what she or he perceives as salient reasons, some of them being in their own character self-regarding. The possibility of integrity depends on maintaining a sense of oneself as an autonomous acting subject, so far as possible in full command of one's own course of life. *Self-respect* is in this way one significant aspect of respect for persons universally, and as important in its place as due respect for the other persons one interacts with in the course of a lifetime. Nobody should suffer herself or himself to become a doormat for others or for any other, yet again everyone should show due consideration to and for others. Self-respect is the golden mean here. Selfishness is the vice of over-favouring one's own wishes, aims, projects and aspirations in competition with those of others. Here, one encounters the classical virtue of 'temperance', meaning a sense of when 'enough is enough', and a readiness not to take more than a reasonable share of anything for oneself. A Smithian reflection upon ideal impartiality is the best, perhaps the only, safeguard against this in the privacy of one's own reflections. The social, interpersonal response of critical friends and advisers is perhaps even more useful, though those who by position and fortune have succeeded in accumulating an entourage of flatterers and sycophants effectively (and perhaps of semi-conscious intent) deprive themselves of this vital recourse.

Diligence and industry are also general and auxiliary virtues to whatever else one tries to achieve. Little good is ever achieved without hard work. Willingness to work hard even in discouraging circumstances and when faced with boring tasks is essential to carrying through any plan of life to any kind of fulfilment. Like everything, this can be carried too far, into a fanaticism of single-minded effort, and obsession with one element in the good that shuts out all others—contrary to the demands of reasonableness. On the other side, the temptations of idleness are always available to seduce one from the efforts to which one's better self is committed. Laziness is a vice to which everyone is exposed, the more so because taking suitable periods of rest from endeavours is also required for the successful exercise of diligence on resuming the task. Sloth, we remember, is one of the 'seven deadly sins'.

Finally, we all must acknowledge the dominion of luck over all that we try to do. Not everyone can succeed at everything, and not everyone's failures are their own fault or anyone's fault. Those who have exercised all due diligence in pursuit of reasonable aims may sometimes achieve but small returns for their efforts, by contrast with others who for no greater effort have had the luck to reap rich rewards. A temperate readiness to be satisfied with enough even at a relatively meagre level can prevent the canker of envy eating at one's soul and embittering one's world view. *Patience* in the face of ill-luck is an admirable characteristic and one that everyone should cultivate.

The foregoing deals with what seem to be auxiliary virtues, in the sense that they are of service whatever one is embarked upon doing. They are of service both in respect of doing one's duty and in respect of doing one's best beyond the call of duty. The qualities we have considered are of value to people in their own endeavours and are valued by their neighbours in all circumstances. The life of a person who cultivates these qualities is one that goes on better than that of one who neglects them, or pursues their opposites, or deviates to any great extent from the golden mean in any case. They predispose one to worthwhile uses of freedom. In essence, however, they emerge as answers to the question 'How?' They express how we ought to go about pursuing whatever we pursue, but do not tell us what to pursue. We turn now to the 'What?' question. What ends are worthy of human attention?

3 Good ends

Life itself is a precondition of any other aim for a person, and much of anyone's efforts will always contain a concern for staying alive and for securing a livelihood for oneself and any dependants. For ordinarily fortunate human beings in postindustrial societies this has ceased to be a matter of perpetual struggle dominating all practical attention. Many people are able to achieve the needful simply through the expenditure of wages or salaries on housing, housekeeping and household necessities. This presupposes some kind of employment or adequate personal savings or social insurance during periods out of work, and involves the exercise of suitable diligence and industry in holding down whatever job, business or professional engagements one has.

The contemporary division of labour means that activities in the support of life are spread out among the primary food-producers on land and at sea, the distributors and retailers of food, the providers of energy to cultivate, harvest, transport, and finally cook it, and ultimately the consumers. They live in houses as tenants or owners, with or without mortgage-supported loans, and thus depend in various ways on house-builders, repairers and decorators, specialists in kitchen and bathroom fittings, real estate agents and lawyers, bankers, insurance companies and mortgage companies. They maintain communication links both through telephone and through internet and depend still to some extent on postal services collecting and delivering letters and parcels. The contemporary economy is indeed an elaborate network, dependent on the security provided by the several states and, at a particularly increasing rate in Europe, by supra-state confederations and international organizations. Central to such an economy is an adequate body of private law, embedded in state legal systems alongside public and criminal law—even in contemporary circumstances of global capitalism the state plays this essential role. Indeed, no one is an island, and each person's sustenance of life and shelter in reasonable comfort along with family and/or friends depends on the engagement of untold and unknown many others in the sustenance of theirs.

And yet there is more. Life requires *health*, and a multiplicity of agencies and activities in contemporary societies is engaged in the provision of health services. This is done both directly in the way of patient care and indirectly through agencies of public or private health insurance, the building and maintenance of health centres and hospitals, and the manufacture and distribution of therapeutic drugs and all manner of medical and surgical sundries. The most successful of contemporary efforts in the direction of distributive justice are found where, by one means or another, health care is made available to all people who need it on the basis of need, not ability to pay.

Obstetric services and paediatric medicine have become an essential part of the *transmission of life* from one generation to the next, and again legal and social institutions concerning family life formalize the framework for the custody, care, rearing and education of children. Biologically, a union of male and female is necessary to this. Sociologically there is a weight of evidence that the traditional two-parent nuclear family, especially when nested in a broader extended family network, remains the most stable and successful basis for the transmission of life and human values—culture and traditions, both familial and societal—through the generations. Contemporary egalitarianism has challenged the all-purpose traditional heterosexual marriage and demanded recognition of gay marriage with extension of normal parental rights to adopting partners in non-traditional unions. There is an obvious risk here of adopting policies that treat babies as though they were family accessories a bit like pet animals—which everyone is entitled to acquire and rear, and which provide a valued outlet for the nurturing qualities of many people. Nevertheless, there are so many instances of the successful rearing of children into remarkable adults through far-from-standard family backgrounds that a broadly tolerant attitude makes sense on this point.

Here, the matter concerns adoptive parenthood for children who for whatever reason do not have two natural parents available to look after them. What needs always to be stressed, however, is that one deals in this context with the rights and interests of children, in face of which the rights of adults take second place, even their equality rights. So far as concerns taxation and inheritance regimes there is no reason whatever to deny to adult partners in homosexual unions, whether styled 'marriages' or (more appropriately, it seems to me) 'civil partnerships', the same rights as obtain between heterosexual partners in marriages. For here there are no children's rights that could possibly trump the claim of adults to similar treatment despite difference of sexual orientation.

Looking broadly over these considerations about life and its sustenance and transmission, one can see many elements that delineate possibilities for reasonable life-plans. To be engaged in some way with a family, and to help it support the acquisition of maturity and independence by its younger members, while giving mutual love and support to all those involved, is an undoubted aspect of human good fortune. It is one good that all humans have reason to embrace so far as good luck and sensible conduct make it available to them. In a nuclear family, at least one parent needs to have or find employment (including successful self-employment). Single persons also need work, and may find valued companionship in their workplace as well as beyond it. Having a job may also be for many people the means through which they exercise their independence and autonomy as creative beings, even in the context of a perhaps quite hierarchically regulated workplace. The 'dignity of labour' is not always a pious fiction. Planning a career path is not a realistic option open to everyone, but for those who have suitable skills, qualifications, and opportunities it is a valuable exercise of practical reason in all the ways considered so far. Some careers, such as those of social workers, health professionals of all kinds, and educationists enable people to engage in work that is geared to ensuring the lives and health and personal development of many others. To care for life and for health in all the ways in which humans can do this is always a reasonable exercise of human effort and talent. It extends beyond human life to care for animals and the living terrestrial environment. Whoever does this as a job may find in it the necessary means to sustain her or his own life, but the motivation to most of what such people do is essentially other-directed, and (e.g., in case of immunization campaigns) often irreducibly community directed.

Education and educational institutions are not only part of the system for passing essential *knowledge* to new generations. They are also much concerned with new enlightenment, exploration, discovery, in a word, research. For all the part that luck and contingency play in each human life, the universe is not an arbitrary place. To pursue a sound understanding of it in all its dimensions and aspects, from the inwardness of human culture, history, biology, and psychology through to the ultimate questions of cosmology is a matter of absorbing interest to humans. Certainly, knowledge and information have considerable economic value and hence are instrumental goods from the point of view of many actors in the complex contemporary economy, but those who argue that the *value of knowledge and truth* transcends this simply instrumental value surely have the correct view of it.[2] Those who pursue knowledge do not have to justify themselves by proving its usefulness, for the mere pursuit of it makes sense of activity expended to that end. In economic terms, it may not justify anyone paying you to do it, but that is another matter. Those who are committed to learning and to advancing our grasp of the truth have to make themselves useful in other (related) ways to earn the huge privilege of being able also to pursue the truth for its own sake.

Knowing the truth is one thing, communicating it another. *Freedom of communication* is vitally ancillary to the pursuit of knowledge, as is open debate between those of different views. Without communication there is no testing of knowledge claims. Sharing of knowledge is hugely important in human communities. This makes the ever-increasing demand of contemporary capitalism for increasingly tightly defined and sternly policed 'intellectual property rights' highly problematic.[3] There is a good utilitarian justification for ensuring that those who invest heavily in research or in the composition of works of art, literature, or science can obtain a return on their investment before the fruits of it are open to free use by all. But the avarice of mighty corporations and those who control them has pressed these claims far beyond what would be justified in the light of reasonable temperance. There are no natural rights to property, *a fortiori* to intellectual property,[4] only adventitious rights. The claim that some economic actors nevertheless make to natural rights of property in these highly artificial institutions sits oddly with the way in which they use them to impose inhibitions on other people's freedom of speech and inquiry. That is something they might more appropriately regard as a natural right against the state and its agencies. It is certainly well recognized as a fundamental right in Human Rights conventions, charters and declarations.

Anyway, quite apart from serious front-line research, invention, and creative writing in humanities or sciences, there are many valuable and important forms of associated communication. The role of the serious journalist and skilful popularizer is a great one in the dissemination of new knowledge and improved understanding in all domains of creative endeavour. This applies across all media of communication from print in all its forms to electronic. It also applies to the steady updating of school curricula to ensure that children and adolescents are as well exposed to today's knowledge as yesterday's.

---

[2] See John Finnis, *Natural Law and Natural Rights* (Oxford: Clarendon Press, 1980) 59–80.

[3] For a vivid account of the competition between open public endeavour to advance knowledge and private efforts to lock up the same knowledge behind patents and copyright claims, see J. Sulston and G. Ferry *The Common Thread: A Story of Science, Politics, Ethics and the Human Genome* (London: Bantam Press, 2002).

[4] See N. MacCormick, 'On the Very Idea of Intellectual Property: An Essay according to the Institutionalist Theory of Law' (2002) *Intellectual Property Quarterly* 228–239.

We have already reached a point in this discussion at which strictly truth-directed activities shade over into those that are equally or more concerned with *beauty*. Humans do not only communicate information, they capture beauty and seek to express it in music, visual arts and literature of all kinds. They can also be enraptured by the beauty of nature. Composers and performers of great music, painters of fine pictures, architects whose buildings command fine vistas and themselves complement the view in which they stand, poets and novelists, playwrights and those who present and act in great tragedies or comedies, or in grand or light opera, distinctively enrich human experience. To seek out that which is of beauty naturally, or to add to the world's beauty creatively, is an activity which carries its own justification in the experiences it promotes or sustains. Experience akin to the aesthetic can also be obtained occasionally through spectating at sporting competitions where athletes and sportspersons of the highest class are competing.

Apart from sport as spectacle, however, there are *sports and games* and outdoor activities for pure recreation of those who take part, as well as more cerebral activities like bridge or chess. We are inveterate players of games, in which we take pleasure for the sake simply of playing as well as we can, but in which also it is often easier than in other contexts to cement deep friendships. They are also contexts which make it easy to engage closely with those one already loves within a family circle, because, while the game goes on one is concentrated solely on one's interaction with co-contestants and competitors. One is playing to win, but even more to gain the pleasure of fair and friendly competitive or collaborative activity, with no point beyond enjoying the activity itself in the company in which one enjoys it.

In high moments of *aesthetic experience*, whether before natural beauty— a spectacular sunset, a stupendous waterfall—or under the impact of a great symphony or a spectacular painting or a fine play or movie, many people become aware of the sublime (as Longinus first expressed it, and eighteenth century philosophers rediscovered it[5]). It is an experience that does or seems momentarily to transcend space and time and to give the bearer of the experience a sense of perhaps momentary oneness with the universe. *Religious experience* appears to have the same quality and intensity, and perhaps to be a variant on the same thing. One's awe before great religious architecture makes it seem so. Whether or not you believe there is a creator, it must be a mark of great dullness of spirit in a person never to have confronted the wonder of creation and the richness of the created universe. Inscrutable big bang or fatherly creator of all, something brought all this about, and a sense of worshipful wonder is surely appropriate. Whether and how far churches and other modes of organized religious teaching and worship are successful agencies for bringing this to more articulate consciousness is,

[5] S. H. Monk, *The Sublime: a study of critical theories in XVIII-century England* (Ann Arbor: University of Michigan Press, 1960).

in a secular society, a question of autonomous judgement for all of us. The fullest possible religious tolerance, both by states and by religions and denominations *inter se* are what best support the right of individuals to find their own way to the truth in these matters as they come to apprehend it.

The argument of this book, following in footsteps of many predecessors, has laid repeated stress on the value of friendship and of community to all human beings. A solitary or a friendless life is a poor one indeed. *Friendship* entails that what is good for the friend is good for the other. Love for another person is one of the deepest of human emotions, and a deeply humanizing one. My spouse's or friend's successes and happiness are a necessary part of my own. Also in community we can find common goods that are essential to our own good but that cannot be achieved by purely individualistic efforts of all. As I write this I glance out of the window to Braidburn Park in Edinburgh and remind myself how many such common public spaces and other common assets there are, that essentially belong to nobody in particular but to everybody in common. (That is, to all Edinburghers, or Parisians, or New Yorkers, or whatever you find of equivalence to this, wherever you, reader, happen to be.)

This itself brings to attention the importance of the *political as well as the communal*. Maintaining the institutions of a successful community requires politics and maintaining these among autonomous persons requires democratic politics in a constitutional and democratic state. It is an essential part of the human good to seek some involvement in the self-governance of one's society, whether through elective office or political activism at the level of local, provincial or central government—or even at all-Europe level, within the EU—or through pressure group or single-issue engagement, or in some other manifestation of civil society. There is a growing professionalization of politics in western societies that threatens the wellbeing of the body politic. Engaged citizens are the life-blood of a healthy polity. To be a politically engaged and active citizen is to live well and to contribute through one's activity to the common good of one's community and society. No doubt some become puffed up with self-importance and others become corrupt and yet others present only the most misguided conceptions of common good and justice. But in the vigorous exchanges of democratic debate, supported by free and honestly presented media of communication (a case sadly lacking for much of the contemporary press) the truth has the best chance to emerge. The very existence of debate and contention is some guarantee against stasis and ossification.

4 A good plan of life

From the elements that have been quite sketchily presented here, one can build the concept of a good life. A person leads a good life, and makes the best of her or his chances, by seeking to realize in reasonable ways and with independence of judgement some element or part of the good, and, over time, some balanced mix of different goods whose pursuit is mutually compatible. Each needs some overall view of his or her life and its direction or trajectory through time, here somewhat grandiloquently entitled a 'life-plan'. In such a plan, intrinsically worthwhile aims and objectives are conceived and adopted as ends, acknowledging that there are auxiliary virtues that have to be cultivated for successful pursuit of these. As well as independence of mind, one has to develop self-knowledge, courage, reasonableness, technological competence, considerateness for others, politeness, self-respect without selfishness, diligence and a will to hard work, along with patience in the face of adversity and ill-luck. These are virtues one can try to develop while at the same time pursuing some of the goods wrapped up under such headings as life and health, education and learning, good communications, aesthetic values, religious experience and activity, recreational activities, friendship and political activity. These goods thus delineated do not amount to a complete or definitive list, though surely nothing that directly conflicts with any of them would find a due place in an expanded list.

The essential point is that one who seeks to lead a worthwhile life has to engage in some way with one or more of the goods identified, or some other similar and compatible good. That person has to try to cultivate the auxiliary virtues, especially those most required to meet the opportunities and difficulties of emerging situations and dilemmas. We have reason to act, and reason to do one thing rather than another, wherever there is an opportunity to realize some good in the world on the basis of a coherent plan for, or outlook on, the development of our lives. We must also, of course, fulfil basic moral duties and be faithful to the obligations enshrined in our many and varied engagements with other persons. It is in the sphere of moral freedom that our responsibility for pursuit of the good takes hold. Laziness and dissoluteness—pleasures of the table, the bottle, or even the hypodermic syringe—may tempt one to tarry aside or stray away from any engagement with the good, but that way lies self-destruction, not self-fulfilment. Vices are those dispositions that obstruct a commitment to the good, or actively subvert it.

The obligation of fidelity to engagements is indeed a constraint on our moral freedom. Yet, as was noted at several points in the previous part of the argument, our ability to pursue goods in the way of life or health or aesthetic activity or learning or communications or anything else depends greatly on our ability to make such engagements. Contracts and promises and informal understandings and much else are essentially involved in establishing the practicalities, usually involving co-operative or at least collective activity, of actually achieving anything. Freedom is not inert, but can be self-limiting, for the most beneficial exercise of freedom may often be the making of a suitable binding agreement with another person or persons, whether an individual, a partnership, or a corporation. This is one characteristic way in which, as was noted at the very beginning of this book, for any person the domain of practical reason comes to contain many other-regarding reasons for action.

There are legal rules that say we must keep our contracts and that specify what this keeping of a contract amounts to, properly interpreted. There are rules that define our basic duties to each other, at least those that figure in the law of torts and the criminal law. But there are no rules that tell us how to act for the best where we are free to act for the best. That is the point of being free. Likewise there are no weighing scales that tell us how much heavier one good is than another so that we may weigh them and reach the right answer how to act for the best. This does not deprive of use the metaphor according to which, in a dilemma, we have to weigh the pros and cons of each available course of action. What it means, however, is that, for each of us, within all that is plainly and objectively good, there is a task of constructing a personal conception of a path through life fitted to one's own opportunities and emerging talents or abilities and geared to reasonable realization of some constellation of goods. Inside such a life-plan, one can answer what is for the best. Outside it, what is for the best is that everybody be advised to get on with establishing such a plan.

5 But how do you know?

A writer who has reached this point in arguing about how people should try to live well faces an obvious and inevitably asked question: 'How do you know? How can you say what is good for me? This is just your subjective idea dressed up as objective advice.'

The best answer looks again to Adam Smith's argument from the impartial spectator. Each human being as an active subject pursues some goals and aims that somehow can be related to larger overarching ends. Each can to some extent enter sympathetically into the commitments of others and can feel empathetically their satisfaction at aims achieved and their disappointment over failures. To begin with, we naturally find this easier in relation to those who are close to us by family ties, close friendship, or neighbourhood, but with greater reflection broader sympathies become possible. But where ends are or appear evil, that is, negations of goods such as we have explored, we sharply withhold sympathy, especially in cases of success. We find ourselves at ease with, and ready to applaud, those who exhibit the auxiliary virtues in the pursuit of an intelligible range of goods in an apparently reasonably planned way of life. This way of considering matters leads to a kind of intersubjective ground for approval. There are infinitely many ways of leading a good life, and it is no one's business to lay down the law for anyone else about how they should live. It is sufficient in a moral perspective that each person must see to the basic duties and all of that person's voluntarily undertaken obligations. In positive law, likewise the law prohibits crimes and makes provision for civil remedies in cases of civilly wrongful and harmful activities. It provides the public law institutions of distributive justice as well. There is no rule other than a universalizable, indeed universal, permissive norm that leaves to everyone's choice her or his own use of moral freedom. But that does not extend to activities that embrace evil, for these prove to be prohibited as violations of basic duties or of engaged obligations.

Like anyone else, I may have committed partial errors in some part of my exposition of these matters, and to that extent my subjective proposals fall short of objective truth. The solution to that is for others to correct my argument, not to dismiss the possibility of any such argument, or the relevance of intersubjective approaches to truth that aim at humanly relative but otherwise objective conclusions. Whoever engages in this argument by that very act of engagement reveals a similar commitment to aiming for objectively sustainable conclusions that show the weakness of rival views.

Practical reasoning is a way of establishing well grounded preferences both in respect of how to live one's own life and in respect of the advisable way for others to lead theirs. In its deontic aspect, it establishes what are our duties and how we come by, and must stand by, our obligations. One way to express what it does is to say this: it reveals the structure and (in part) the content of people's reasonable preferences. We do not just happen to prefer whatever we happen to prefer from the menu of opportunities factually open before us. To establish what is worth doing or having is a matter of practical reason. Having established it, we have achieved a set of reasoned preferences. If we did the job well, they are also reasonable preferences. It is proper for each person to go about seeking to fulfil their reasonable preferences, and to continue with the reasoning processes that yield such preferences as serial elements of a developing and unfolding plan of life.

At this point, we are able to establish renewed and much improved links with contemporary economic theory. Not illegitimately, economists have largely left the concept of preference as a kind of theoretical black box. They discuss how to satisfy preferences, and to maximize their satisfaction, not what makes them reasonable in the first place. Adam Smith in his *Moral Sentiments* supplied the tools which, with remarkably little adaptation, facilitate re-establishing the bridge between moral and economic theory. This book is such a bridge.

10

Judging: Legal Cases and Moral Questions

1 Judgements, legal and moral

This book's theme concerns how humans can apply reason to the solution of practical problems, seeking a satisfactory resolution of the question what it is right to do in a given situation that presents a problematic character to the person who is or persons who are in this situation. Reasoning leads to judgement, judgement to decision, and decision to action, it has been suggested. Accordingly, those elements in the thought of Kant and Kantians which stress the legislative role of the will in moral reasoning may be considered after all misleading. Among the commonly recognized branches of constitutional government, the judicial seems to be the one which functions through a method most akin to that of a sound moral reasoner, though there may indeed be grand moral debates which to some extent parallel legislative debates. Examples can be found in debates about issues such as the death penalty, the legitimacy or not of progressive income tax, the acceptability of stem-cell research involving human-animal cloning, the appropriateness of awarding punitive or exemplary damages in the law of torts or delict, the legal prohibition of homosexual acts,[1] and the legal recognition of gay marriages.

For each person who enters reflectively into such a grand debate, there has to be prior reflection on the apparent rights and wrongs of the issue. One merit of good debates is that all participants in the discourse can and should use the exchange of opinions as a way to test and revise, if needs be to abandon, starting positions. The final judgement of the issue what is right or wrong if it is a sincere one must take account of the whole discourse that has gone before. Nevertheless, as a member of the legislature or as an ordinary voter in elections or referendums, the citizen must make up her or his own mind on the rights and wrongs of the issue put to the vote. The law-making will has to express a judgement of the person who casts the vote, if voting is indeed the act of an autonomous and self-commanding person. We cannot, it seems, escape the necessity for judgement.

In the higher courts of all states that live within the rule of law, it is a requirement (whether of strict law or of profoundly respected convention) that judges

---

[1] H. L. A. Hart, *Law Liberty and Morality* (London: Oxford University Press, 1963) and P. Devlin, *The Enforcement of Morals* (London: Oxford University Press, 1965) afford a grand example of such a debate.

must back their decisions with some statement of reasons. The judicial opinion that accompanies the decision, whether the opinion of a single judge or the collective opinion of a bench of judges, has to show the justification for the decision reached. It explains the judgement by showing why it is right according to law to decide the case before the court in this way rather than some other way. An earlier published book in the present series of books,[2] and a predecessor volume,[3] contain an elaborate account of the elements of such judgements and the sense in which judgements containing such elements can genuinely amount to justifications for decisions of the momentous kind law courts have to make.

The question now to be posed concerns the relationship between legal and moral judgement. Clearly, both involve forms of practical reasoning—what Robert Alexy calls the 'special case thesis'[4] holds good, for legal reasoning is definitely a subset of general practical reasoning. But is it also a subset of moral reasoning, or are legal reasoning and moral reasoning parallel and closely related but different forms of practical reasoning? Legal reasoning clearly must proceed in a highly institutionalized setting. Moral reasoning, though it often has to have close regard to the institutional context of a moral decision, has as its goal to form the autonomous will of the moral agent, in a context in which the value of any institutional obligation is also open to question. Judges enjoy autonomy of a kind under the doctrine of the independence of the judiciary, yet they are indeed bound by the provisions of constitutions and statutes and they must have regard to—in some cases indeed they are bound by—precedents. All these are certainly relevant in an appropriate setting to a well-founded moral judgement, but the element of the 'binding' is absent in this case.

An advantage for the student of these matters that arises from the institutionalization of legal judgements is the public availability of legal judgements containing full statements of the opinions of the court as a whole or of the several judges who compose the court. It is easy to read and possible to analyze the kinds of arguments judges present as persuasive or indeed sometimes as compelling towards a given conclusion. None of this is so easy as respects moral decision-making. But there may be a possibility of turning published legal judgements to use for purposes of moral analysis. Suppose that we say: 'what is in issue in a legal case is often if not always also a morally significant question'. Then we could go on to ask how the moral question might be answered ignoring the legal-institutional constraints that led the judges to the decision they made in the case. This may be an effective way to tease out further similarities and differences between these two closely related forms of practical reasoning. The two cases for extensive consideration, the *Conjoined Twins* case, and the case of *Donoghue v Stevenson* are

---

  [2] N. MacCormick, *Rhetoric and the Rule of Law* (Oxford: Oxford University Press, 2005).
  [3] N. MacCormick, *Legal Reasoning and legal Theory* (Oxford: Clarendon Press, 1978; 2nd edn., 1994).
  [4] R. Alexy *Theory of Legal Argumentation* (trans. R. Adler and N. MacCormick) (Oxford: Clarendon Press, 1988).

ones I have elsewhere reviewed in depth as legal decisions. Now I reappraise the issue morally, and seek to highlight any contrast with the legal approach.

2 The conjoined twins[5]

This section of the chapter reconsiders the tragic case that I discussed at length in *Rhetoric and the Rule of Law*, concerning conjoined twins conventionally called 'Jodie' and 'Mary', to disguise their actual identity. At birth they were conjoined at thorax and abdomen and only Jodie had a fully functioning cardiovascular system. Mary was never able to oxygenate her own blood by her own breathing and was dependent on Jodie for the circulation of oxygenated blood that kept her alive. The strain on Jodie's cardiovascular system was such that she would survive only a few weeks or months unless an operation were performed to separate her from her sister. But if Jodie and Mary were separated surgically, Mary would certainly die as an immediate result, for want of oxygenated blood. Jodie, on the other hand, would survive and could then undergo a series of difficult operations to restructure her body in something approaching normal form, though she might always require the use of a colostomy bag and would probably never be able to walk in a fully normal way. The paediatric physicians and surgeons in charge of the case considered that the separation operation followed by the other operations were unequivocally in Jodie's best interests and ought to be performed provided it was lawful to do so.

But could it be lawful? If Mary were actually alive at the time of the operation,[6] she would certainly die as a result of it. The operation would kill her. The price of Jodie's survival was an operation that would inevitably kill her twin sister Mary. On the other hand, the price of Mary's immediate survival was that, for want of the operation, Jodie and she would die together after a slow and lingering process as Jodie's heart and lungs gave out under the strain of breathing and circulating blood for two growing infants. Mary's short-term survival would result in both Jodie's early death and her own. An operation would save Jodie, at the certain cost of Mary's death; a failure to operate would, within a fairly short time span, save neither.

The twins' parents, devout Catholics who lived in Malta but who had come to England for the birth of the twins in view of the known risks of a difficult confinement, expressed it as their wish that 'nature should take its course'. That is, they wished to give the little twins as much love, care, and support as possible during a life that could only be a short one. They did not wish drastic surgical

---

[5] *Re A (children) (conjoined twins)* [2001] Fam 147: [2000] 4 All ER 961.

[6] The case proceeded on the footing that this was so, but whether Mary had been born alive according to the legal definition of 'live birth' might have been treated as more (than) questionable. See J. K. Mason, 'Conjoined twins: A Diagnostic Conundrum' Edinburgh Law Review 2 (2002) 1–9.

intervention that would leave one dead and one still considerably disabled, in circumstances in which they would have difficulty looking after her back in Malta. They felt that the children God had given them were ones destined by divine providence for a short life and that their dignity as little human beings was best respected by accepting the situation as it was without any surgical intervention.

The medical personnel of the hospital where the twins found themselves were strongly in favour of performing the operation since they believed Jodie's life could be saved and that a series of operations over several years would result in her being able to live a reasonably normal life. Each of the twins was made a ward of court in order that the interests of the children and the parents could all be fully considered and properly represented. Bishops entered the argument and submitted *amicus curiae* briefs that reminded the Court of the morally and theologically unacceptable quality of any decision to preserve one person's life at the cost of destroying another's. The doctrine of double effect had no application here, since the operation to separate the twins could not be said to further any interest of Mary's. This was not a case of an operation which could have some desirable effects from Mary's point of view, albeit shortening her life. The only beneficiary of the operation would be Jodie.

Setting aside for the moment any discussion of the case as a legal one, can any moral judgement be formed about the rightness or wrongness of performing such an operation, and, if so, how? The Smithian approach involves starting from the particular case, and considering the relations and interests of all the parties. The babies have limited consciousness and awareness of their situation, but they are live human persons with limited present capacity, and with some potentiality to develop, Jodie more than Mary. Only Jodie has a prospect of survival into adulthood, and thus of development as a fully competent moral person. This is a possibility, not a certainty, but it is possible only on condition of the hospital staff carrying out the operation to separate her from her sister. If that happens, Mary will die instantly, and, if not, she will die, along with Jodie at a future date measured in weeks not months (far less years).

Whatever happens, the primary carers for the children are their parents, though with much assistance from the hospital staff, especially in the event that the operation is carried out. Jodie will undergo a series of operations over several years, and will end up with the possibility of an independent life, but with various deformities of a more or less serious kind. Supporting her through all this, while also grieving for a lost child in the early stages, will fall on the shoulders of her parents, though (as with all parents of all children) their own survival and continued ability to provide care cannot be guaranteed.

They wish the operation not to be performed. If it goes ahead by order of the court, it goes ahead against their expressed wish. The care they will provide for Jodie thereafter will be under the cloud of their distress over the separation operation. If the operation goes ahead, Jodie will at some time learn that her continuing life was achieved through the sacrifice of her sister, a sister, however, who could by no means have survived beyond early infancy, and whose survival to that date would have been fatal for Jodie.

Whatever one says and concludes in a case like this, the need for maximum information is clear, and the limits on relevant and important information are stark. Nobody can know how things will work out if the operation is performed.

3 The parents' opinion

The legal setting of this case results in our having much fuller access than would be normal in other circumstances to an extended statement of the opinion that the parents offered about the problem as they saw it. It is material to the present argument to quote this extensively:[7]

We have been spoken to on many occasions by all the treating doctors at St. Mary's Hospital and we were fully aware of the difficulties... We have been treated with the utmost care and respect at St. Mary's Hospital and we have no difficulties or problems with any of the medical staff that are treating (us).

They did not, however, agree with the opinion of the medical personnel in favour of carrying out the separation operation:

'We have of course had to give serious consideration to the various options as given to us by our daughters' treating doctors. We cannot begin to accept or contemplate that one of our children should die to enable the other to survive. That is not God's will. Everyone has the right to life so why should we kill one of our daughters to enable the other to survive? That is not what we want and that is what we have told the doctors treating Jodie and Mary. In addition we are also told that if Jodie survives and that is not known at all, then she is going to be left with a serious disability. The life we have... is remote... with very few, if any facilities. [This] would make it extremely difficult not only for us to cope with a disabled child but for that disabled child to have any sort of life at all.

... there is a small hospital where you can receive emergency treatment but certainly they do not have the staff or facilities to cope with someone with serious ongoing difficulties. Any treatment would have to be undertaken (some distance away) where there is a hospital and a further hospital is being built which should be completed in about three years time. However if specific treatment is required it may be necessary for us to go further afield and indeed come back to St. Mary's Hospital in Manchester for further treatment. That is how we came to St. Mary's Hospital in the first place to ensure that our babies had the best possible treatment.

These are things we have to think about all the time. We know our babies are in a very poor condition, we know the hospital doctors are trying to do their very best for each of them. We have very strong feelings that neither of our children should receive any

7 [2001] Fam at 162–3, [2000] 4 All ER at 985–7.

medical treatment. We certainly do not want separation surgery to go ahead as we know and have been told very clearly that it will result in the death of our daughter, Mary. We cannot possibly agree to any surgery being undertaken that will kill one of our daughters. We have faith in God and are quite happy for God's will to decide what happens to our two young daughters.

In addition we cannot see how we can possibly cope either financially or personally with a child where we live, who will have the serious disabilities that Jodie will have if she should survive any operation. We know there is no guarantee of survival but she is the stronger of the two twins and if she should survive any surgery then we have to be realistic and look at what we as parents can offer to our daughter and what care and facilities are available to her in our homeland. They are virtually nil. If Jodie were to survive she would definitely need specialist medical treatment and we know that cannot be provided. Jodie would have to travel, on many occasions, possibly to England to receive treatment. It concerns us that we would not have any money for this treatment and we do not know if this is something (our) government would pay for.

This has meant that we have also had to give very careful consideration to leaving Jodie in England, should she survive, to be looked after by other people. We do not know if other people would be willing to look after such a seriously disabled child, but we do know that this is something that if we had any other choice we would not even give it consideration. It would be an extremely difficult, if not impossible decision for us to reach, but again we have to be strong and realistic about matters and understand that certainly Jodie would receive far better care and importantly the required medical treatment should she continue to reside in England as opposed to her being taken home. We do not know whether it is possible or feasible for Jodie to remain in England. We do not know if it is possible or feasible for her to be fostered by another family so that we can have an involvement in her upkeeping or whether she would have to be adopted and we could have no contact with her at all. That would break our hearts. We do not want to leave our daughters behind, we want to take them home with us but we know in our heart of hearts that if Jodie survives and is seriously disabled she will have very little prospects on our island because of its remoteness and lack of facilities and she will fare better if she remains in this country. . . . So we came to England to give our babies the very best chance in life in the very best place and now things have gone badly wrong and we find ourselves in this very difficult situation. We did not want to be in this situation, we did not ask to be in it but it is God's will. We have to deal with it and we have to take into account what is in the very best interests of our two very young daughters.

We do not understand why we as parents are not able to make decisions about our children although we respect what the doctors say to us and understand that we have to be governed by the law of England. We do know that everyone has the best interests of our daughters at heart and this is a very difficult situation not only for us as their parents but also for all of the medical and nursing staff involved in Mary's and Jodie's treatment.'

The view of practical reasoning advanced in this book argues a decision-maker has to be as well informed as possible and to seek to enter as far as possible into a sympathetic (empathetic) sharing of the emotions as well as the judgements of persons engaged in an issue calling for moral judgement. The Kantian ideal of trying to decide on the basis of an acceptable universal law has (it is argued) to be supplemented with a Smith-like engagement with the sentiments of those affected, for the sake of finding a guide to what is acceptable as a shared basis for judgement and action.

The extensive quotation just given is therefore very helpful as a lead in to expressing a judgement that exemplifies this approach. I therefore now offer my own opinion—it would not be possible to do this impersonally—it really has to be done in the first person.

Even several years after the event I find myself sharing the parents' grief and distress at the situation in which they found themselves. They face the early death of at least one of the babies. Mary's death will be accelerated on one possible solution of the dilemma, namely performance of the operation that will kill her. That operation may (though it will not certainly) save Jodie's life. The quality thereafter of Jodie's life will be problematic, though the medical and surgical prognosis was reasonably hopeful about the possible outcome of a series of operations. A further problem will concern the possibility that she can during such a period of treatment be cared for by her parents. They cannot provide much specialist care in Malta and they are not in a position to move permanently to England. The parents are appalled at the prospect of causing Mary's death and they are appalled by the prospect of trying to care adequately for Jodie, or providing suitable surrogate care, if the operation does go forward, with all its foreseen aftermath.

In a countervailing way, a sense of common humanity and human potentiality enables me to understand that Jodie's chance of life is drained by the innocent conjointure of her sister Mary on to her. She could live and breathe for a long time but that Mary uses up too much of her oxygen, and will do so the more as they grow larger. There is a sense in which non-intervention amounts to standing by while Mary innocently causes Jodie's death. There much of sorrow and pain attached to that, and it weighs to some extent against the parents' distress. Are the parents actually being selfish in preferring their own convenience to their daughter's potential for life? On the other hand, Mary's heart and lungs are not and cannot be made strong enough to enable her to breathe for herself and oxygenate her blood adequately to sustain vital functions. Whatever distress and pain we impute to her or imagine sympathetically on her behalf, could we really go along with a demand by her or on her behalf for continuing support by Jodie when this support will in due course cause Jodie's death and Mary's at the same time?

I have to come to whatever judgement I reach in the context of a background set of principles and assumptions. These I have derived from experience, from prior judgements of my own, from reading[8] and from discussion with all those with whom I have at one time or another confronted issues of life and death. One principle seems to me of real importance, namely that where parents are concerned and conscientious, they ought to have a prior say in questions concerning

---

[8] See in particular Z. Bankowski and J. MacLean (ed), *The Universal and the Particular in Legal Reasoning* (Aldershot: Ashgate, 2006).

treatment of their children, the younger the more so. I do not deny that parental selfishness, fecklessness or sheer callousness frequently justify an override, and indeed a removal of children from parental care to some safer situation as fit as possible for their safe upbringing. Where such an override is not justified, it is likely that natural parents will always care more and more conscientiously for their own children than anyone else will or can, although there are indeed many examples of highly successful infant adoptions. Children's interests are best served, even when they are not particularly well served, by their being embedded in a family in which in their early years their parents have the primary say about how they are to be looked after.

On this assumption, I cannot see any sufficient reason in the conjoined twins' case to override the parents' view. It is a difficult matter of balanced sentiment and marginal judgement. To impose a decision about the children over the head of the parents is morally unacceptable. This seems to me to express a reasonable application of the Smithian categorical imperative:

'Enter as fully as you can into the feelings of everyone directly involved in or affected by an incident or relationship, and impartially form a maxim of judgement about what is right that all could accept if they were committed to maintaining mutual beliefs setting a common standard of approval and disapproval among themselves.'

That then leads on to a subsidiary imperative:

'Act in accordance with that impartial judgement of what it is right to do in respect of the given incident or relationship.'

Whether or not the reasoning I engaged in does exemplify and does help to vindicate this 'Smithian' approach, I stand by the conclusion I reached.

4 The legal judgement

Unfortunately, this places me at odds with the legal decision reached by the Court of Appeal of England and Wales. The judges there concluded that the operation must be performed and gave orders for it to be so done over the head of the parents' wishes. Critical to this decision as a matter of law was the overriding duty the law imposes on judges in cases involving children to treat a child's interests as paramount. In this context they held that they must weigh equally the right to life of each of the twins. The differential worth of any treatment to Mary by comparison with its worth to Jodie justified the conclusion that the operation that would end Mary's life could legitimately be performed in the interest of Jodie's likely life-chances. Since it could be done, it must be done. Such an individualism of children's interests, though well understandable in contexts of parenting that is inadequate or worse, may be questionable from a moral point of view in other family situations. But it is, at present, undoubtedly the law.

Even so, Lord Justice Ward did not find it easy to dismiss the parents' view, and he treated them with great respect:[9]

'It is a laudable feature of this case that despite holding such different views about the twins' future, the parents and the hospital have throughout maintained a relationship of mutual respect. Th[is is a] highly commendable attitude of the parents...'

However, he went on to itemize his disagreement with them:

'In their natural repugnance at the idea of killing Mary they fail to recognise their conflicting duty to save Jodie and they seem to exculpate themselves from, or at least fail fully to face up to the consequence of the failure to separate the twins, namely death for Jodie. In my judgment, parents who are placed on the horns of such a terrible dilemma simply have to choose the lesser of their inevitable loss. If a family at the gates of a concentration camp were told they might free one of their children but if no choice were made both would die, compassionate parents with equal love for their twins would elect to save the stronger and see the weak one destined for death pass through the gates.

This is a terribly cruel decision to force upon the parents. It is a choice no loving parent would ever want to make. It gives me no satisfaction to have disagreed with their views of what is right for their family and to have expressed myself in terms they will feel are harshly and unfairly critical of them. I am sorry about that. It may be no great comfort to them to know that in fact my heart bleeds for them. But if, as the law says I must, it is I who must now make the decision, then whatever the parents' grief, I must strike a balance between the twins and do what is best for them.'

I confess freely that at this point I share the potential resentment of the parents in the face of his Lordship's words. The concentration camp analogy does not move me towards a warmth of approval of what is being said and done here. Beyond that, it is not appropriate here to expound at great length the legal reasons and reasoning that led the Court of Appeal to the conclusion that the operation must be authorized and carried out with all due expeditiousness. I have done that elsewhere. Suffice it to say that many arguments of principle were weighed and considered from the standpoint of family law, of medical law and of criminal law. The issue whether the operation would necessarily involve murder was considered and that conclusion rejected. Acknowledging that his final holding in the case had to have a universalistic character, Ward LJ nevertheless deliberately kept it as narrow as possible, in the following terms:[10]

'In my judgment the appeal must be dismissed. Lest it be thought that this decision could become authority for wider propositions, such as that a doctor, once he has determined that a patient cannot survive, can kill the patient, it is important to restate the unique circumstances for which this case is authority. They are that it must be impossible to preserve the life of X. without bringing about the death of Y., that Y. by his or her very continued existence will inevitably bring about the death of X. within a short period of time,

---

[9] [2001] Fam at 192–3, [2000] 4 All ER at 1009–10.
[10] [2001] Fam at 204–5; [2000] 4 All ER at 1018.

and that X. is capable of living an independent life but Y. is incapable under any circumstances (including all forms of medical intervention) of viable independent existence.'

In none of what he said did he claim or purport to be giving a moral judgement superior to that of the parents, or to be second-guessing the Bishops in matters which he considered to belong to their rather than his own expertise. As he made clear, his duty was to the law and to come to the best conclusion he could concerning what the law mandates in this case and any like cases, even if in the narrowly drawn category just described.

In the setting in which all these matters arose for decision, necessarily the legal judgement rendered anyone's moral judgement inoperative as far as concerned actual performance of the operation. Hospitals within the National Health Service (and indeed outside of it as well) and the surgeons, physicians, nurses and other staff who work there have to treat their patients within the law, and as required by it. The requirement of the law is especially clear when, as in this case, a court has weighed carefully a request for an operation to be ordered and decided that the request is justified, and made orders accordingly. As a generality, it is always true, where legal authorities must reach a decision on a morally significant matter, that the practical implementation of the legal decision may render the moral decision inoperative in terms of immediate action. But this is not unqualifiedly true, for at least three reasons.

First, there may be on-the-spot conscientious refusal or even conscientious resistance to the implementation of the legal decision (though in a case like that of the conjoined twins this is not a serious possibility, nor a desirable course of action). Secondly, there may be moral critique of the legal decision that will lead to its being reconsidered by the same legal authorities at a later date. Such is the analogy between moral reasoning and judicial reasoning that judges may come in later decisions to reinterpret the law in ways that diminish or elide the difference between law as judicially declared and some well-argued moral account of the salient issues in the case. Moreover, those who disagree morally with a judicial decision are very likely to, and are often well placed to, construct a technical-legal critique of a judgement such as that of the Court of Appeal in the *Conjoined Twins* or that of the House of Lords in the *Anthony Bland*[11] case. This, though motivated by moral disagreement, may be a better mode in which to seek reconsideration of judicial decisions than direct moral critique. Third, one may embark on a programme of 'critical morality' seeking to raise legislators' consciousness about a problem and to motivate new legislation to alter the established law about a matter. The long-term work of the Abortion Law Reform Association led eventually to reform in UK Abortion Law with the Abortion Act of 1967. Critique of this from the opposite end of the moral spectrum by the Society for the Protection of the Unborn Child has not succeeded in reversing that law, though the debate is ongoing and there have been modifications to the statute over the years. The issue of assisted suicide remains on the agenda as an

---

[11] *Airedale NHS Trust v Bland* [1993] AC 789; [1993] 1 All ER 821.

aftermath of the case of *Diane Pretty*[12] whose plea for her husband to be allowed to kill her to save her the final (to her) unbearable horrors of motor neurone disease was rejected by the courts as unfounded in law. Many other instances, from homosexual law reform through issues of men/women equality, race discrimination and incitement to racial or religious hatred, to the question of the fair balance of risks in developing new therapeutic drugs or food and drink products, or other consumer protection issues, might be cited.

Moral opinions are very often highly relevant to law, or at least to law reform. Moral opinions and moral arguments can in general be powerful motors toward legislative change, and the courts of law are very far from inhabiting a moral vacuum such that shifting interpretations of law over time do often reflect engagement with public moral debate.

What never happens is that legal change (or legal stasis), by judicial decision or by legislative enactment, cancels the validity of the conscientious judgement of any issue by a moral agent. Autonomy in moral judgement means that each person is responsible for her/his view of what is good and bad, right and wrong and can never be overruled on that issue. This is distinct from the issue of what a public agency or authority may be required by law to do in a given dilemma, an issue which certainly has both moral as well as legal relevance—but not moral conclusiveness. Certainly, people can and should reflect deeply whether their minority opinion on some matter is an aberrant eccentricity rather than a clearer insight than that of the majority, or of the judiciary, into a moral truth. Over time, dearly held moral convictions can come to be revealed to their holders as unwarranted, even superstitious, hangovers from less enlightened times. But that is to do with persuasion, with the weight of arguments, not with the power of the state. In moral issues, the state has none, though it is subject to the moral scrutiny of the whole citizen body in a democratic polity.

5 The snail in the opaque bottle

Donoghue v Stevenson,[13] the second case for present discussion, is one I considered at very great length in *Legal Reasoning and Legal Theory*,[14] in which it played the

---

[12] *R. (Pretty) v DPP and Home Secretary* [2001] UKHL 61, [2002] 1 A.C. 800. The difference between the legal and moral aspects of the case was stressed in para 2 of his speech by Lord Bingham of Cornhill: 'In discharging the judicial functions of the House, the appellate committee has the duty of resolving issues of law properly brought before it, as the issues in this case have been. The committee is not a legislative body. Nor is it entitled or fitted to act as a moral or ethical arbiter. It is important to emphasise the nature and limits of the committee's role, since the wider issues raised by this appeal are the subject of profound and fully justified concern to very many people.' The European Court of Human Rights also dismissed the case as a matter of law: see *Pretty v UK* no. 2346/02 ECHR 2002 III (29.4.02).

[13] [1932] AC 562; 1932 SC (HL) 31.

[14] Oxford, Clarendon Press (2nd edn, 1994) 42, 69–70, 80–85, 108–28, 148–9, 157–60, 224–5, 251–4.

part of a running example. Subsequent work by other scholars has revealed details of the personal and social history of the parties to the case and issues involved in it in a way that may further facilitate taking a parallel look at the moral arguments relevant in the case.[15] This gives another interesting opportunity to compare moral with legal judgement.

The case concerns events that on Sunday 26 August 1928 befell Mrs May Donoghue (née McAllister[16]), whose marriage in wartime circumstances in 1916 had run into difficulties and who had recently separated from her husband Henry Donoghue. She left her home in a poor part of the east end of Glasgow city centre, and, with a friend, took an electric tram car ride to the nearby burgh of Paisley, at that time separated from Glasgow by a strip of open countryside that has long since disappeared. Whatever else they did in the course of afternoon and evening, by about 8.50 p.m. the two friends ended up sitting in a café in Wellmeadow, Paisley, owned by Mr Francis Minghella. The friend, whose name and even whose gender have disappeared from the record (though in the law reports it is assumed the friend was a woman), bought a refreshment for both of them. She chose for herself a 'pear and ice' (presumably, a scoop of Minghella's ice cream with a tinned half-pear on top). She bought for May Donoghue what is known in the West of Scotland as an 'ice drink', namely a scoop of ice cream in a glass, with a fizzy soft drink poured over it. What Mr Minghella supplied was a glass with a scoop of ice in it, with a bottle of ginger beer provided along side of it. He poured some of the ginger beer over the ice cream, and May took some sips of it. In due course she poured more of the ginger beer into her glass, at which point the remains of a decomposing snail floated into view. The ginger beer was contained in a dark glass bottle that made its contents invisible to external inspection. (Because ginger beer was brewed in the bottle, there was a residue of yeast and ginger at the foot of the bottle, and opaque bottles masked this.) The bottle bore the name of a local manufacturer, David Stevenson of Glen Lane, Paisley, whose brewing and bottling plant happened to be quite near to the café.

May took a nasty turn on seeing the snail, and we may be sure the café proprietor's attention was drawn to this event. Worse was to follow. She became quite sick with gastro-enteritis in the following days, and after the immediate shock and nausea on the day itself she had to consult a doctor on 29 August eventually being admitted to the Glasgow Royal Infirmary for emergency treatment for gastro-enteritis on 16 September. She lost several weeks of her relatively ill-paid work as a shop assistant.

[15] P. T. Burns with S. J. Lyons, *Donoghue v Stevenson and the Modern Law of Negligence: the Paisley Papers* (Vancouver, B.C.: University of British Columbia, for the Continuing Legal Education Society of British Columbia, 1991). I refer here especially to papers in that volume by M. R. Taylor, 'Mrs Donoghue's Journey', pp 1–24, and W. J. McBryde 'The Story of the "Snail in the Bottle" Case', pp 26–56. See also A. F. Rodger, 'Mrs Donoghue and Alfenus Varus' (1988) 41 CLP 1–22.

[16] Not 'M'Alister', as the Law Reports incorrectly record Mrs Donoghue's maiden name; see McBryde 'The Story…'.

She consulted a Glasgow lawyer, Walter G. Leechman, who was also a city councillor and a political radical, much engaged in efforts to protect poor people against exploitation by manufacturers and others. He took up her case on what appears to have been a 'speculative fee' basis, and in due course a summons was lodged suing David Stevenson of Glen Lane, Paisley, for the sum of £500 as compensation for nervous shock and loss of earnings and for pain and suffering due to gastro-enteritis. The legal ground stated for the action was that Stevenson as manufacturer of ginger beer had owed her a duty of care as a consumer of it and was in breach of this duty. It was averred in one condescendence of the summons that the bottle store at Glen Lane, where bottles were kept prior to filling, was unsanitary in character and bore visible signs of snail trails (a detail which suggests that Leechman's firm had done some 'detective work' themselves in preparing the case).

The recitation of facts here derives entirely from the legal papers and proceedings in the case, hence it gives a somewhat one-sided version of events. Even in the one-sided version there are significant details, including a denial by the defender that the bottle as described in the Donoghue pleadings was of a kind he had ever issued, since it allegedly had a metal cap and an adhesive label stuck on it. Behind this may lie another fact known from other litigation of the period involving manufacture of aerated waters in Scotland.[17] At the time there was a penny deposit on each bottle sold, giving consumers an incentive to return emptied bottles to retailers. Bottle exchanges existed to return bottles embossed with a manufacturer's name to that manufacturer for re-use. But this was a voluntary arrangement in the trade and there was nothing in law to prevent other manufacturers, or even very small-time entrepreneurs, acquiring and using a bottle embossed with someone else's name, and bottling their own preparations in it. It seems likely that had matters gone to trial on the facts, Stevenson could have challenged the assertion that, just because the bottle bore his name, he was necessarily responsible for the ill-prepared contents of that bottle on that occasion.

We have to take it, then, that the facts recited belong to the class of alleged rather than to that of proven facts, for reasons that will appear shortly. Nevertheless, they say quite enough to enable us to pose a problem for moral judgement and to apply, for example, 'impartial spectator' reasoning to the case. An Adam Smith, one can be confident, would have had no difficulty entering sympathetically into the shoes of May Donoghue. We can all imagine, with a quiver of revulsion, pouring a drink from an opaque bottle and discovering the contents to have been contaminated by animal remains like those of a snail or a small mouse.[18] The kind of gastric illness that could result from such an event is familiar to us, as are the pain and debilitation attending it, with resultant unfitness for work.

---

[17] See *Leitch & Co v Leydon* 1930 SC 41; 1931 SC (HL) 1.
[18] The reference is to *Mullen v A. G. Barr and Co; Mc Gowan A. G. Barr and Co* 1929 SC 461, where there was allegedly a mouse in a bottle of lemonade.

What of the alleged perpetrator? We need not suppose that David Stevenson acted deliberately or recklessly to harm May Donoghue or anyone else like her. But we can surely say that mass production of articles of drink or of food carries obvious risks to consumer health, and that only the manufacturer can take precautions to prevent realization of these risks. This applies especially to cases of products issued in bottles or other packaging materials that prevent inspection of the contents until they are in actual use. If we considered that there had been a serious want of care in the preparation or packaging processes managed by Stevenson, we would find it difficult to enter sympathetically into any claim by him that May Donoghue's accident was no fault of his. Except if it were to turn out, for example, that the bottle had been used by a different manufacturer on this occasion, or that the pursuer was unable to prove the alleged facts about the snail, an impartial spectator would come down on May Donoghue's side. Being aware of the sentiments and emotions and physical events occurring in this case, the impartial spectator would conclude that a poor woman suffering illness and loss in this way was owed some compensation by the one person who, by due care, could have prevented it from happening.

To try to formulate a possible covering rule for such a case, as suggested through the device of the 'Smithian categorical imperative' earlier in this book, would be a little more difficult. This might show the advantage attaching to Smith's view that general rules are constructed by induction from individual cases, not constructed a priori to deal with the first in a series.[19] On the other hand, as the legal parallel suggests, it would be unsatisfactory not to have at least some tentative formulation in mind for a working rule that could show when liability for harm is appropriate in such a case, and when not. (We shall in due course consider how the judges did this.) One way or the other, anyway, the case looks relatively easy from a moral point of view, just in terms of relations between Stevenson as manufacturer and Donoghue as consumer. Of course he ought to give her reasonable compensation—and then he ought to clean up his act for the future. The materials for a confident moral judgement are discoverable in the legal pleadings, and the judgement is a straightforward one.

6 The legal problem

Why then was the case so difficult and epoch-making a decision in legal terms? (It is generally conceded to have been the most important decision of the twentieth century dealing with the principles of liability for the tort of negligence, or with the place of fault or *culpa* in the Scots law of delict. It retains saliency even into the twenty-first century.) A part of the answer to the point about difficulty

---

[19] Cf S. J. Burton, *An Introduction to Law and Legal Reasoning* (Boston and Toronto: Little Brown and Co, 1985) 11–24, on how to read cases.

may concern the very issue of legal institutionalization of liability in cases involving allegations of negligence. The legal concept of negligence requires identifying somebody who owed a duty to someone else to take reasonable care to avoid harming them. The problem was to say when and how such a duty of care arose. In a world of rapidly advancing industrialization, there withered away any probability of prior personal relations between manufacturers and consumers. Railway carriage manufacturers, for example, do not know who will ride on trains made up of these carriages after purchase by an operating company. Yet if the axles are defective and there is a crash many people will be injured.[20] Can we make the manufacturer an insurer of all these risks? Or should it be a matter of contract between manufacturer and train operating company to cover risks of defects in carriages, and of contract between train operating company and passengers to set conditions of liability for injury in the event of accidents?[21]

If the decision is made to hold manufacturers liable for want of reasonable care, how will this actually work as a legal regime, for example in soft drink manufacturing? Is there not a risk of a spate of 'gold-digging' actions in which whoever happens to have contracted some stomach complaint can take a case against a convenient target manufacturer and either force an expensive settlement or draw them into a potentially ruinous course of litigation? What would be the prospect of any payment of expenses in the event of the poor consumer losing such a case? The moral simplicity of the Stevenson-Donoghue relationship might begin to look difficult and fraught with risk once you try to fit it into the institutional framework of law and legal proceedings for damages in civil cases.

Anyway, for either or both of these reasons (and doubtless others like them), the law relating to compensation for harms of this kind was, as of 1932, complex and difficult and lacking in clear principles. One or two precedents, regarded as of low authority, had essayed statements of general principle about the grounds of liability for negligence or fault in general. But the majority of the precedents denied any general ground of liability, confining the duty of care to cases of articles highly dangerous in themselves like guns or gas stoves, and certain other special categories. At the highest level of civil jurisdiction in the UK, the House of Lords, there had been no clear decision either for or against a more general duty of care and accordingly for or against liability attaching to breach of it through failure to take reasonable care. The preponderant opinion among academic commentators at the time was that no such liability existed and that the consumer's primary remedy was either in contract law, or non-existent. Counsel who eventually took May Donoghue's case all the way to the House of Lords

---

[20] There was a disastrous railway accident on the Versailles Railway around 1840 where the cause was a defective axle. This example found its way into the dissenting speech of Lord Tomlin in *Donoghue*.

[21] Typically, train companies inserted in their tickets conditions that strictly limited their liability for injuries, so in the heyday of 'privity of contract' there was cold comfort for injured passengers.

in forma pauperis[22] were indeed engaged in a speculative enterprise, and their eventual victory was an epoch-making event when, against the odds, they carried the day.

As was mentioned above, the facts of the case never came to proof at law. David Stevenson elected to challenge May Donoghue's case by way of a 'plea to the relevancy' of her case. Rather than go into the issue whether she could prove her injuries and what caused them, or could prove the drink in the bottle was of his manufacture, or that he had failed to take due care, or anything else, he simply challenged her on the law. At law, he claimed, someone in his position owed no duty to someone in Mrs Donoghue's. If no duty of care, no duty to breach; if no breach of duty, no liability for negligently causing harm—end of story. One probable reason why the Stevenson team took this course of legal action was because they were acting with the support of a trade association of soft drinks manufacturers. All of them had a common interest in achieving a clear and preferably a negative answer on the question of a manufacturer's liability in such circumstances. In the end, however, the answer was the reverse of that for which they were hoping. May Donoghue won in the debate at first instance in the Outer House of the Court of Session; then on appeal to the Inner House, she lost on a 2-1 split in the court's opinion. Finally, in the House of Lords, a masterly leading opinion by Lord Atkin backed up by high quality speeches of Lord Macmillan and Lord Thankerton settled the law in favour of manufacturer's liability for failure to take care, against thunderous dissents from Lords Buckmaster and Tomlin.

(After her victory in the Lords, it remained for the Donoghue team to prove their case on its facts, and the case went back to the Court of Session for that purpose. Before proceedings got under way, however, David Stevenson died. His executors in due course reached an agreed settlement of May Donoghue's claim for a payment of £200, and Stevenson's carried on as a family business for a further quarter-century before being taken over by a conglomerate. So the snail was never proved to have existed, nor the bottle to have been actually filled by Stevenson—the facts remain 'alleged' ones.)

The highly technical legal aspect of the reasoning in the case shines clearly in all the Lords' speeches. Much of the discussion concerns the interpretation and evaluation of precedents. Such discussions include attempts to expound and clarify underlying principles that help unify the precedents into a coherent body of law. This has always to be done while allowing that some may appear anomalous in the light of whatever is the favoured principle, and will be to that extent disapproved and weakened as significant precedents for the future. Unsurprisingly, the precedents that the majority treated as anomalous were treated by the minority

---

[22] That is, on the basis that the appellant's proven poverty allowed a special procedure whereby the appeal could be heard without any security for costs of the appeal being deposited, and with counsel arguing the case essentially in the public interest as well as for the sake of the poor litigant.

as the favoured ones, and vice versa. Yet despite the technical legal quality of the reasoning, there is, particularly in the speech of Lord Atkin, a strong recognition that the legal issue runs in parallel with, and ought to be considered against the background of a moral question. That question concerns the moral basis of the law of torts—why ought one person ever to compensate another for harm suffered? An answer to that question can in his view guide towards the correct legal answer, since the law must be presumed to have been developed by judges and legislators who are themselves moral agents. Hence, though it is necessary to 'aim off' to allow for the positive and highly institutionalized character of the law of England or Scotland, reflection on underlying moral principles will be essential. It is necessary for formulating a credible general principle of legal liability to give coherence to the law of negligence, with all its massive array of precedents and commentaries. By coincidence, Lord Atkin, very shortly before commencing to hear the arguments in *Donoghue v Stevenson* had presented a Holdsworth Lecture in the University of Birmingham, in which he advanced just such a view, suggesting that the law of torts did and must have a moral basis. Here is a key passage in his lecture:[23]

'It is quite true that law and morality do not cover identical fields. No doubt morality extends beyond the more limited range in which you can lay down the definite prohibitions of law; but, apart from that, the British law has always necessarily ingrained in it moral teaching in this sense: that it lays down standards of honesty and plain dealing between man and man.... He is not to injure his neighbour by acts of negligence; and that certainly covers a very large field of the law. I doubt whether the whole of the law of tort could not be comprised in the golden maxim to do unto your neighbour as you would that he should do unto you.'

Certainly, the argument of the present book, especially in this chapter, endorses Lord Atkin's suggestion as to the relatedness-but-difference between morality and law, moral reasoning and legal reasoning as subsets of practical reasoning. (It is also pleasant to take note of yet another judicial allusion to the 'golden rule', or 'golden maxim', notwithstanding Kant's rather dismissive view of it.)

When it came to the concrete case, in *Donoghue v Stevenson*, where the issue was what in law could justify a ruling in favour of manufacturer's liability in the situation envisaged there, Lord Atkin developed his point thus:[24]

'At present, I content myself with pointing out that in English law there must be, and is, some general conception of relations giving rise to a duty of care, of which the particular cases found in the books are but instances. The liability for negligence, whether you style it such or treat it as in other systems as a species of 'culpa,' is no doubt based on a general public sentiment of moral wrongdoing for which the offender must pay. But acts or omissions which any moral code would censure cannot in a practical world be treated so as

---

[23] See Lord Atkin, 'Law as an Educational Subject' (1932) *Journal of the Soc. Of Public Teachers of Law* 27 at 30.
[24] [1932] AC 562 at 579–80.

to give a right to every person injured by them to demand relief. In this way rules of law arise which limit the range of complainants and the extent of their remedy. The rule that you are to love your neighbour becomes in law, you must not injure your neighbour, and the lawyer's question: Who is my neighbour? receives a restricted reply. You must take reasonable care to avoid acts or omissions which you can reasonably foresee would be likely to injure your neighbour. Who then, in law, is my neighbour? The answer seems to be—persons who are so closely and directly affected by my act that I ought reasonably to have them in contemplation as being so affected when I am directing my mind to the acts or omissions which are called in question.'

That is all very well as a general principle, and as showing the limitations of institutional law contrasted with autonomous morality, but it is still much too broad and open-textured a principle to justify a decision in the instant case. To get to a sufficiently precise ruling may be more problematic—problematic, yes; but not insuperably so:[25]

'It is remarkable how difficult it is to find in the English authorities statements of general application defining the relations between parties that give rise to the duty [of care]. The Courts are concerned with the particular relations which come before them in actual litigation, and it is sufficient to say whether the duty exists in those circumstances....And yet the duty which is common to all the cases where liability is established must logically be based on some element common to the cases where it is found to exist.'

When one comes down to the instant case, the difficulty seems less acute:[26]

'[I]n the case now before the court I cannot conceive any difficulty to arise. A manufacturer puts up an article of food in a container which he knows will be opened by the actual consumer. There can be no inspection by any purchaser, and no reasonable preliminary inspection by the consumer. Negligently, in the course of preparation he allows the contents to be mixed with poison. It is said that the law of England and Scotland is that the poisoned consumer has no remedy against the negligent manufacturer. If this were the result of the authorities, I should consider the result a grave defect in the law, and so contrary to principle that I should hesitate long before following any decision to that effect which had not the authority of this House.... There are other instances than of articles of food and drink where goods are sold intended to be used immediately by the consumer, such as many forms of goods sold for cleaning purposes, where the same liability must exist. The doctrine supported by the decision below would not only deny a remedy to the customer who was injured by consuming bottled beer or chocolates poisoned by negligence of the manufacturer, but also to the user of what should be a harmless proprietary medicine, on ointment, a soap, a cleaning fluid or cleaning powder. I confine myself to articles of common household use, where every one, including the manufacturer, knows that the articles will be used by other persons than the actual ultimate purchaser— namely, by members of his family and his servants, and in some cases his guests. I do not think so ill of our jurisprudence as to suppose that its principles are so remote from the ordinary needs of civilised society and the ordinary claims it makes upon its members as to deny a legal remedy where there is so obviously a social wrong.'

[25] [1932] AC 562 at 579.   [26] [1932] AC 562 at 582–3.

The three long quotations convey the whole gist of Lord Atkin's argument. The rest consists of essential lawyer-like work reviewing the precedents and explaining why some deserve more respect in the light of the elaborated 'neighbour principle' than do the others. The argument as a whole exhibits three principal desiderata for good legal reasoning.[27] These are:

- Coherence: the ruling in the instant case should square with some broader principle that makes sense of the relevant body of law in the light of a reasonable evaluation of it;
- Consistency: the ruling must not contradict any binding established rule of law; but this does not exclude care in explaining and distinguishing apparently adverse precedents, or seeking reasonable interpretations of statutory provisions;
- Consequences: the decisions mandated by the ruling in question should be more acceptable in evaluative terms than those that would be mandated by the opposite view—for example, the law should not mandate denial of a legal remedy where there is an obvious social wrong.

It is particularly in relation to the former two desiderata that legal diverges from moral reasoning. For legal systems contain a vast and ever-increasing volume of authoritative texts—precedents, statutes, EU regulations and directives, international conventions and the like—that give their special character to arguments concerning coherence and consistency in law. These are not virtues entirely absent from or irrelevant to moral reasoning. But the latter knows no single authoritative rule-book and lacks the deeply institutional character of legal reasoning. Even where a judge's decision conforms closely to what she or he considers the underlying moral merits of a case, and, all the more, where there is a divergence between what is justifiable legally and what seems right morally, there is strong analogy but no perfect identity between the reasoning appropriate to legal and to moral judgement respectively. But both are genuine cases of judgement, not of legislative rule-making nor of pure emotional reaction to a situation.

7 Ratio and ruling

In the initial discussion of the *Donoghue* problem looked at purely in moral terms, we noted that someone engaged in pure Smithian 'spectator' reasoning might find it difficult with confidence to enunciate any covering rule for the situation. Perhaps asking for anyone to apply a categorical imperative of any kind,

---

[27] These three desiderata were proposed in N. MacCormick, *Legal Reasoning and Legal Theory* (1978; 2nd edn 1994), and followed up in N. MacCormick, *Rhetoric and the Rule of Law* (2005).

even a Smithian kind, is a demand too stringent? The point is difficult. On the one hand, if one cannot figure even tentatively any kind of general norm that accounts for the case, is one not being arbitrary? On the other hand, one may be more confident of the actual judgement than of any generalization one can yet formulate. At least, it seems, the approach through a version of the categorical imperative encourages us to avoid arbitrariness and sets at least a standard of aspiration for well-formed moral judgements.

Here again, one may detect a significant analogy with legal reasoning, certainly as practised in UK and most Americano-British jurisdictions, where judges do obviously try to clarify a decided ruling or (in US usage 'holding') on the point of law specifically in issue. There are clear examples of this in *Donoghue v Stevenson* both in the majority speeches and in the dissenting ones. Lord Macmillan, who agreed with Lord Atkin, and whose speech in the case has comparable power, concluded:[28]

'I have no hesitation in affirming that a person who for gain engages in the business of manufacturing articles of food and drink intended for consumption by members of the public in the form in which he issues them is under a duty to take care in the manufacture of these articles. That duty, in my opinion, he owes to those whom he intends to consume his products.'

Lord Tomlin, dissenting, said this:[29]

'[I]f the appellant is to succeed it must be upon the proposition that every manufacturer or repairer of any article is under a duty to every one who may thereafter legitimately use the article to exercise due care in the manufacture or repair. It is logically impossible to stop short of this point.'

The legal context, including the context provided by elaborate arguments of counsel addressed to the highest courts on one side and the other of any seriously contested case, facilitates the sharpening of rulings like these. They are, of course, rulings that cover the instant case and spell out its implications as a direct precedent for the future. Precisely because of the precedential impact of such a decision, the argument from consequences acquires real saliency. They illustrate the way in which attempts to apply rigorously some variant of the categorical imperative would bear on our moral reasoning if we were ideally equipped for it, as we sometimes come close to being. But again, we need to observe the institutional quality of legal reasoning, and to note that this idea of making a 'ruling' on a disputed point ties up with a lot of technical learning and controversy about the character of the '*ratio decidendi*' of any precedent[30] in law. Heaven forfend that this controversy be transplanted to moral deliberations!

---

[28] [1932] AC 562 at 620.   [29] [1932] AC 562 at 599.
[30] Compare N. MacCormick, *Rhetoric and the Rule of Law*, 152–61; and see L. Goldstein (ed), *Precedent in Law* (Oxford: Clarendon Press, 1987), esp chapters 1, 3, 6 and 7.

8 Objectivity?

The very existence of dissenting opinions in the published law reports of those countries where public judicial dissent is permitted shows that our questions may seek objective answers, but that our answers are never untouched by subjectivity. A Smithian would probably be inclined to expect this. Spectator reasoning can help us to achieve a common position with all of our fellow human beings, or at least with neighbours, even Atkinian neighbours. But it never takes us the whole way. Again, one can illustrate the point rather vividly with one last long quotation from *Donoghue*, where Lord Buckmaster repudiates the majority view in strong terms:[31]

'In *Mullen v. Barr & Co.*, a case indistinguishable from the present excepting upon the ground that a mouse is not a snail ... Lord Anderson says this:

In a case like the present, where the goods of the defenders are widely distributed throughout Scotland, it would seem little short of outrageous to make them responsible to members of the public for the condition of the contents of every bottle which issues from their works. It is obvious that, if such responsibility attached to the defenders, they might be called on to meet claims of damages which they could not possibly investigate or answer.

In agreeing, as I do, with the judgment of Lord Anderson, I desire to add that I find it hard to dissent from the emphatic nature of the language with which his judgment is clothed. I am of opinion that this appeal should be dismissed, and I beg to move your Lordships accordingly.'

Where then does this leave any claim about objectivity in legal reasoning?

We are back to one of the points discussed in relation to moral autonomy. There are divergences of opinion on deep issues even among reasonable people. Each can only act on his or her own opinion, after listening with all due attention to points on the other side. Yet what is sought is a common reasonable rule for all— what is sought is indeed an objective ground of judgement. How then to cope with disagreement? In institutional settings like law courts, an obvious answer is to settle disagreements by voting, and let the majority opinion prevail. There is also, however, an important opportunity to appeal to time and history. Had Lord Anderson and Lord Buckmaster been correct about the 'outrageous' effect of the decision in favour of manufacturers' liability, the outcome of Donoghue would have been a crisis in food and drink manufacture. No doubt the legislature might have had to intervene to alleviate the load on manufacturers. But it did not happen so. Indeed, over the years the legislatures of most civilized countries have steadily raised the standards required of those who manufacture goods for consumption. So time can prove a person or a judge wrong, and as moral persons we need also to be alert to new evidence that ought to affect our hitherto settled

---

[31] [1932] AC 562 at 578, quoting Lord Anderson in *Mullen v Barr and Co* 1932 SC 461 at 479.

views, while legal systems need to have institutional means for rectifying precedents that prove unworkable.[32] The aspiration to objectivity[33] among a mass of subjective opinions remains a reasonable one.

9 Conclusion on legal and moral judgement

This chapter has had two aims. First it has sought to compare moral judgement as it might apply to leading reported legal cases with a view to seeing elements of convergence and of divergence. Does a moral assessment of the facts of the matter simply replicate the legal, or is a different approach possible and appropriate? As for this, we have seen that both where the moral conclusion diverges from the legal conclusion and where it converges with it, there are differences in the appropriate reasoning, and these are intimately bound up with the relative institutionalization of the context for legal reasoning. In this sense, legal reasoning is a different instance of practical reasoning from moral reasoning. Neither is a mere subset of the other, though there are important analogies and similarities between them.[34]

Second, it has sought to test out the suggestion in an earlier chapter that discussion of the categorical imperative should focus more on adjudication than on legislation if a legal model is desired to cast light on moral reasoning. For this purpose, the conclusion is clear: notwithstanding important differences, the analogy between moral judgement and legal judgement fully makes out the case for developing our understanding of the categorical imperative in this direction. It may be claimed as an advantage for the 'Smithian' version of the categorical imperative that it runs in that line of development.

---

[32] See, for example, the treatment of *Anns v Merton LBC* [1978] AC 728 in *Murphy v Brentwood District Council* [1991] 1 AC 398.

[33] See also N. Stavropoulos *Objectivity in Law* (Oxford: Clarendon Press, 1996) for a masterly overview of issues concerning objectivity.

[34] R. Alexy *A Theory of Legal Argumentation* (R. Adler and N. MacCormick trans) 211–220 advances the 'special case thesis', according to which legal reasoning is a special case of general practical reasoning, not simply a subset of moral reasoning. 211–20.

11

Practical Reason, Law, and State

1 The broad view: this book in context

This chapter concludes, not only a book, but a quartet of books, on 'Law, State, and Practical Reason'. The philosophical scope of the quartet has been large. It has covered a general theory of law as 'institutional normative order', a discussion of sovereignty, statehood, and nationalism, an inquiry into legal reasoning as a discipline involving both logic and rhetoric, and finally in the present book a study of practical reasoning in law and morality.

Its central point is an interpretative-analytical account of law as institutional normative order, one of the most salient elements in the self-organization of states. Yet it has also insisted that institutional normative order, that is law, characterizes many other forms of social and political ordering among human beings, not only states. State-law is a particularly important kind of law, but not the only kind. States are typically viewed as entities endowed with sovereignty, and sovereignty has often been considered essential both to democracy and to law. Yet in the contemporary world, the all-purpose omnicompetent sovereignty of states is questioned and even challenged. Especially in Europe, it seems highly questionable to attribute omnicompetent sovereignty to any member state of the European Union. It would, however, be well wide of the mark to suppose that the EU has itself replaced its members as a kind of sovereign federation or super-state. It is a matter for discussion whether this is a welcome development or a cause for dismay and alarm among European lovers of democracy.[1]

If law depends on there being always a law-giver, dismay and alarm might be the appropriate reaction. Loss of sovereignty equals loss of law—loss, that is, of one's own final law-making authority. For the institutional theory of law, however, this sovereignty argument rests on a fundamental error. The error is that it takes norm-giving to be prior to norm-using. This is completely wrong. The latter is prior to the former.

---

[1] J. H. H. Weiler, *The Constitution of Europe: 'Do the New Clothes have an Emperor?'* (Cambridge: Cambridge University Press, 1999) 264–85; cf. N. MacCormick, *Who's afraid of a European Constitution?* (Exeter: Societas/Imprint Academic, 2005) 50–58 and, in an opposed sense, P. Allott, *The Health of Nations: Society and Law beyond the State* (Cambridge: Cambridge University Press, 2002) 161–228.

To give the priority to norm-giving is to suppose that humans can lead ordered lives only if someone lays down norms or commandments telling them how they are to order their lives. If this were true, there could be no natural human languages. But there are such languages, so it is not true. People are able to interact in co-ordinated ways without being told to do so. Interactively and spontaneously, they can construct and come to share the kinds of mutual beliefs that are at the heart of any common standards of behaviour we have, including common patterns of speech. These can, of course, include co-ordination by common acceptance of a common authority for making further norms and regulating some kinds of tricky situations. Authority, however, presupposes norms that confer it; so not all norms result from authoritative acts.

Persons in authority, especially those who consider themselves to be bearers of sovereignty (their own monarchical authority, or that of the state or the people or the nation as collective entities) always have a tendency to claim absolute authority. '*Après moi le déluge*' said the French King (Louis XV) to his people—'get rid of me and you get chaos'. Hobbes had earlier said much the same thing to the English—'grant absolute sovereignty or put up with the war of all against all'.

There is always a reason to refuse absolutism. Human beings are autonomous moral agents—at least, they have the capacity to be such, and they achieve the fullness of their humanity in achieving autonomy and self-command. This need not imply a hard-necked refusal to attend to the authorities, whether the referee in a game of football, the conductor of the orchestra, or the sovereign Parliament in Westminster or Ottawa. Institutional obligations are real obligations in most normal circumstances, based on mutual trust and personal commitment. But, morally speaking, the agent can never surrender the last judgement nor what is sometimes called the primacy of conscience: 'This act is required by authority, but I consider it wrong so I may not and will not comply.' Possession of this last judgement is the mark of a morally mature human being. Lose it, and we lose the distinctive mark of our humanity. We slide down the road marked with the warning signs of Stanley Milgram's experiments[2] that ends in the gas chambers of Auschwitz, the killing fields of Laos, the slaughter of Srebrenića.

Claims of this kind are always open to challenge. The challenge says that the supposed autonomy of each person is simply a mask of anarchy. It is a licence for arbitrariness in conduct and thought. The challenge ignores the place of practical reason in the moral life of the self-governing individual. Arbitrariness is the last vice of which a reasonable person is likely to be guilty. People who act and live in accordance with reason may be suspected of a lack of spontaneity, or criticized for being somewhat hide-bound and obsessed with rules and principles, but not for being merely whimsical. They face a danger of ignoring the emotional and sentimental dimension of human life. They reason away the passions. That is indeed

---

[2] S. Milgram, *Obedience to Authority: an Experimental View* (New York NY: Harper and Row, 1974).

a risk. One might even toy with the apophthegm that 'too much Kant leads to too much cant'. But that would depend on a too one-sided reading of Kant. Here, a corrective to that dependency has been found in the sentimentalism-coupled-with-impartiality that we find in Adam Smith's theory of moral sentiments, in turn adjusted to allow for the insights of Kant. Somehow to marry together the insights of two giants belonging respectively to the Scottish and the German enlightenment and to make this vivid for now, not only for then, is the trick we must bring off. That has been a main effort of the present book.

For the trick to come off, it is essential to have a serious understanding of the interaction of reason, argumentation, judgement, and decision. *Rhetoric and the Rule of Law* attempted an exhaustive account of these matters in the context of positive law, mainly but not only state law. In that context there is also scepticism to be confronted. Law is obviously a rhetorical discipline, especially in its courtroom manifestations. But is it rhetoric only? Is it only rhetoric in the vulgar and adversative sense—a matter of dressing up with plausible arguments a decision whose true account lies in undisclosed motives? Or can we study it as rhetoric in the sense of the elements of persuasiveness? Not all argument in law (or indeed in astrophysics) is strictly logical and demonstrative in the technical sense of the term 'logic'. Certainly, some of it is—much more than casual observers of law are inclined to admit.[3] But many of what are offered as reasons in legal arguments, whether of counsel putting forward a case or rebutting someone else's, or of judges stating an opinion in support of their decision, lack demonstrative character. They are persuasive without being logically compelling. What then is this persuasiveness—is it rational persuasiveness, or are we just back at appealing to emotions or to baser interests? At the heart of this lies the deeper question whether one such argument is ever really any better than another, or whether the choice between them is finally an arbitrary one.

For anyone interested in the question whether reason can be applied to solving practical, as distinct from theoretical questions, and, if so, how it can, law is a grand field of study. For lawyers and judges do a great part of their arguing in public, and they (judges in particular) place on public record the arguments that they find convincing in the context of deciding what to do in deciding cases. Of course they do not, and cannot, tell all. There must be many relevant reasons that they never mention in their judicial opinions. What is important is to give the big reasons, the telling ones, not every possible fragment of a reason that might be relevant. To justify a decision, one has to show sufficient reason for taking it, and that need not be every reason that there possibly is in its favour. That is obvious and unobjectionable, but it has potentially a dark side. For sometimes a judge might suppress what seems to her the best reason in favour of a decision, or what

³ See *Rhetoric and the Rule of Law*, 49–77 and compare N. MacCormick 'A Reply to Comments on *Rhetoric and the Rule of Law*' in (2008) 59 *NILQ* 43–44, responding to G. Sartor, 'Syllogism and Defeasibility' (2008) 59 *NILQ* 21–32.

is in fact her actual motive in deciding the case as she does. To cover her tracks, she might construct a 'façade reason' that will sound convincing in law but that will mask the true balance of the arguments. There could be at least three temptations towards this. First might be reasons of state: she is persuaded that the public safety or the maintenance of an essential military alliance requires that a certain notorious defendant be convicted, or that the appeal of such a person against conviction be rejected. Second might be reasons of deep personal beliefs: she thinks the death penalty is wrong and inhumane, but within the realms of what can reasonably be decided by a democratic legislature. As judge in a 'death penalty state' she always finds some reason to avoid a conviction or allow an appeal or some mitigating circumstance that justifies a conviction of a lesser form of homicide. She never discloses that her real reason is moral objection to the death penalty.[4] The third case is corruption, either of a crude monetary kind or in some more subtle form of personal or political favouritism. Reasons can be given for her decisions, but the reasons she publicly avows do not tell us why she decides as she decides.

Legal systems in which any more than a few judges are even reasonably open to suspicion of acting in any of these three ways are in deep trouble, and the more the suspicion of 'façade reasoning' grows, the worse it gets. Yet every lawyer knows how difficult it really is to be sure that the reasons given are the true ones, and every courtroom lawyer knows that all judges have their own personalities and predilections. So there are good and bad ways of pleading a case before this judge or that one. An ideal world of perfect judging exists nowhere, but some states approximate better to it in the conduct of most of their judges than do others. This makes very important an ongoing socio-legal critique of bar and bench, for without critics practice can become slack. A fearless and independent bar whose members are not beholden to government or to business interests or to the judges themselves is also a condition of maintaining honest adjudication.

There also remains an important role for the analysis of judicial reasoning as genuine practical reasoning genuinely directed at justifying the decisions the judges make. It would be as big a mistake to suggest that all published judicial opinions are mere 'façade reasoning' as to suppose that none is. The published opinions of the judges and of the courts, as considered briefly in Chapter 10 and at length in *Rhetoric and the Rule of Law*, are a mine of valuable examples and evidence for students of practical reasoning, since they contain statements of what a judge is deciding. This is supported by a full and carefully argued account of what the judge considers makes it right to decide in this way, for or against this litigant or accused

---

[4] Compare John Grisham's interesting and sympathetic account of a judge facing this dilemma, in his novel *The Appeal* (London: Century/Random House, 2008) at pp 173–5. That the judge envisaged in the novel and in the text above considers it a legitimate decision for a democratic legislature to provide for a regulated form of death penalty is crucial to the argument. For otherwise she would only be able to observe the law at the cost of violating her own moral autonomy, or *vice versa*.

person. Different legal systems, one must concede, vary in the degree and extent to which they allow or encourage expanded and discursive accounts of decision-making.[5] There is a wide gap between the multiple-opinion report of a House of Lords decision (or a decision of the forthcoming (2009) 'United Kingdom Supreme Court' that will replace the judicial committee of the House of Lords) on an appeal in Scots or English law, and the tightly drawn and narrowly allusive '*motifs*' of a decision by the French *Cour de Cassation* for example. Yet both have value and interest as indications of how to justify a decision in this or that legal setting.

Where, as in the present book, one's focus is more on the moral reasoning of the ordinary moral agent, the legal model is an interesting source of possible comparisons. Admittedly, there could easily be a risk of letting the analogy so dominate the principal field of study that one ends up with a far-too-legalistic conception of moral reasoning.[6] If the book has fallen into this trap, it will be despite strenuous efforts by its author. Whether these efforts have succeeded, however, is for the reader to judge. Meantime, having located the concerns of this book in the broad themes of the series to which it belongs, this final chapter must proceed to tie up some remaining loose ends that connect the present work with its predecessors. These concern: universal and particular in moral judgement; the place of autonomy in moral reasoning; the issue about 'natural law'; the virtues of the law-abiding person; the question of how to live; and the problem of life and death.

2 Universal and particular

There has been a great deal of discussion whether or not Kant's claim about the universalizability of moral judgements is well-founded or not. Some argue for the essential particularity of moral decision making.[7] We are not legislators as we make our way through life, law makers who lay down 'universal laws of nature'. We are not even beings who behave 'as if' we were doing this, and then applying the determined rule to the particular instance and acting accordingly. There may be various more or less popular summary accounts of the whole duty of human beings. Actually, however, there is no authoritative moral rule-book akin to the Laws of Golf as promulgated by the Royal and Ancient Golf Club of St Andrews, or the *Code Civil* and related codes of the French Republic, or the *Corpus Juris Civilis* of Justinian. Legalistic moralism[8] would be the result of pretending there were such a thing, and moral agency would be enfeebled, not strengthened by such a pretence.

[5] D. N. MacCormick and R. S. Summers *Interpreting Precedents; a comparative study* (Aldershot: Dartmouth, 1997).
[6] Judith Shklar, *Legalism* (Cambridge, MA: Harvard University Press, 1986); Z. Bankowski, *Living Lawfully* (Dordrecht: Kluwer Academic Publishers, 2001) 43–59.
[7] Notably J. Dancy, *Ethics without Principles* (Oxford: Clarendon Press, 2004).
[8] Compare again Shklar and Bankowski cited above, n 6.

The argument in the present book is that judgement, not legislation, is focal for morality just as it is important (but not all-important) in law. As a moral judge of my own conduct and that of my neighbours, I cannot but implicitly consider the universalizable implications of what I am inclined to decide. It is relevant to be aware what norm supported by mutual beliefs could be shared by all who are affected by a situation or incident where decision is necessary—I do actually apply a kind of reasoning that was summed up in the 'Smithian categorical imperative'. If I judge at all, I have to judge in that way, whether or not the formulation offered of the Smithian categorical imperative captures perfectly how we have to do it. If we do not judge, we fail to engage morally with the situation.

Someone may say that spontaneity is the best response to human problems—go with the flow and act how it feels right without further reflection.[9] But that is itself a moral judgement about how to live. It may for some contexts be good advice (that is advice that is good for anyone and for everyone in these contexts, of which one might be the inner sanctum of a loving relationship with another person). If so, there are reasons why it is good advice, and these reasons can and should be produced under challenge. It seems like very bad advice for other contexts if you tell me that spontaneity is *always* the best response. Surely sometimes reflection is called for. Do you really want to spend five years qualifying as a Scottish solicitor or to work for three years writing a book, just in response to the feelings of a long-ago moment, taken without ever being subjected to reasoning or reflection? I think not. In considering the proper place for spontaneity, and in considering difficult decisions where spontaneity is not enough, the mutual analogy of morality and law supports a common conclusion. Universalizability is essential to justification. There cannot be good reasons for a legal or a moral decision that are not (however defeasibly and with whatever scope for future exceptions and qualifications) universal in application. Chapters 3 and 4 of the present book bring to a conclusion the issues discussed in chapter 5 of *Rhetoric and the Rule of Law*, and further pursued in a companion volume by Zenon Bankowski and James MacLean.[10]

3 Moral autonomy and institutional law

Chapter 5 of the present book wrapped up an issue left trailing from chapter 14 of *Institutions of Law*. There, a distinction was drawn between the institutional character of positive law and the individual autonomy that characterizes moral

---

[9] Here springs to mind Bernard Williams's famous 'one thought too many' point about the man who, before he saved his wife in an accident, had to decide he was justified in saving her rather than someone else equally needy. See B. Williams, *Moral Luck* (Cambridge: Cambridge University Press, 1981) 16–19.

[10] Z. Bankowski and J. Maclean (eds) *The Universal and the Particular in Legal Reasoning* (Aldershot: Ashgate, 2006).

agency. Human beings in the territory of a state are heteronomous in face of the state's law and the commandments it imposes on them, but they are autonomous as moral agents. This gives each person the final say as to whether or not it is right to knuckle under to legal norms where one considers them to be morally unacceptable. But such norms are likely to be enforced against moral dissenters whatever they say, and the more openly they protest the more likely they are to face the enforcement. This contrast between the institutionality of law and the autonomy of moral agency justifies the conclusion that there is an important conceptual gap between positive law and morality. This argument was deployed in *Institutions of Law*, subject to a question left open concerning how exactly to make out the philosophical case for the view that morality presupposes and engages autonomy, and depends on what Adam Smith calls self-command. That question is now answered, so far as it lies within my power to answer it.

The answer does not undermine an important point established *in Questioning Sovereignty*,[11] namely, that we are all 'contextual individuals'. Our individuality expresses a junction-point between genetic inheritance and social, including familial, context. We acquire the name we have, and come to self-consciousness as the bearer of that name, only in a context of interaction with others. It is to the person whose self-understanding and sense of identity emerges from this process that we can ascribe autonomy in the Kantian sense. It is that contextual individual which can develop the capability of 'spectator reasoning' and the capability for self-command, and this development may itself depend partly on the presence of propitious social circumstances. It is to that individual, interacting with others of like kind that the Smithian categorical imperative gives relevant guidance.

4 Natural law

A very large number of questions can be clustered together under the rubric of 'natural law'. The most important concerns whether or not there is a common human nature shared by all men women and children everywhere and at all times, and whether that nature itself engages values and norms. Or is it merely the case that most human beings in most places seem to have a capacity to issue more or less arbitrary commands to each other, or to receive them under some threat of sanctions for disobedience? Notwithstanding cultural variability in all its extremes, the case proposed here favours the claim that there is a universal and intrinsically normative human nature. Chapter 3 made this point on the footing that humans are speaking animals. (So far as we are aware, they are the only speaking animals, but the presence of others would not disturb the essential point about humans.)

[11] N. MacCormick, *Questioning Sovereignty* (Oxford: Oxford University Press, 1999) 178–82.

You can't speak without norms of grammar,[12] though of course you do not need to know these as pre-formulated rules; and you can't speak outside of a community. Speech in community requires mutual trust and makes humans essentially trust-valuers. This is no longer a matter of pure anthropological speculation. It can also be backed by a well-founded proposition of human genetics. It is known what in the genome makes possible the development of speech by each human child, and it is known in what circumstances (being reared in a speech community) the child's experience activates the relevant gene. A theorem that follows is this: *humans are norm users before they can become norm-givers*. The corollary is that voluntarism of the kind espoused by Bentham (see Chapter 6) and Austin is false.

Kant counselled us to formulate moral judgements 'as if' the maxim of our acting would become through our will a 'universal law of nature'. The best reading of that delphic phrase becomes now clear. Our judgements should take account of our nature—following Smith, whether or not Kant would have agreed, this nature of ours is expressed to a very great extent through the 'sentiments' or emotions and passions that are aroused in human interaction. In the light of our mutual understanding as passionate beings we must see what norms of judgement we can live by as common norms. What is right for us to do and what it is good for us to do are matters that do depend on and refer back to our common human nature. To that extent there is 'natural law'.

But the particularists are right on one vital point. There is not a rule-book[13] written into our nature or 'inscribed in our hearts'. The moral rules and principles we have worked out are, as Smith argued, established inductively by reflection on actual judgements of the kind we confirm by reference to 'impartial spectator' reasoning. Any such inductively established rules are bound to be culturally specific to a considerable extent, and anyway they are always open to critique and revision. Natural law is not a 'brooding omnipresence in the sky',[14] from which we can read down the ideal set of rules for the state of which we are citizens. If belief in natural law required belief in such a perfect pre-ordained code, it would be a false belief. By contrast, if you mean by 'natural law' that humans have in their nature a propensity to norm-guided and in that sense law-like behaviour, it is a correct belief. It is also correct that it is not arbitrary in any given setting what are the grounds of judgement we can genuinely will 'as if a universal law of nature'.

The transition made in their different ways by Smith and Kant from the protestant natural lawyers' vision of law that was a 'dictate of reason' written in the hearts

---

[12] For an even deeper-going view of the significance of grammar for the possibility of thought, see G. Pavlakos, *Our Knowledge of the Law* (Oxford: Hart, 2007).

[13] See J. Dancy, *Ethics without Principles* (Oxford: Oxford University Press, 2004) 118–39 for refutation of views that there might be some stock of given moral principles from which all moral reasoning proceeds.

[14] The phrase, of course, is that of Oliver Wendell Holmes, Jr, applied to the common law in his case. See his opinion in *Southern Pacific Co v Jensen* 244 US 205, 222 (1917).

of human beings is crucial for human self-understanding. By evolution we have come to have a complex neurophysiology and psychology such that we can both act and reflect—impartially reflect—on our acting and can express judgements and mutual exhortations about it. The methodology of our self-construction of moral norms by which to live and moral conceptions of the goods it is worth pursuing, is well captured by some formulation of the categorical imperative. Here the preferred version has been the 'Smithian categorical imperative' but the deep point remains sound even if that superficial formulation proves open to objections. Natural law is not a set of rules established *a priori*. It is at most a set of inductive generalizations justified according to the methodology of their derivation through practical human experience in determinate social settings.

In any tolerably constitutionalist state, whether or not a democratic one, the legislature that has enacted positive laws and the judges who have established any precedents that are binding will normally both regard these as being morally justified laws, and represent them in such terms to the subject population.[15] In this they will usually also have the support of the professional commentators on the law. Robert Alexy and I have both drawn attention to the apparent oddity, if not indeed self-contradiction, if a law-maker were to say: 'I hereby decree that the following unjust law shall be in force in my realm...'.[16] Those responsible for maintaining and upholding a system of positive law are themselves moral beings upon whom it is incumbent to treat fellow human beings with due respect and concern. A good society is one in which human beings as autonomous moral agents can live together in peace and harmony, within a framework of 'obedience, freedom and engagement'. The proper vocation of the law-maker and the judge is to try to create and sustain the framework of a good society. Laws ought to be just and to be conducive to the common good of a good society so understood. No serious commentator on law, politics, or morality could doubt this. The problem is achieving it.

The positivity of positive law does not, however, presuppose that the law-makers and judges have yet, fully, or even at all, achieved these objectives. They may have made a bad and pretty unjust job of it all. They are still law-makers and judges, and what they have imperfectly made are still laws or precedents. By analogy, authors ought to write only original and interesting books. Many fail, but are still authors. They still did produce this ordered succession of words containing some meaning, however obscure, that bears some relation to the title of the book and the genre in which it is represented as belonging. The positive or posited character of positive law depends on its institutional character in a way fully expounded in the companion volume to this one, called *Institutions of Law*. Validity of legal

[15] See G. Barden, 'Rhetorics of Legitimacy' *European Journal of Law, Philosophy and Computer Science* 2 (1998) 47.
[16] See G. Pavlakos (ed) *Law, Rights and Discourse: the Legal Philosophy of Robert Alexy* (Oxford: Hart, 2007), papers by N. MacCormick 'Why Law makes No Claims' (59–67 at 63–7, and Alexy 'Thirteen Replies' 333–66 at 333–5.

enactment is institutionally determined and what is validly enacted is presumptively a rule of law, subject to its interpretation by the judges and subject to any
possible challenge in respect of constitutional requirements, satisfaction of inter-
nationally institutionalized human rights conditions, or the like. The aspiration
towards justice and the common good that is definitive of the legislative and judicial roles considered in relation to their final causes is not perfectly reflected in the
material cause of the laws they make and authoritatively interpret. The positive
laws that we find in every state of the United Nations are as they are because of
decisions taken within the states and in the context of their own politics, whether
democratic, oligarchic or dictatorial. Some are a dreadful mess, others less so,
some much less so, some even reasonable and acceptable for the most part. None,
we may be confident, is wholly without flaws.

Positive law is not therefore ever an achieved embodiment of natural law, in
either the unsustainable or in the sustainable sense of that term. So far as concerns the unsustainable sense, it is obvious that positive laws do not and cannot
mirror the ideal rule-book, for there is no rule-book to mirror. In the sustainable sense, natural law is not an abstract rule book but the kind of law or system
of laws that, for a given socio-political context and at a given level of economic
development, would fully satisfy the constraints of the (Smithian) categorical
imperative and tend to procure a genuinely common good. Positive laws do not
automatically satisfy this test just because they are valid laws, and are thus always
open to the stern gaze of critical morality, in the light of which some are objec-
tionable. In this sustainable sense of 'natural law', positive law does not necessarily match up to the standard its final cause entitles us to demand of it. There is a
conceptual gap between positive law and natural law, likewise between positive
law and ideal morality. This does not imply, far less entail, that in positive law
anything goes. There are extremes of injustice and irrationality which again and
again it has proved to lie within the *de facto* power of governments to enforce and
make happen. But these lie so far beyond anything encompassed within the final
cause of legislation or of adjudication that no person in any capacity should concede to them the appellation 'law'. In this extreme sense, *Iniusta lex, nulla lex* is
true, except that one should add the scare quotes and superlativize the adjective:
Iniustissima 'lex', nulla lex. Not every so-called law is really a law, and absolute
injustice is outside the realm of law altogether.[17]

5 Should a moral agent be law-abiding citizen?

The discussion of natural law leads on easily into the question of obedience. The
autonomy of the moral person entails always a final judgement by that person
concerning what it is right to do in any situation in which doubt is present. Yet

---

[17] For a more extended argument to this effect, see N. MacCormick, *Institutions of Law*, ch 15.

people are not moral obsessives. They do not devote every moment of waking life to wrestling with moral problems, for they would live no real life if they did. Much of the time humans 'go with the flow', observe the ordinary moral virtues, are tempted by and sometimes seduced into the ordinary moral vices, but largely keep within the confines of a customary or conventional morality according to the individual's internalized understanding of that. Their life is largely shaped by habits and routines and it is not too frequently that one is forced up against the question whether there is something amiss, or even seriously wrong, with what habit and routine prompts either in a general way or in a particular case. Nevertheless, our autonomy requires us to be on the lookout for the trouble case and to wrestle with it when it turns up. That is the price of moral maturity. We must stand ready to be our own impartial spectator and judge. So what does this have to say about obedience to the law of the land, in whatever land you find yourself?

The image of the good, law-abiding citizen floats into view. Such a person pays taxes promptly and does not spend weary hours devising clever schemes that slip on to the right side of the blurred line dividing (illegal) tax evasion from (lawful) tax avoidance. When driving, she observes speed limits pretty faithfully and never 'jumps' traffic signals. She respects her neighbours' property and keeps her contracts and other engagements without giving thought to the risk of being sued if she does not...and so on. 'What a dullard!' you may think, 'What a timid town mouse!' But are you sure about that? Certainly the virtues of civility can be drab compared with the exotic drama of a more 'bohemian' existence. But are they not real virtues nonetheless?

The argument for spontaneity in action and for a readiness to expose convention and law to coruscating criticism is an argument founded in autonomy and is to that extent a very powerful one. Driving a sports car at 220kph in a zone with a 100kph speed restriction is hardly, however, an advertisement for the splendours of moral autonomy. It looks more like reckless selfishness, a display of rather pathetic false machismo and immature arrogance. Doing just as you please and displaying your contempt for the mere conventionality of others is no admirable conduct, though once in a while the dramatic act of illegal or unconstitutional protest can focus public attention on some standing injustice that demands reform. This may not quite justify so violent an act as (for example) the act of John Brown and his rebel party in seizing the US armoury at Harper's Ferry by force of arms during the slavery controversy that preceded the American Civil War, though a long-popular song dismisses so pusillanimous a doubt. For many, John Brown's soul does indeed go marching on and is still needed for the inspiration it can give. Those Scottish protesters who removed the Stone of Destiny, an ancient symbol of the Scottish people, from Westminster Abbey to a secret place of refuge in Scotland in 1950 have less on their conscience, but also made their point.[18]

---

[18] For an account of this escapade, see I. Hamilton, *Stone of Destiny* (Edinburgh: Birlinn, 2008).

A serious regard for the autonomy of persons does not normally give countenance to the use of raw violence in however good a cause, except where every possible other avenue is permanently closed. Experience teaches that violent exercises or seizures of power typically lead to 'strong arm' government, dictatorial rule that may not be mitigated till generations have passed. It is the ordinary person, the 'little man' unable to fight his corner in such circumstances that is then the loser. Kant was surely right that it is under the 'laws of freedom' that autonomy and thus the full moral life for all or most persons can flourish. This does mean that there has to be a body of law, both criminal and civil, that lays down the basic duties and provides both for punishing wilful violations of them and for remedying harmful breaches of them. There must also be private law concerning contracts and other engagements and institution-arrangements, including those defining property rights of all kinds. Insufficiently noticed by the eighteenth century inspirers of the present book, there must also be a considerable body of public law. This must not only provide for the organization of the state and its agencies, but must also enable them to undertake necessary interventions in the way of securing social or distributive justice and various forms of environmental protection. Generally speaking, the domain of justified freedom is that which lies beyond the principles of obedience and engagement, and outside the duties of citizens under public law. Only when things are going badly wrong does moral liberty include the liberty to violate law in order to protest its wickedness. But when they are, it is the duty of all good persons to rally to the side of the protester, thereby making more likely some response by the authorities or some shift in political support towards the side of those who angrily demand reform. Sometime, it is an even better idea to write a really good and forceful book.[19]

Why it really matters to be law-abiding, but not slavishly law-abiding, is because of the obvious proposition that law has to be largely self-policing and self-administered by citizens. 'Mutuality of restrictions' is a great motive to conformity with laws that impose reasonable restrictions. You observe them in my favour even when it would be more convenient not to, and I observe them in yours when the boot is on the other foot, and so on for many, many actually and potentially interacting citizens. These are the conditions for mutual civility under law. Where this prevails, people go about their daily life and ordinary business unarmed and without fear of each other. They fulfil their mutual duties and obligations, not without occasional controversy as to what exactly this requires of them, and even with occasional resort to authoritative

---

[19] E.g., Herbert Hart's *Law Liberty and Morality* with its huge impact on homosexual law reform, or Alan Herbert's novel *Holy Deadlock* that satirized out of public credibility the pre-1939 English law of divorce. See also R. Gordon, *Rehumanizing Law: A Narrative Theory of Law and Democracy* (Edinburgh: Edinburgh University PhD thesis, 2009) for illustration of the relevance of Upton Sinclair's novel *The Jungle* (New York NY: Doubleday, Page & Co, 1906) to developing consumer protection law and that of Rachel Carson's *Silent Spring* (Boston, MA: Houghton Mifflin, 1962) on the development of environmental protection law.

interpretations of such questions. They try to avoid violating the criminal law, and when accused of some lapse in this they do not waste police and court time by insisting on a 'not guilty' plea when they consider the charge to be justified and just. When expectations of such mutuality begin to break down, alarming trends appear. Guns become more and more prevalent in use among criminals. Young people come to feel obliged to carry knives for self-protection, and all too often resort to pre-emptive use of them in threatening situations, fetching up facing murder charges.

Truly, the civility of civil society is a very great collective achievement of all those states whose citizens have brought it about by mutual self-restraint and by voluntary compliance with reasonable laws. This also requires unremitting political criticism of those laws that are unreasonable, and a realistic prospect of securing reform of these. In such circumstances each person has a real prospect of acquiring a capacity for self-command and thus developing into a fully autonomous moral agent with all the scope for due spontaneity that moral freedom provides.

It is not dull to be law-abiding, it is sensible, and it is almost always just. But there is no universal or absolute obligation to obey any law just because it is a valid law, regardless of its content.

6 How to live: no recipe

This book makes a contribution to moral as well as legal philosophy. It may have disappointed readers who think philosophers should tell them how to live. This would manifest a longing for the rule-book conception of morality and a hope for some philosophical insight into its contents. Alas, the philosopher's rule book, like the philosopher's stone, does not exist. The Smith/Kant revolution in moral philosophy leads to a new level of understanding. Here, we can think through the method and the structure of moral thought and understand why the moral agent must rely on self-command and act autonomously, not like an inexperienced cook with a Delia Smith recipe book for good actions and right decisions.

One can resort to pure imagination, or to works of drama and imaginative literature or to history, or to the Law Reports. One can consider, to an extent not to be overdone, the contents of our own abstract introspection. By reference to such resources, we can display moral issues to ourselves and air them before an audience or a readership. We can discuss how it seems right to come to judgements and decisions in such settings. An author can and often should explain the opinion he has formed about them. But as a proponent of autonomous decision making the author has no business to prescribe answers to the reader or hearer. The discursive quality of moral thought is most clear in this. One may present ideas as to what is the most attractive conception of some public or private virtue or value—justice, democracy, liberty and equality come to mind as possible candidates for such treatment.[20] The philosopher's work is not, however, that of the political polemicist though some people are indeed good in both roles.

Some denounce this claim that there is a difference between the role of philosopher and that of polemicist. Ronald Dworkin, for example, considers that it involves claiming a strange philosophical capability to transcend earthly existence and find an 'Archimedean Point'. This is located in the empyrean somewhere well above the dust of real moral and political debate. From it, the long-nosed philosopher looks down on mere mortals and advises them whether their opinions have any foundation or not. Since this Archimedean Point does not exist, the philosopher either has no job or just has to hunker down among the polemicists and tear into the same arguments with them. This is a teasing critique, but not a just one.

Let us recall what was Archimedes' own point about his 'Point'. It illustrates a principle of mechanics concerning leverage. It depends on the physical principle that a lighter weight can shift a heavier one using a lever, provided that the fulcrum of the lever is placed sufficiently far from the point of incidence of the lighter and sufficiently close to the heavier. A light weight with a long enough lever moving through a large arc can shift a heavier through a proportionately smaller arc. So, if a mere human being could get far enough from planet Earth, and could find a suitable fulcrum, he could move the earth just by pushing on a lever, provided a long enough lever were available. This is a very persuasive and vivid argument in physics. It is, of course, a counterfactual argument since the necessary fulcrum point is immaterial and no lever long enough could possibly be constructed. But if it is counterfactual, how can it be true? What justifies extrapolating from the behaviour of tangible physical objects used in experiments to non-tangible objects used in thought? What makes the conclusion persuasive, or true?

You may be inclined to say that it is just obviously true, or, in terminology applied by Ronald Dworkin to political arguments, it is the most 'attractive' argument one can construct in relation to the subject matter. It certainly is attractive, but not in any ineffable way. Reflection on the methodology of physics and the application of mathematical models to physical problems can teach us what is attractive, not only about this, but about many analogous arguments across wide fields of physics and other natural sciences. Methodology may involve metaphysics, but not in any disreputable way, as Kant showed in applying transcendental reasoning to the very possibility of arguments from causation and for the application of mathematics to physics. Others have followed where Kant led. Likewise, we can discuss why some forms of argument lead to persuasive conclusions in practical matters like those involved in legal or moral judgement and in political arguments. This is material to the arguments the same people, or other people,

---

[20] Such is the treatment of them advocated in R. Dworkin, *Justice in Robes* (Cambridge, MA and London: Harvard University Press, Belknap Press, 2006) 156–162, and in chapter 6 at large. One has to tread carefully the line between philosophical analysis and political polemics.

advance in their character as polemicists. But the philosopher has no business to pretend to superior wisdom in practice over the non-philosophical polemicist. People with real moral problems to solve should go to wise counsellors with much experience in matters of the kind causing the problem. They should be guided by them, but not directed, far less commanded. And they should put the philosophy books aside till a quieter day.

7 Confronting life and death

This book has drawn a perhaps too sharp distinction between the animal and the ideal values that are the components of human good, whether pursued individualistically, in an other-directed way, or for the sake of community. There is real difference between the tangibles that support life in a way that matters to us much as it matters to all members of the animal kingdom, and the intangibles that we construct in art and thought and contemplation of the universe around us, in all its wonder. So far as we can currently be aware, this interest in the intangibles is exclusive to ourselves within the animal kingdom, which justifies the terms used to make the contrast. But nothing would change in the basics of the argument if it turned out that some animals—whales might be likely candidates—also have some appreciation of intangibles albeit in terms that would be barely translatable into human thought.

Some might consider this all too flat a view. 'Life' they might say, 'comes before and after all else. Without life there is nothing else to value, no right and wrong to be concerned about'. According to this objector, the one absolute value must be life, and the one fundamental principle of practical existence is to hang on to it as long as you can. *Perseverare in esse suo* is a universal and supreme value of animal existence in all its forms, as much for humans as for others.

In one sense this is plainly true, in another, it is highly questionable. It has been urged throughout the present book (but particularly in Chapters 2 and 9) that in our ordinary life we do have to look first to what is vital for our own and for our families' and close friends' and neighbours' survival (and, preferably, survival in reasonable comfort), before we start worrying about higher or remoter things. This is indeed a matter of practical priority, and indeed reflects the fact that one can pursue nothing else when dead and that comprehensive bereavement of one's nearest and dearest is a practically and morally enervating experience. But once one is securely alive, life alone hardly justifies itself. There are other worthwhile things to do apart from securing survival, and if there were not, life itself would lose its savour. Life is of value as a keystone in an arch which requires other stones for its sustenance. The metaphor needs a cautionary rider—most of these stones are non-material and intangible. Thus qualified, it is a valid metaphor.

Overvaluation of life can lead to a disproportionate and even superstitious fear of death. Death is not the opposite of life, but its natural outward boundary. The sense of living for a limited time is one of the incentives we have to reasonable industry and diligence. We pass this way only once, and if we do not make the most of it, the loss and failure will be ours alone. This is not a visitation by malign fate but another of the intrinsic elements of our normative-as-well-as biological nature. Approaches to geriatric medicine that would seek to facilitate for future generations an apparently limitless or greatly expanded life-span derive from a false conception and valuation of life, and betoken a dubious attitude to intergenerational justice. Speaking from the standpoint of my late sixties in age, I have to say that there is justice that my generation should, later or sooner over the next not-more-than-thirty years be ready to step permanently aside in favour of the grandchildren and (perhaps) great-grandchildren's generation and their successors. Three score years and ten is no longer an 'allotted' though it is still a reasonable span, and what one has not done within that span, one is not very likely to do later. Those who have deferred gratification beyond such a point are apt to find they have forgone it, even if they remain physically in reasonable shape. Easing the pains and fears of death for the elderly is a great mercy. Trying to abolish them can be no more than a silly illusion.

There is a profound sense of unfairness and tragedy about the death of young people, whether from accident or from cancer or wasting diseases like multiple sclerosis. These contrast somewhat with deaths arising from risky sporting activities like sailing or mountaineering or motor-racing. Testing one's skill and endurance against big risks is itself one school of courage and a theatre in which to demonstrate a mixture of courage and high skill in one's chosen activity. Whoever takes high risks has to be aware of the down-side as well as the up-side, and that things can go badly wrong when least expected. The exhilaration of risky pursuits would be missing were this not so. The domestic risks that can manifest themselves even in well run households and cause deaths in, say, gas explosions, have far more of the tragic in them, especially when younger people are their victims. In all cases, there is of course profound grief for those left behind, most especially parents who do not expect to bury their own children, and young offspring and spouses face a bitter loss, too, in all cases of premature death.

Fate, however, is not unfair. 'Fate' is only a personification of whatever happens, especially of untoward things that happen. Nor is God unfair, since He does not intervene arbitrarily in the creation. Being omnipotent and omnibeneficent, He could only have set up the best possible universe from the beginning, with the seeds of evolution in it. Diseases have evolved along with the people whom they plague. Miraculous or malevolent divine or other superhuman interventions are not to be given any credence in the light of practical reason. (All this is *a fortiori* true for those who deny the existence of a God.) If there is any remediable injustice in untimely death it is because of a failure by human beings in their constitutional states to do enough in the way of insurance against it. Most particularly this ought to cover need-based health services and medical research services that establish the causes of and possible cures for the illnesses that plague younger people. Substantial recent progress with, for example, breast cancer illustrates the right way forward. Of course 'ought' implies 'can', so no blame attaches to the present incompleteness of medical knowledge and expertise available in the cause of evening out the life chances of different individuals and families in some way more meaningful than cash assistance in cases of destitution through illness. The point, however, is not to get bogged down in political polemics about health services. It is simply to underline that the issue of life and death, and of the distressing character of premature death by contrast with death in old age at the end of a full life, poses issues of justice between generations. Apart from that, death is not the negation of life, but, when it comes in season, its consummation, and should be accepted with gratitude as such. It is part of natural law in its sustainable sense that human morality has real connections with human mortality.[21]

8 Conclusion

'Can reason be practical?' We return to the question with which the book opened, and give it an answer that is loudly affirmative. Nothing is more important to the leading of a successful human life than that one apply reason and intelligence to the course one takes through life. This applies both to observing the common moral and legal norms that bind us to other people and define our duties to and engagements with them, and also to seeking to do the best we can with the opportunities that come our way in the domain of moral freedom.

The first main chapter addressed the question whether the author of this book had any good reason to write it—a reason or reasons good enough to justify the expenditure of much time and effort on research, reading, and writing. Whatever be the truth of that, this concluding section may not improperly pose the converse question to the reader. Was it worth the effort of reading right through to this point? Has reading the book informed and enlightened you upon matters in which you are interested? Has it given new insight into the truth about human reason in morality and law? If not, has it provoked you to attempt an improvement on the ideas advanced here, with a view to getting better at the truth of these deep matters? The answers you give to these questions may lead you to conclude that 'yes' is indeed the answer to the question 'Can reason be practical?' for they are of interest only to someone who supposes it may be.

---

[21] See also T. Nagel, *Mortal Questions* (Cambridge: Cambridge University Press, 1979) 1–10.

Index